Cod Fishing
The Complete Guide

COD FISHING:
The Complete Guide

Dave Lewis

The Crowood Press

First published in 1997 by
The Crowood Press Ltd
Ramsbury, Marlborough
Wiltshire SN8 2HR

British Library Cataloguing in Publication Data

A catalogue record for this book is available from the British Library.

ISBN 1 86126 017 2

Dedication

I would like to dedicate this book to my wife Alison and two young children, Amy and Luke

Picture Credits

All photographs by the author
All line-drawings by Andrew Green

Typeset by Phoenix Typesetting, Ilkley, West Yorkshire.
Printed and bound in Great Britain

Contents

Foreword

Having fished for cod with Dave Lewis in numerous locations as far away as Denmark, and shared some memorable hauls on feathers, rubber eels, pirks, bait and – believe it or not – on trolled plugs and spoons, I have no hesitation whatsoever in stating that within the following pages, whether beach, pier or boat orientated, the reader could have no better guide in furthering their knowledge of this popular species. For not only is Dave one of Britain's most successful anglers, his methodical and practical approach benefits from a lifetime's experience including a navigation profession in the merchant navy. You want to catch cod? – then read on.

John Wilson

Introduction

It was one of those all too infrequent windless days which boat anglers long for, the surface of the sea was mirror calm and the only sounds were those of the tide gently gurgling past the anchored hull. Hopes were high that day. The anglers knew they were fishing at the peak of the autumn cod run. They knew they were fishing with one of the most experienced charter skippers in the business. They knew they had the best bait for the job . . . they also knew they were going to catch cod. Yes, hopes and the anticipation of a cod thumping on the end of their lines were high that cold and frosty morning.

The sun had barely started its daily ascent above the horizon and was, as yet, still a bright red glow of promise in the eastern sky. Almost motionlessly, the group of anglers were either standing or sitting in the cockpit of the charter boat. The air temperature was still several degrees below freezing and with each exhaled breath, puffs of condensation rose above their heads in the still morning air, like billows of smoke from a factory chimney. Gradually the dawn progressed and the sun climbed steadily into the sky providing the first warmth of the day, which quickly melted the thin veil of frost and ice covering the decks and railings.

Occasionally one of the anglers stepped forward and picked up his rod to retrieve the terminal rig, rebait, then cast out. The general scene aboard was one of solitude, with just the continual and good-humoured banter between the anglers, accepted as part and parcel of a day's fishing. After a while the boat's skipper emerged from the warmth of his wheel-house carrying six steaming mugs of tea which were gratefully received, and, for a short while, managed to reduce the onboard humour to a minimum, each angler savouring the warming brew.

Suddenly one of the anglers leapt forward and snatched his rod out of its perch on the railings, and quickly started retrieving the bow of slack line which was hanging taut in the tide. Steadily the rod tip started to bend over as the tension caused by the grip lead holding fast on the seabed increased. Then, for a few moments, all went slack as the lead sprang free. Still the angler wound furiously, as yet not knowing if the fish was still there.

Then once again the rod started to bend and the angler's face erupted into a huge smile as he felt the fish thumping on the end of his line. Slowly he inched his prize out of the murky depths and back against the tide, towards the surface and the waiting landing-net. All eyes aboard strained at the water for that first glimpse of the first fish of the day.

First to show was the shockleader, indicating that the fish was just 20 feet below the surface hanging vertically beneath the boat, using all its power to break free. Then, all of a sudden, a huge white belly emerged out of the coloured water, and seconds later a cheer went up as the skipper lunged forward and netted

A 12lb cod in pristine condition.

the fish. With his prize now safely aboard, the angler held his fish high for all to admire, approximately 12 pounds of fighting fit cod in the absolute peak of condition. With fins erect and bristling in the bright morning sunshine, the fish was a pristine example of the most sought-after species of saltwater fish in the North Atlantic.

For me and thousands of other anglers the above scenario sums up the magic of cod fishing. The prospect of catching few other species of fish would drag grown men out of a warm bed, often many hours before dawn in the dark depths of winter, to face many hours on boat or beach; and often with only a minimal chance of success.

Yes, the cod is a true angler's fish, often plentiful, often caught in good numbers. The average size of cod compared with many other species is high, and when caught on balanced tackle cod fight well. What is more, the cod is an extremely attractive fish, it 'looks like a fish ought to look' and no more so than when taken fresh out of the sea. And, finally, few fish are quite as delicious as a freshly caught cod. What more could an angler ask from a fish?

For most of my life I have been a fisherman, and a high percentage of my fishing effort over the years has been concentrated on the pursuit of cod. I do not know how many cod I have caught. Certainly many thousands of fish, the biggest of which have topped 30 pounds. I have pursued cod from both beach and boat, and in almost all of those countries where the species is caught. I have personally caught cod by just about every recognized angling method in the sea, and, through the pages of this book, I hope to pass on some of the tips and knowledge that I have either been taught, or learnt for myself over the years.

1 The Life-Cycle of the Cod

LOCATING COD

The cod is one of the few species of fish which both shore and boat anglers based in the British Isles can fish for throughout a full twelve months of the year. The life-cycle of the cod is such that at some time or other there will be fish within the angler's range somewhere around the coast, because at different times of the year cod migrate to and from different areas. These migrations are governed by two factors: feeding and breeding.

Anglers today are lucky as these seasonal migrations of cod have been well researched and documented over the years, and those times of the year when fish are present in numbers at any given venue are generally well known. Given a minimum of research it should be possible for even the novice angler to determine more or less exactly when, where, and also how to catch cod. What is more, it is often possible to predict the size of those fish which are generally available.

Let me give you an example. I am based in south-east Wales and my local patch for catching cod is the coast of the Bristol Channel running from Swansea Bay in the west to the Severn Bridge in the east. I know that the first codling start to move into this area in September, occasionally late August. These first fish are invariably located by anglers fishing the upper reaches of the estuary

around Redwick and Goldcliff, and they are usually small fish weighing between 1 and 4 pounds.

As the season develops both the size and the

A typical early season codling, caught by an angler fishing the mud flats at Redwick in south Wales.

9

quantity of fish caught increase to the season's peak just before Christmas. By now fish are being caught throughout more or less the entire region, and the average size of fish caught will have risen by several pounds. Double-figure specimens are now common. The best of the fishing is generally over by the New Year, though this is often the time of year when the biggest fish of all are caught. By March locals fishing the area know the season is all but over, though cod are often caught right through the spring months. Such precise predictions are easily made by boat and shore anglers in most of the venues around the country where cod are caught.

If you are new to fishing any particular area and wish to catch cod, I suggest you start by contacting your local tackle shops. They should be able to tell you when, where and how to fish. They will also be able to point you in the direction of local sea angling clubs, which are always an excellent starting block for new anglers. The pages of specialist sea angling magazines such as *Sea Angler, Boat Angler* and *Improve Your Sea Angling* carry extensive news coverage of the best fish caught in different areas, and regularly feature profiles on the most productive venues.

DEPLETION OF STOCKS

It has never been easier to locate cod, which is just as well as the species is far less abundant today than it was even ten years ago. It is no great secret that cod are one of the most valuable fish in the North Atlantic, highly prized as a source of food. This has resulted in almost constant persecution on both sides of the Atlantic. Indeed, the value of cod is so high that countries have fought over fishing rights, as in the infamous 'Cod Wars' of the 1970s, a dispute between Britain and Iceland over who owned the fishing rights on certain grounds.

On the western side of the Atlantic this relentless persecution resulted in cod being fished almost to extinction, certainly to the point where they are now not considered as a commercially viable species. The once famous Grand Banks fishing grounds off Newfoundland are sadly all but devoid of cod today, a result of bad fisheries management and excessive commercial pressure. In the eastern Atlantic overall numbers of cod are also vastly reduced from what they once were, but thankfully there are still sufficient cod swimming in the seas of Northern Europe to satisfy the needs of most rod and line anglers.

Commercial fishing is controlled by a system of quotas which determine the total allowable catch, TAC, in different areas. In theory, when the numbers in any given area either fall or increase, the TAC is adjusted accordingly. Unfortunately, in recent years the method by which the data is used to calculate TACs has been found to be inaccurate. This was one of the primary factors which allowed the massive overfishing and consequent collapse of the Grand Banks fishery.

Despite all of our sophisticated technology and the attempts by some of the most eminent marine biologists in the business, we are still unable to calculate accurately just how many cod are present in any one area, and probably never will be able to. The simple fact remains that anglers and commercial fishermen who have been around for a few years all report the same story, a reduction in catches. Ultimately this cannot be allowed to continue.

Obviously, commercial fishermen are mostly to blame for this decline. A large modern trawler can probably wipe out in one sweep more cod than all of the rod and line anglers fishing the same area could in an entire year. However, anglers cannot allow themselves to be totally exonerated from blame. In certain areas anglers' rod and line fishing regularly account for enormous catches of cod per

A trawler sets off for a day's fishing. Commercial fishing has drastically reduced the number of cod swimming in the sea.

day, catches of fish which are measured in thousands of pounds and often including fish which are in peak breeding condition, and stuffed full of roe. Some of these anglers then openly sell their catch on the open fish market.

Quite simply, anglers must be educated into taking only those fish which they realistically need for the table. And, as soon as they start selling fish, they should expect to be counted alongside the ranks of commercial fishermen. Indeed, on several occasions in the 1980s this was the case. The fisheries authorities imposed a total ban on landing cod, a ban which included rod and line caught fish. Not surprisingly, many anglers protested, but what defence have they to offer when shown pictures of thousand of pounds of cod caught on rod and line and sold?

LIFE-CYCLE

Thankfully the cod is a fast-growing species of fish, with a very high reproduction rate. Over the years numbers of fish in different areas have peaked and fallen, marking either the success or failure of a past year's spawning. A female cod produces somewhere in the region of eight million eggs, only a tiny fraction of which survive. It only takes a minute difference in the survival rate of a year's spawning to make an enormous difference in the resulting numbers of fish. It is almost always the case that a lean year or two cod fishing in one area will be followed by several years when fish are abundant, and vice versa.

Around the UK most inshore migrations of cod are associated with feeding, as the fish

11

A year or two when fish are scarce in any one area will often be followed by a few seasons when fish are abundant.

move into inshore waters to pack on weight prior to spawning, which usually occurs during the first couple of months of the year. This is partly the reason why the largest fish of the year are often caught right at the back end of the season, i.e. just prior to the fish migrating back offshore into deeper water to breed. Naturally, therefore, conservation-minded anglers should consider returning these heavily pregnant fish, which in any case generally make poor eating when compared with smaller specimens.

Following spawning, the fish often return to inshore waters, once again driven by the urge to feed and recover body weight lost during the rigours of spawning. This is the reason why many areas receive two distinct runs of fish, with a short gap of a month or two in between. Cod caught immediately after spawning are generally in a very lean condition and almost worthless as a table fish. It makes sense to return fish which are obviously in a post-spawning condition.

When cod are one year old they are about six inches long, and feed heavily on small fish and shrimps and just about anything else which is edible. These small immature fish are often caught in large numbers by anglers, who should treat them with great care and return them unharmed as soon as possible. By the end of their second year these fish will have packed on a lot of weight. Now they will measure up to 16 inches, with an average weight of about 1½ pounds. The legal size limit for taking codling in the UK is 14 inches.

At about three years old codling weigh

A plump 4½lb codling. This fish would be about three years old.

between 4 and 6 pounds, at which age about 25 per cent of fish reach spawning maturity. By the time these young fish are four years old the biggest fish will weigh over 10 pounds, and somewhere in the region of 60 to 70 per cent of fish are mature. It is worth noting at this stage that anglers in most areas class fish of less than 5–7 pounds in weight as codling, and bigger fish as cod.

Sadly, very few cod live to five years old, another reflection on the near constant and heavy commercial pressure which the fish are exposed to throughout their lives. Five-year-old cod average around fifteen pounds in weight. From now on, cod add approximately four pounds of body weight per year, a factor which depends very much on the availability of food, which itself is generally a reflection on where the fish live. Fish in the North Sea and Irish Sea are slow growing when compared with those fish which live in the western approaches to the English Channel, though in this instance these slower-growing fish tend to be more prolific.

2 Natural Food and Baits

The cod is both predator and scrounger. Throughout its life-cycle the average cod will feed on a wide selection of different types of natural food, ranging from live fish such as sand-eels, sprats, herring, whiting and pouting, to mopping up huge quantities of shellfish and marine worms following gales. Crabs make up a major part of the diet of inshore cod; indeed it is unusual to gut a cod caught from any inshore mark which does not have the remains of a few hard-back crabs in its stomach. Prawns and shrimps are another major food source, especially in those areas where these are abundant.

When targeting cod, or any species of fish for that matter, the angler's primary objective should be to try to use whichever bait most closely resembles the food the fish are feeding on at the time. In other words, the angler should strive to 'match the hatch'. That said, I doubt whether any hungry cod would swim past any suitable offering; it's simply a case that success will be far more consistent when the angler is using a bait which the fish are actively searching for.

In clear water, cod feed primarily by sight, and this is when the use of artificial lures can be productive. In the coloured water typical of many inshore marks, cod tend to rely more on their incredibly keen sense of smell to locate their food. Throughout the winter months in places like the Thames Estuary and Bristol Channel, the water is often so heavily coloured that visibility is more or less nil. Obviously when faced with such conditions, the angler can only expect to catch cod if his bait is emitting a strong and attractive scent trail.

Like most species of fish, cod use their lateral line to help detect prey. The lateral line picks up tiny vibrations given off by fish etc. swimming through the water. A fish in distress, easy prey, will send out a very strong signal which the cod will detect and then home in on. Thus the use of livebaits, which will be discussed in more detail later, can be deadly, particularly for the larger fish.

Whenever an angler is using a natural bait for cod he should constantly ensure that it is as fresh as possible. The vital fish-attracting juices are very quickly washed out in the tide, especially when the tide is running fast, which will often be the case when fishing for cod. No natural bait, with the single exception of a live-bait, should be left unchecked for more than 20 minutes. When fishing in a very fast run of tide I always try to reel in and freshen up my baits at least once every quarter of an hour, especially when I am using baits which quickly become washed out, such as blow lugworm and mussel.

On retrieving a bait it might well look untouched and attractive to the human eye, but I can assure you it will make a vastly inferior bait to a fresh one, certainly as far as the cod are concerned. To highlight the importance of bait quality, allow me to offer an example.

A group of anglers are fishing for cod aboard a charter boat. Eventually and perhaps following an hour or two of inactivity, one of the group gets a bite and lands a nice fish. He unhooks his cod, rebaits and casts back out. The other anglers have sat intently watching their rod tips for any sign of a bite, scared to reel in and change their bait just in case they miss a shoal of fish passing through. In the meantime, the angler who caught the first fish catches another. The others are now even less inclined to reel in, often calling the succesful angler lucky, especially when he rebaits, casts out and takes a third fish!

I regularly witness the above scenario on charter boats, and often the successful angler doesn't know himself why he is the only one catching fish. The answer is really very simple: he is the only angler whose bait is emitting an effective scent trail which, naturally, any feeding fish in the area are going to locate and home in on first.

There is no getting away from the fact that bait is expensive, that is for the vast majority of anglers who are not fortunate enough to live near the sea and who are unable to collect their own. Supplying sufficient bait to fish effectively throughout the full duration of a typical ten-hour charter boat trip is certainly not cheap. However, the level of fishing will invariably fluctuate throughout the tidal cycle, with the cod only feeding strongly at certain times of the day and states of tide. When bait is scarce it makes sense to concentrate what bait you do have over the most productive times of the trip.

You can, of course, still fish at other times, by using a cheaper bait such as squid, fish or a livebait, instead of costly worms or peeler crabs. Any good charter boat skipper should be able to anticipate when the fish are most likely to feed. If the fish start to feed outside these anticipated times, you can always reel in and change your bait.

The exact times when cod feed vary considerably in different areas; indeed, there is often considerable variation on different marks within the same area. The ebb tide might be most productive in one spot, the flood tide on another perhaps just half a mile away. In my experience I have found that any distinct change in the run of tide affects how the fish feed, for example, when the ebb tide starts to ease towards low-water slack, or the first run of a flooding tide following low water. Local knowledge is essential and should always be sought whenever possible.

LUGWORM

Lugworm are probably the most consistent and widely used natural bait around the country, for cod. There are, in fact, two different species of lugworm, the common blow lug and the larger black lug. Black lug, 'blacks' as anglers usually call them, are by far the better bait, being larger, tougher and often more attractive to the fish than blow lug.

Blow Lugworm

Blow lug can be dug from many beaches and estuaries around the country. Their location in the sand or mud is given away by their classic coil on the surface and their blow-hole, which marks the location of the worm's U-shaped burrow. The worms are easily dug using either a fork or a spade, depending on the consistency of the ground they are living in. If the worms are living in hard sand then a fork is usually the best tool, while a spade is often preferable when digging worms living in wet sand or mud. The best type of fork to dig worms with is a potato fork with four flat tines.

Prime cod baits: blow lug left, black lug right.

Blow lug cast and blow hole marking precise position of the worm's U-shaped burrow.

Digging worms is easy enough when a colony has been located, but there is a certain technique which the angler will have to master before he will be successful. Usually it takes three or four digging sessions before any bait digger starts to acquire the necessary 'knack'.

It is easiest to dig worms where there are a lot of worms living in a relatively small area. When this is the case the angler can dig a trench through the area where the greatest concentration of casts are showing, picking out worms as they are uncovered. This technique can be adopted using either the fork or a spade. It is important to pile up the sand excavated out of the trench in such a way that it forms a dam, directing any surface water away from the trench. This will help prevent the trench from filling up with water.

When an area is more sparsely populated with worms they will have to be dug singly. The actual depth that the worms lie in the sand varies according to temperature and the consistency of the beach, but in general they will be lying between 1½ and 2 spitfuls deep. The head of the worm lies facing the blow-hole, and tail towards the cast. Start by drawing an imaginary line between the blow-hole and the cast, then place the fork at 90 degrees to this line, in a position approximately midway between the hole and the cast, and facing the hole. Remove just half a spitful of sand. Now move the fork back to a position just behind the cast and carefully remove a full spitful. Often the worm will be uncovered at this stage; if not you should find it when you remove a second spitful from the same position. Always dig slowly as you will risk breaking the worm if you dig too quickly.

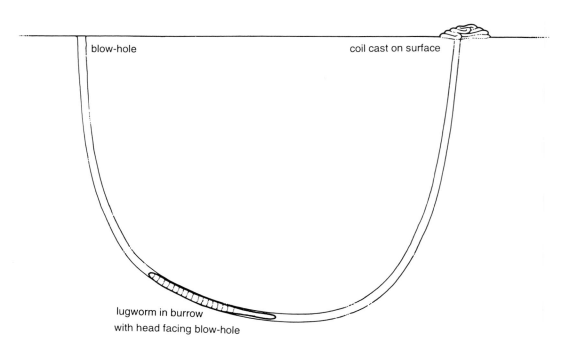

blow-hole

coil cast on surface

lugworm in burrow
with head facing blow-hole

A cross-section of a beach showing a lugworm in burrow.

Selection of live baits kept in good condition in an old domestic fridge.

The technique I use with a spade is similar, though I rarely use a spade now as I find a good fork sufficient at over 90 per cent of the venues where I dig lug. A spade is, however, very useful when trenching worms in very soft mud and sand or when digging individual worms which are not lying too deep.

It is essential that blow lug are kept cool and moist because they die off very quickly if they are exposed to direct sunlight or allowed to 'stew' in their own juices in a plastic container, especially on a warm day. Always separate broken worms from healthy worms. Broken and bleeding worms are all right to keep if they are going to be used for bait more or less immediately, but they will very quickly kill off healthy worms if they are stored in the same container.

As soon as possible, wash the worms off in cool clean sea water, never fresh water as this will kill the worms. I store my worms in an old fridge set at around 4°C, lying in flat trays lined with newspaper. It is important to check the worms regularly and remove any which are dead or dying. Change the sea water on at least a daily basis, using replacement sea water at the same temperature.

When I am going fishing I wrap the worms in clean dry newspaper, and usually carry them in a freezer box along with several frozen gel packs to help keep the worms as cool as possible. It is best when carrying a large quantity of worms to wrap them in several small-sized packs, rather than bunch the whole lot together in one. By this method, it is possible to remove packs of worms as and

19

Top-quality freshly dug blow lug.

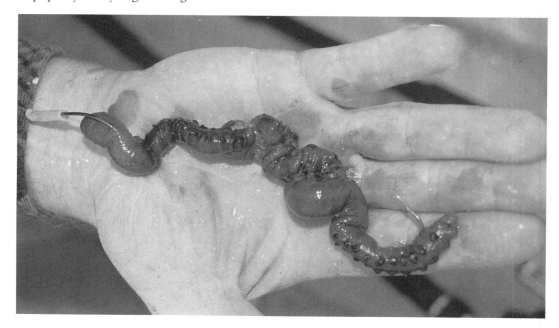

Blow lug correctly mounted onto a pennel rig.

when they are required, which will help to keep the remaining worms in the very best possible condition, especially when fishing in hot weather or when it is raining.

Blow lug are at their best when used within three days of digging, but they are most efficient when used the same day that they are dug. Occasionally it is possible to dig blow lug which are almost as tough as the larger blacks, but in general blow lugworms are little more than bags of water, which very quickly lose their juices and subsequently their attraction to fish.

Black Lugworm

Good-quality fresh black lug are without question my own favourite bait for cod. Over the years I have used blacks on hundreds of occasions, so much so that I am much more confident when using black lug than when using any other bait. Up until very recently it was argued that black and blow lug were actually two of a kind, the same species which simply displayed different characteristics according to location and age. Anglers knew different, and today the scientists finally agree that the species are totally individual. The black lugworm is the undisputed king of the lugworm, certainly as far as cod are concerned.

Blacks are not as generally available as blow lug. They tend to populate the extreme low-water marks on those beaches where they are found, and as a result it is only possible to collect them over the low-water period on spring tides. They live at a much greater depth in the beach, and their casts are not as distinct as those made by the blow lug. The cast of the black lug, despite being a much larger worm, is much smaller and tends to consist of a small and often almost perfectly formed 'catherine wheel' coil of sand, about the size of a 2p coin. There is a small blow-

hole, but rarely is this visible until you start to excavate the worm.

There are two ways of extracting black lug from their deep and near-vertical burrows, which often extend as much as three feet down into the sand. The first method is digging, which is extremely arduous and messy work. The second is to use a bait pump to literally 'suck' the worm up out of the sand.

A trenching spade is the best type of spade to dig black lug with. The technique is to dig down the burrow until the tail of the worm is located, by removing horizontal slices off the surface of the sand. The first slice is taken below the cast, which should expose the actual burrow leading down through the sand. The angler now removes successive slices until he exposes the tail of the worm. Next he has to reach down, grab the worm by the tail, then carefully manipulate it free, taking great care not to snap it in the process.

A few years ago bait pumps started to appear in British tackle shops. At first many anglers tried to use pumps for collecting blow lug, and soon discovered that they were next to useless, due to the fact that the blow lugworm lives in a U-shaped burrow. Then a few anglers attempted to pump black lug, and once the basic technique had been mastered it was found that they were ideal for the purpose. Today there are several pumps available on the market; the Australian-made Alvey pump, marketed in the UK by Leeda, is by far the best that I have used.

The pump is used to suck out cylindrical columns of sand, starting at the cast on the surface and following the burrow down to the worm. It is important to remember that great success with a bait pump does not come instantly, and the angler should be prepared to persevere with mediocre results for his first couple of attempts. However, when the technique has been mastered, the results will pay very quickly for the initial outlay on the pump.

Pumping black lug using the excellent stainless steel Alvey bait pump.

Black lug are a lot easier to keep than blow lug. Kept in flat trays and covered with clean sea water or laid out on clean newspaper, 'blacks' are easily kept for well over a week. Some anglers 'gut' their blacks by gently squeezing them as soon as they can. If I intend using the worms within a day or so I try to keep the worms intact, thus retaining as many valuable fish-attracting juices as possible. If I anticipate that I will not be using the worms for a while, I gut them.

Black lug also keep well when salted and stored in a freezer, unlike blow lug. To salt blacks, they should first be gutted and left to lie on clean dry newspaper or kitchen roll until most of the excess blood and moisture has been absorbed. Next, straighten the worms out on a second piece of paper and lightly sprinkle them with salt. After about an hour replace the paper again and give the worms a second application of salt. Finally, roll the worms within a coil of clean newspaper, making sure that individual worms do not come into contact with each other. I have kept blacks lug preserved in this way for many months in my freezer.

Whenever I fish for cod using frozen black lug I do so with total confidence. I always try to ensure that I have an ample supply of frozen blacks in my freezer by the start of each cod season, so I have a ready supply of bait from which to draw, allowing me to fish at short notice. More often than not I fish frozen blacks as part of a cocktail bait in conjunction with another bait such as squid, razorfish or blow lug. Frozen correctly, blacks really do make a very durable and effective cod bait.

RAGWORM

There are several species of ragworm used by anglers in the UK, but it is really only the large red or king ragworm, and the smaller white rag which are worth using for cod. I know you can catch cod on harbour rag, I have done so myself, but it's just that this species of worm tends to be too small to be of any real use to the serious cod angler.

Ragworm can be dug from the inter-tidal zone on many beaches. They favour a mix of mud and sand, especially where there is a high consistency of shell grit and gravel. Due to the rocky nature of the ground where rag are normally found, a fork with pointed tines tends to be the best tool to use to dig them with. Ragworm do not throw out a cast like lugworm, but a small pin prick of a blow-hole can often be seen on the surface, indicating the entrance to the burrow. Digging a trench

Digging king ragworm.

Top-quality fresh king ragworm.

through an area known to be populated by ragworm is the usual method of digging for them.

Ragworm are a much hardier species of worm than either of the lugworm species, and with a minimum of care they can be kept in a usable condition for up to a fortnight, or longer if they are kept in an aquarium. As with lugworm, it is essential that ragworms are kept cool and moist once they have been dug. For short-term stowage I do not keep ragworm in sea water. A light layer of the sand or mud from which they have been dug and then a top layer of cool moist seaweed, will keep the worms in perfect condition for several days. Kept in this way or wrapped in newspaper soaked in sea water, ragworm will keep for up

to two weeks in a fridge set at about 4°C. It is important to check the worms daily and change the sand or newspaper in which they are kept.

It is also very important that too many ragworm are not crowded together in one container. Ragworm are equipped with a vicious set of pincers mounted at the head which they will use to attack each other and inflict nasty open wounds, or even cut other worms in half. Once a worm has been cut it quickly becomes infected and starts to die. Damaged and sick-looking worms should always be kept separate from the remaining healthy stock.

For longer-term stowage, provided that the worms are in the very best of health when you obtain them, ragworm can be very successfully kept for much longer periods in an aquarium. To tank ragworm you will need either a glass fish tank or a sizeable plastic fish box, filled with very clean sea water. Put about three inches of clean coral sand in the bottom of the tank, into which the worms can burrow. It is important to aerate and filter the water continually, and if it can be chilled to around 4 or 5°C then so much the better.

Once again, it is very important not to cram too many worms into one tank, to prevent them from attacking and damaging themselves. The sea water should be completely changed at least once a week, more frequently where possible. Any worms which look in less than perfect health should be removed immediately, or they will very quickly contaminate and kill the rest of your stock.

There has been a lot of debate among anglers regarding the effectiveness of tanked worms, sceptics saying that the worms lose a lot of their fish-attracting juices during the tanking process. I suppose that to a point this must be the case, ragworm certainly shrink when tanked, but I have personally caught plenty of cod on worms that I have kept in tanks for several weeks. That said, given the choice between freshly dug and tanked worms, I would personally opt for the freshest bait available every time, regardless of what type of bait.

A few years ago Sea Bait, a firm based in the north-east of England, started offering farmed ragworms for sale through tackle shops. Over the years I have used Sea Bait farmed ragworms on many occasions, having been

Sea Bait farmed king rag, a very effective cod bait.

sent the worms specifically to evaluate their effectiveness. In all honesty I have nothing but praise for the quality of Sea Bait ragworm and, yes, I have caught plenty of cod, including fish weighing well into double figures, when using them. One of Sea Bait's biggest selling points is that their worms are always of a consistent size and a very high standard. Provided the angler takes suitable care of the worms after he has bought them, they keep equally as well as wild worms.

PEELER CRAB

Peeler crab is one of my favourite baits for cod. Just about every cod I have caught from inshore marks, that is marks within three miles

of the coastline, has had crabs in its stomach. Peeler crab is an especially good bait to use over rough ground marks; after all, crabs are probably exactly what foraging cod are looking for over rough ground. There are three different types of crab which are of interest to the cod angler when they are in the peeling stage: the common or green shore crab, which is abundant more or less everywhere, and the larger edible crabs and velvet swimming crabs, which are generally only found near the low water mark on open coastlines.

So what is a peeler crab? Crabs are classified as crustaceans with an exoskeleton. In other words, it is the crab's hard outer shell which both supports and protects the delicate internal body organs. In order to grow, crabs first develop a new shell beneath the existing

Peeler crab in the peak of condition for use as bait.

one. This takes place once or twice a year, depending on the weather.

At first the new shell resembles little more than a very thin membrane, but gradually it develops until the crab has formed a complete new shell beneath its hard outer shell. The outer shell then becomes weak and brittle as a result of the crab extracting calcium from it, which is then used to help develop and strengthen the new shell. When the new shell is completed the crab is ready to lose its old shell. At this stage the crab is known as a peeler, and is extremely vulnerable to predators. Prior to peeling, the crab crawls away into a safe area, usually beneath a rock or deep amongst the fronds of kelp and seaweed, and starts to shed its old shell. At this stage the crab draws water into its body, causing it to swell, and this splits the already weakened outer shell. At this stage the crab is in prime condition for use as bait.

Gradually the crab works its way out of the old shell, and is left as a soft jelly-like blob. There is a certain degree of speculation which suggests that during the peeling process the crab emits a strong scent and body juices which are attractive to feeding fish. Many species of fish find peelers irresistible and whether this is due to the crab sending out attractive juices, or simply because they are easier to eat when soft matters little to the angler. The simple fact remains that peeler crabs are a very effective bait, and obtaining a supply of them is well worth the effort and cost. The soft shell gradually hardens off, over a period of up to five days.

Peeler crabs can be distinguished from hard backs (crabs which are not ready to peel) very easily. The simplest way for the novice to identify them is by gently twisting the last segment of one of the crab's legs. If the crab is a peeler the outer casing of the leg segment will fall easily away, revealing a perfectly formed new leg beneath. If it is not, then a white sinewy strand will be revealed, and the crab should be carefully returned.

Common or Green Shore Crabs

As has been mentioned above, common or green shore crabs can be found on almost every shore. They tend to be particularly prolific around areas of rock, in deep gullies, beneath patches of sea weed, around the base of breakwaters, piers and groynes, and in estuaries.

The first shore crabs start to peel in large numbers as soon as there is an appreciable rise in sea and land temperatures, usually around late April and early May. This first peel, or moult as it is often known, is sometimes followed by a second peel in late August or September. However, in many areas crabs can be found in the peeling stage throughout the summer months. In the extreme south-west of the country peeler crabs can often be found throughout the winter, especially within the tidal rivers of the Teign and Exe in south Devon.

Any crab which is being held beneath another crab will almost always be either a peeler or a softie, a crab which has already peeled. The carrying crab will be holding on to the peeler waiting for it to shed its shell in order to mate with it. As the peeling stage advances the shell starts to crack along the seams at either side. With practice, many anglers can identify a peeler just from the colour and texture of its shell.

Common shore crabs can be kept for a very long time, with a minimum of effort. I have kept large quantities of peelers for up to a month, with a minimum of losses. Keeping shore crabs in the peeling stage is easy: by storing them in an old domestic fridge, set at around 5°C, the crabs will remain cool, which retards the peeling process. I keep my crabs in plastic containers deep enough to prevent the crabs from escaping. Common shore crabs should be kept by keeping them covered in moist fresh seaweed, or newspaper dampened with sea water. It is important to ensure that the crabs' gills do not dry out, as if this happens they will very quickly die. To prevent this, give the crabs a daily drink of sea water, chilled to the same temperature as the crabs. All they need is a swift dunk in and out of the sea water; any longer and they will start drawing in water in order to continue the peeling process.

The crabs should be checked daily and any dead crabs removed. Eventually the urge to peel becomes too much for the crab and it literally starts to force its way out of the shell. The angler will now have to use that crab for bait within a day or so, or freeze it for future use. To freeze crabs, many anglers simply wrap them in cling film and place them in a freezer. Crabs frozen this way do work as bait, but I have found that they are vastly inferior to crabs which have been frozen correctly.

It is important that only healthy crabs are frozen for future use, as dead or dying crabs will be next to useless when they are eventually thawed out. To freeze a crab, first peel the crab completely, removing as many pieces of shell as you can, along with the gills or 'dead man's fingers', which are located on either side of the crab. Personally I discard the legs. These are too small to be of use to the cod angler, but worth keeping if fishing for smaller species such as flatfish. Next, gently run the crab under a cold water tap and dab it dry on a piece of kitchen roll; then place it on a metal tray in the freezing in compartment. Placing the crab on a metal tray speeds up the freezing

Peeler crab correctly mounted onto a hook. Note that the point of the hook is well exposed.

Small codling caught on peeler crab.

process. Frozen crabs are best used within six months, but I have caught cod on frozen crab up to a year old.

Edible and Velvet Swimming Crabs

The peeling biology of these two species of crabs is identical to the common green shore crab, but both generally peel only once a year, between the end of May and August.

Collecting both edible and velvet swimming crabs is usually much more difficult than common shore crabs. Both species are only located on or very near the low-water mark on the open foreshore. They do not show the

same tolerance towards brackish and coloured water as the shore crab. The sort of areas to look are along exposed rock headlands and foreshores, areas where there are vast expanses of rock intersected by deep gullies and crevices. Rock pools are excellent places to look. Gently lift any slabs of rock lying in the pool, and the crabs will be found lying beneath.

Both species often hide deep among the cracks and crevices within the bed rock, and extricating them is not easy. Many anglers make themselves a 'crab hook' by putting a 90-degree bend into the end of a narrow steel rod about 3ft long. The rod is then attached to half of an old broom handle using jubilee clips. To use the crab hook, gently manipulate it into the crack or hole; if a crab is hiding there you will clearly be able to feel it, and hear its claws grating against the hook. Very carefully use the hook to manoeuvre the crab to within your reach.

It should be noted that there is a minimum size for taking edible crabs. This varies from area to area, but is generally in the region of 4 inches. Several anglers have been fined for taking quantities of undersized crabs.

Keeping edible and velvet swimming crabs in the long term – for more than a day or so – is a lot more involved than keeping shore crabs. If you intend using the crab for bait within 24 hours then simply keeping it cool and moist will be adequate. For long periods, you will need to set up an aquarium fitted with both an aerator and a filter. If the crabs are to be held at the peeling stage, you will need a cooler as well. I have mounted a plastic central heating tank into an old domestic fridge. A small airpump and filter are placed in the tank, which is filled with very clean sea water. The tank is chilled to about 5°C, and I have successfully kept both edible and velvet crabs by using this set-up for several weeks.

Both of these species make excellent frozen baits; indeed, they are often far superior to common shore crabs for cod. They should be frozen in exactly the same way as detailed for shore crabs. I always try to ensure I have an adequate supply of frozen crab in my freezer prior to every cod season. Not only is frozen crab efficient at catching cod, it is ideal for those short-notice trips when conditions fall just right, when for whatever reason no other baits are obtainable.

FISH

Fish form a large part of the diet of cod, especially the likes of sprats, herring, pouting, poor

cod, sand-eels and whiting. In general, many anglers do not use cuts of fish specifically for cod, but many cod, often good ones, are caught each year by anglers fishing for other species. My own personal-best cod from south Wales, a fish of 21lb, came on a chunk of frozen mackerel. But I have to be honest here and admit that at the time I was actually fishing for rays!

I feel sure that if more anglers were to experiment with using fish baits during the cod season, and tried them alongside the more usual black lug and squid baits, then a lot more cod would be caught on fish. The baits which would be worth trying include mackerel or herring head and guts; indeed, a sizeable chunk from more or less any species of fish would be worth trying.

Cuts of fish are also useful for boosting the attraction of artificial lures. I have enjoyed great success with cod when using pirks, muppets and feathers, tipped with a long thin fillet of fish, usually mackerel. The addition of a strip of bait undoubtedly helps to boost and enhance the overall attraction of the lure, especially when the fish are in a finicky mood.

Livebaits

Livebaits are a different matter altogether. For many years anglers have known that a livebait is a deadly bait for cod. Why is it, then, that so few anglers use this very effective and cheap bait? My own favourite livebaits for cod include whiting, pouting and poor cod, but this is more of a reflection on the species of bait fish obtainable in the Bristol Channel during the cod season.

As will be seen later, cod are prolific at different times of the year in different areas, and whichever species are available in those areas – perhaps mackerel, herring or sand-eels – would be worth trying. I know several anglers

Luke Lewis, the author's son, holds a poor cod. These make excellent livebaits for large cod.

who fish the famous Eddystone Reef off Plymouth specifically for cod, using live sand-eels, and they catch a lot of fish. There is certainly plenty of room for experimentation as far as livebaits and cod are concerned.

It is a good idea to fish for livebaits using small bits of fish mounted on fine-wired hooks; then slowly retrieve the bait fish to the surface and very carefully unhook it. This will help ensure that it remains alive and active for as long as possible. Fishing a livebait from a boat is easy. The bait fish is either lip hooked or bridle rigged (tie the fish to the bend of the hook by threading a small loop of line through its lips, and lower gently to the seabed). Presenting a livebait at range from the shore is a totally different matter. The answer is to use a self-hooking livebait rig, which is described in the chapter on shore fishing.

SQUID AND CUTTLEFISH

Squid

Wherever cod are caught on natural baits,

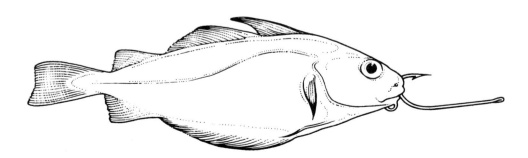

A simple way of attaching a live pouting to the hook. Live bait consistently attract the very biggest cod.

squid are invariably one of the most popular choices with many anglers. The most commonly used type of squid is the frozen Calamari squid, imported from California. These are generally available in boxes weighing either 1lb or 5lb, and from most tackle shops or fishmongers. They are an extremely cheap bait to buy, when compared with, say, worms.

I tend to stock my freezer periodically with a couple of dozen 1lb packs, which I buy from the local fishmongers. The price per pound is slightly less when buying the larger 5lb packs, but I find the smaller boxes are far more convenient. For cod fishing I invariably take four or five individual boxes, which I keep frozen in a coolbox. I can then thaw packs out one at a time as I need them, so reducing waste.

Once defrosted, squid should not be refrozen and used at a later date. Squid are at their best when they are snow white in colour; baits which have not been correctly frozen or refrozen turn pink and make vastly inferior baits. It is worth noting that the best baits are those which have been allowed to defrost naturally. Many anglers defrost their squid quickly by soaking them in a bucket of sea water, but for whatever reason these are often not as effective as those which have been defrosted slowly; perhaps squid lose a lot of their juices when defrosted quickly?

Calamari squid range in size from about three to six inches. They can either be used whole, when targetting big cod, or cut into slices and used to boost the attraction of other baits.

A one-pound box of Californian calamari squid.

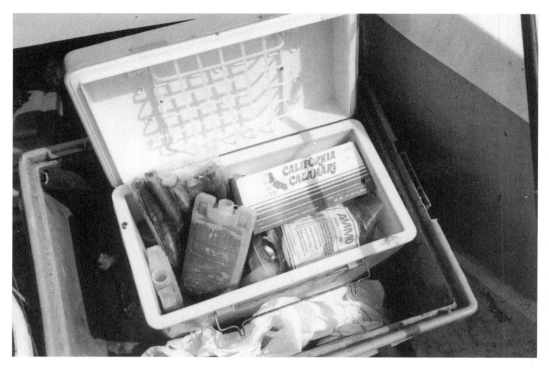

Boxes of frozen squid and other baits stored in a cooler box.

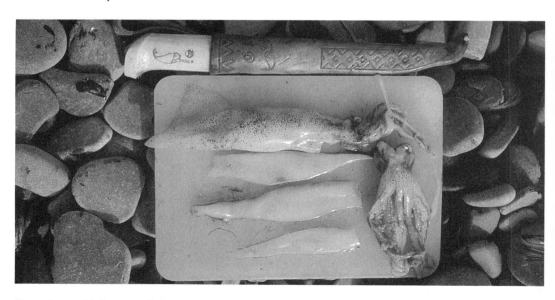

Preparing squid for use as bait.

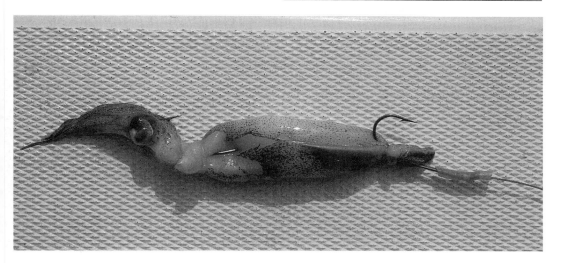

Whole squid mounted onto a pennel rig. This is one of the top baits for large cod.

Lugworm or ragworm tipped with a strip of squid can be a particularly effective cocktail bait to use in coloured water. The squid serves three very important functions: firstly, it adds extra scent to the bait; secondly, the white strips of squid add a degree of visual attraction, which undoubtedly helps fish to locate the bait in coloured water; lastly, a strip of squid helps to keep the hook points clear and exposed, preventing the main body of the bait moving during casting and possibly masking the hook points. A lot of fish are lost each year due to hook points ending up buried in a blob of bait. When casting baits, a light lashing of fine knitting elastic helps to keep the squid on the hook and in the correct place.

On occasion, it is possible to catch various species of squid in European waters, usually by accident when using mackerel feathers or pirks. Large squid are also available at fishmongers. If you do manage to catch a large quantity of squid these will make equally effective baits for cod, provided they are frozen as soon as possible. However, fresh squid available through fishmongers tend to

Black lug and squid cocktail, a classic cod bait.

33

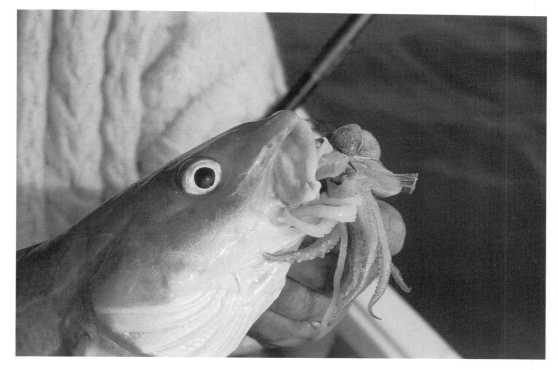

A codling caught on squid.

be considerably more expensive than frozen Calamari squid, and certainly, in my experience, not worth the additional expense.

Cuttlefish

Cuttlefish are equally effective for cod as squid, some anglers claim more so. Along the south coast of England cuttlefish are a frequent by-catch in nets, and with little if any commercial value they are readily available directly off the boat in many fishing ports, either free of charge or for the cost of a few pints. Wherever possible, obtaining a supply of cuttle for freezing and use as bait at a later date is advisable.

There is one other point worth noting about cuttlefish. Most anglers will be familiar with the animal's hard white backbone, which is often found washed up on beaches. Whenever cutting cuttlefish up for use as bait, great care should be exercised to prevent the filleting knife from slipping on the bone and cutting your fingers. I am talking from hard-earned experience here!

SHELLFISH

There are many different types of shellfish available in Northern European waters, and as far as I know they can all be used with varying degrees of success for cod. A few types of shell-fish can be bought through tackle shops or fishmongers; others the angler will have to collect for himself. By and large, most types of shellfish make better baits when used as fresh as possible. The only exception is razorfish, which do remain an effective bait when frozen correctly.

Mussels

Mussels are readily available in many areas, and a very popular bait with many cod anglers. Mussels can be picked in large quantities from the inter-tidal zone, especially in the vicinity of rocks, around the base of harbour walls, pier supports and groynes on beaches. The trick is in locating a patch of large mussels; avoid the more prolific seed and middle-sized mussels, which are of negligible use to the cod angler.

Probably the hardest part of using mussels for bait is extracting the soft meat from the tightly sealed shell. Once again, it is all too easy to slip with a razor-sharp filleting knife and cut yourself. The answer is to make yourself a 'mussel knife'. A small potato-peeling knife is ideal; simply blunten the blade by running it across a hard stone a few times and you will have the perfect tool for de-shelling mussels.

The actual mussel meat is very soft, and great care has to be taken not to damage it when both extracting it from the shell, and mounting it on to the hook. The correct way to mount mussel meat on to a hook is by gently threading the mussel on to the bend of the hook, starting off by passing the point of the hook through the toughest part of the mussel, the beard. The mussel must now be gently lashed into place using knitting elastic.

An alternative which some anglers have adopted is to make a mussel sausage! A mussel sausage is formed by filling a light mesh tube (used as a finger dressing in hospitals) with shelled mussels, then cutting it into suitable lengths and mounting it on to the hook.

I have found that the best mussels of all to

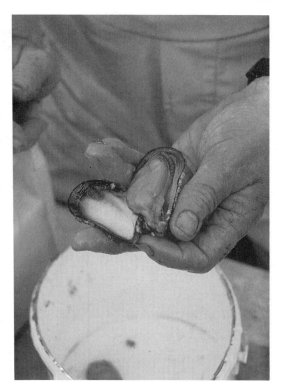

Removing a live mussel from its shell to use as bait.

use as bait are those which are farmed commercially for human consumption. These are often sold alive in fishmongers, and are very cheap to buy when compared to other baits. I have also seen some very large 'green lipped' mussels from New Zealand in supermarkets, which look as if they would make excellent baits.

Razorfish

After mussels, razorfish are the next most useful shellfish for cod bait. Razorfish are located at the extreme low-water mark on open sandy beaches. It is only possible to get

String of lugworm tipped with mussel, a very effective cod bait.

at them for a short period, over low water on the largest spring tides.

Razorfish live in a near-vertical burrow in the sand, generally about 3ft deep. There are several ways of extracting them from these burrows, including digging them in the same way you would black lug, by using a bait pump, or making a purpose-made spear which you prod down the burrow, hook the razorfish and drag it out. All of these methods do work – I have personally tried them all at one time or another – but salting is by far the easiest and most efficient method of obtaining a large supply of razorfish for use as bait.

The razorfish burrow is found by locating the small entrance, or keyhole, on the surface. Occasionally these will be clearly visible, at other times they can be located by a telltale squirt of water which the razorfish ejects out of the burrow from time to time. The 'razorfish shuffle' is by far the best way to locate the razorfish burrows. This involves the angler

Razorfish are often very effective following a spell of rough weather, when many razorfish are ripped out of the sanctuary of their burrows.

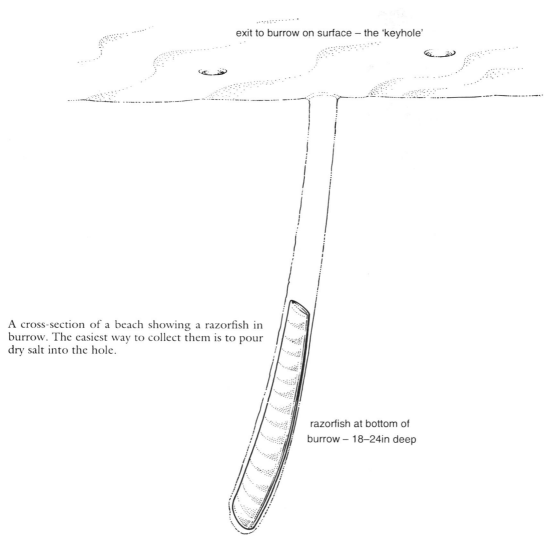

exit to burrow on surface – the 'keyhole'

A cross-section of a beach showing a razorfish in burrow. The easiest way to collect them is to pour dry salt into the hole.

razorfish at bottom of
burrow – 18–24in deep

shuffling backwards across the beach, following a line parallel to the water's edge. As he passes over the top of a burrow the razorfish will eject a squirt of water or simply flood the burrow with water. The angler then either squirts a highly saline solution down the burrow using an old washing-up liquid bottle, or simply pours a thimbleful of dry table or cooking salt into the entrance of the burrow. After salting perhaps two or three dozen burrows, he walks back and starts collecting the razorfish. Many will have completely evacuated their burrows and will be lying flat on the sand, others will be protruding about two or three inches out of the burrow. I regularly manage to collect upwards of 300 razorfish in

A 'salted' razorfish emerges from its burrow.

less than 1½ hours using the dry salt method.

Razorfish can be kept alive for up to a week by keeping them cool and moist and providing them with a twice daily drink of sea water. Alternatively, they can be kept in an aquarium for much longer periods. Whenever they are available alive, razorfish make an excellent bait for cod, but they also remain very effective when frozen. I freeze razorfish in packs of five, by simply placing them into the freezer as soon as possible. Other anglers go to the trouble of shelling the razorfish first, although I see little advantage in this extra effort.

The trick when using frozen razorfish is to ensure that the meat is fully thawed out before you attempt to mount it on to the hook. If the white meat is still partially frozen it will split and crack when you try to bend it and manipulate it on to the hook, making it very difficult to secure.

Razorfish makes a very good bait when used on its own, but it is even more commonly used as part of a cocktail. Razorfish and lugworm is particularly effective, as is razorfish and crab. The big advantage with this species of shellfish is that it is ideal to boost other baits when supplies are limited, as well as being the ideal bait to stock up the freezer with, for use on those short-notice trips.

Other Shellfish

There are many other species of shellfish, all of which can be used with varying degrees of

A large clam, another good bait for cod, though far more difficult to obtain than razorfish.

success by the cod angler. Cockles, especially the large queen cockles, make a good bait for codling. These are often uncovered when digging worm baits. It will be necessary to use up to half a dozen or more at a time, in order to bulk up a decent-sized bait.

Clams can be dug alongside razorfish and lugworms. Unlike razorfish, clams cannot climb out of their burrows, you will have to dig them. A large clam makes an excellent cod bait; they can be frozen in the same way as razorfish, too.

Limpets are another readily available bait, and I have heard of anglers using them with some success for cod. To be honest, if the only bait available to me was limpets, I'd rather not go fishing!

OTHER BAITS

There will always be the angler who uses some weird and wonderful bait to catch a cod. The trouble is that few of these baits work on a regular basis. I remember, once, an occasion when we were floatfishing with live prawns for bass and wrasse; we caught neither on that particular day, but I did catch a plump 3lb codling! Despite many days using live prawns, that single cod remains the only one I have ever caught on a prawn.

Then there are those anglers who claim to catch cod on bacon rind, chicken skin, and who knows what else. I think I'll stick to the main cod baits listed above. These have been tried and tested by many anglers over many years, and work.

3 Artificial Lures for Cod Fishing

There are many different types of lure which are effective for catching cod, ranging from feather-light balsa-wood floating plugs, to enormous great metal pirks weighing upwards of 1½lb. All will catch fish, but only when used in the right situations.

The cod is a voracious predator, and throughout its life it will feed heavily on many different types of prey. When attempting to catch cod using lures it is necessary for the angler first to consider which kind of prey the cod will be hunting for, and then select the lure which most closely resembles that particular species.

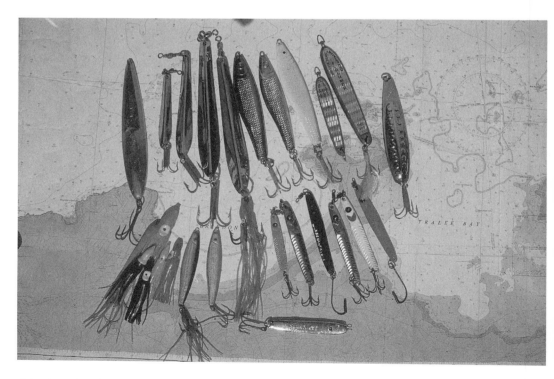

Selection of artificial lures suitable for catching cod.

In practice, the problem of lure selection is usually quite easily solved, as the prevailing fishing conditions such as water depth, tidal flow and sea-bed topography, will almost always dictate which is the most efficient type of lure to use. For example, if you will be fishing in upwards of 300ft of water with a strong tide running, there is little point in trying anything other than a pirk with a minimum weight of 1lb. Conversely, if you were fishing in less than 20ft of crystal clear water with little if any tidal flow, the conditions dictate that you will have to use much smaller and lighter lures.

In the two scenarios given above the lure choice has been more or less decided by the fishing conditions. However, in both cases the angler will almost always be using a lure which imitates the size of fish on which the cod are feeding. In the deep-water situation the cod will probably be feeding on the likes of herring, coalfish, or other large fish, more or less the size of his pirk. In the shallow-water situation the cod will almost certainly be chasing smaller baitfish such as sand-eels, and the small spinners and plugs he will probably elect to use are essentially designed to imitate a sand-eel or small fish.

Many novice anglers initially lack confidence the first few times they attempt to use lures. Confidence in your technique and choice of bait or lure is one of the most important elements of successful angling. If you are not totally confident in what you are doing you will not be fishing to the very best of your ability and thus your chances for success will be reduced. Obviously, if you are new to lure angling it is advisable to do as much research as you can beforehand. Ask in local tackle shops and talk to other anglers. If you are fishing aboard a charter boat, pick the skipper's brains; ask him which are the best types, colours and sizes of lure, and how best to fish them. In many areas the most productive lures

are tried and tested, and you should have little problem in deciding which to use.

Pirks are the mainstay of cod fishing in the north-east of England and in Scandinavia, where anglers concentrate on fishing deep-water wrecks and reefs well offshore. Wherever anglers fish inshore reefs pirks can be equally effective, too, but by and large much smaller pirks tend to be favoured, and many anglers concentrate on using various types of feathers and other multiple strings of lures. Pirks are also effective further south, in the English Channel, but most anglers concentrate on using artificial sand-eels fished in conjunction with much lighter and more sporting tackle.

My advice to the novice angler about to experiment with lures for the first time would be to persevere; success will come eventually. Think fish. When you are pirking do not simply think of your lure as an inanimate lump of metal, bouncing about somewhere way below the boat. Think of it as an injured coalfish falling through the depths, frantically trying to escape from that shoal of cod which it knows are lurking hungrily beneath.

When you are working a set of feathers, try to imagine how a small shoal of whitebait might be reacting. Do not think of your artificial sand-eel as a long thin strip of coloured rubber with a hook shoved into it. It's a live sand-eel, battling to make headway against the strong run of tide; a cream bun of a meal to any hungry cod!

Lure fishing is far more involved than many anglers give it credit for. There is an art to working any lure successfully; yes, even 1½lb of chrome-plated lead. I cannot tell you exactly how to get the very best out of each and every type of lure. All I can say is that if you really believe in what you are doing, if you have absolute faith in the effectiveness of your lure, then you will be more than halfway to success.

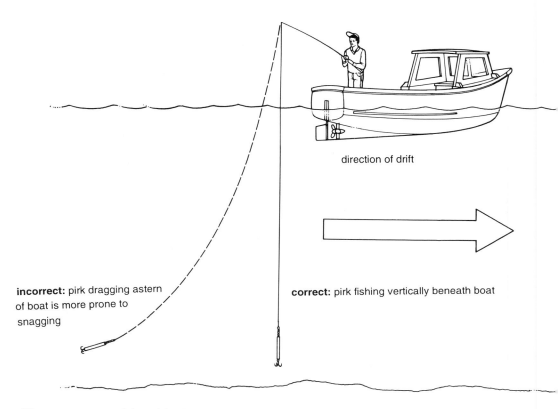

direction of drift

incorrect: pirk dragging astern of boat is more prone to snagging

correct: pirk fishing vertically beneath boat

The correct way to fish a pirk – in as near to a vertical line beneath the boat as possible.

PIRKS

Pirks come in all shapes and sizes, and are probably the most widely used type of lure by cod anglers. With few exceptions, pirks work at their best when they are fishing in as near to a vertical line beneath the boat as possible. In other words, a pirk which is trailing many yards astern of a drifting boat will not be fishing to its greatest effect.

In order to maintain a vertical line it is important for the angler to be using the correct size of pirk, which means the correct weight pirk. The two important factors which need to be taken into consideration when deciding on which size of pirk to use are water depth and the speed of the drift, which, in turn, is dependent on the size and state of tide and the wind. There is no exact formula to follow, other than the deeper the water and the faster the rate of drift, the heavier the pirk should be.

Many anglers believe that the shape of the pirk they use does not matter, but they are wrong. Without any shadow of doubt the very best pirks on the market are those made by Solvroken and Jensen. The shape of these pirks gives them a tremendous fluttering action as they fall through the water, which cod find irresistible. Unfortunately, they are

Selection of pirks used for cod fishing.

very expensive, which is naturally a deterrent to most anglers.

Colour is the other point which needs to be considered. When I am fishing in deep water, let's say water deeper than 100ft, I do not worry too much about the colour of the lures I use, and almost always I stick to plain silver. However, when I am fishing in water less than 100ft deep, especially clear water, I feel that colour does have a considerable bearing on my success rate. To allow for this, I carry a large selection of different-coloured pirks in a range of different sizes and shapes, which allows me to experiment until I find the most successful combination of the day.

It is very important that your lure is fitted with good-quality hooks, swivels and split rings. The better-quality pirks, such as those made by Solvroken and Jensen, are fitted with suitable accessories as standard, but I have

seen several other pirks which are not. The pirks themselves are often very good, it's just that the hooks, etc. are of an inferior quality, and unreliable. Often these are found on the cheaper pirks seen in tackle shops; after all, it is only by cutting back on the quality of fittings used that the manufacturer has been able to undercut the better quality products. The cod is a powerful fish and even a double-figure fish caught in deep water will soon find any weakness in your tackle. Larger specimens will probably smash free without even knowing they were hooked in the first place.

Some anglers rig pirks with three or four single hooks tied to the bottom of the pirk, instead of a standard treble hook. This type of hook, known as a ripper, is not a lure which I favour, as it foul hooks a large percentage of fish. Those anglers who use this technique are invariably those who fish commercially.

A 'ripper', a deadly effective though hardly sporting lure for catching cod. This style of lure foul hooks a high percentage of the fish it catches.

ARTIFICIAL SAND-EELS

Artificial sand-eels are one of the most effective types of lure for many species of fish, including cod. This is hardly surprising as the sand-eel is one of the most important links in the marine food chain. The big attraction with artificial sand-eels, as far as the angler is concerned, is that they often allow him to use really light and sporting tackle under conditions which would otherwise dictate the use of much heavier gear.

Artificial sand-eels come in an equally large selection of different sizes and colours as pirks. My own favourites are the Skal-Li-Wag eels produced by Delta Tackle, in Plymouth, south Devon. The essential attraction with these lures evolves around the action of the tail. The Delta Skal-Li-Wag eels have a very effective tail action which is deadly for a wide range of different species, including cod.

By and large, it is the larger eels which are the most effective for cod, although on occasions I have caught cod on very small rubber sand-eels when fishing for bass. When fishing in very deep water I tend to stick with using black, red or orange eels, but I much prefer to use those which are more naturally coloured when fishing in shallow clear water. The hooks supplied with Delta eels are of a very good quality, though this is far from the case with some other manufacturers. If in doubt, change the hook.

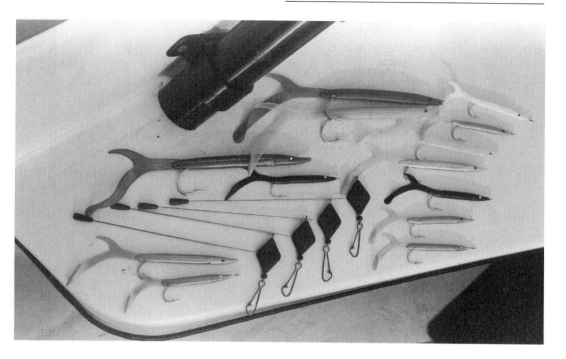

Delta Skal-Li-Wag lures and Knotless Super Spreader booms, excellent sand-eel imitators that are among the best for catching cod.

FEATHERS

Feathers are perhaps the oldest type of lure in the sea angler's armoury. A string of up to six brightly coloured hen hackles is also one of the most productive methods of general reef fishing, as will be seen later, and bait collecting. However, shop-bought feathers are rarely tied using quality nylon and hooks, and as such are totally unreliable for serious cod fishing. On many occasions I have seen an angler drop a set of feathers into the depths and his rod buckle in two as several sizeable fish have smashed into the lures. Unfortunately, the combined weight and pulling from several sizeable fish will almost always result in a smashed trace, and the angler, if he is lucky, ends up with just one or two fish.

The exception to the rule are the purpose-made traces of cod feathers produced by Mustad. These are tied using heavy mono and strong hooks. Personally, I am not a tremendous fan of feathering as a sporting technique, but if you do want to use feathers for cod, I strongly suggest you use a decent set.

These days there are many alternatives to natural feathers in the shops, ranging from bright strips of tinsel to long thin strips of reflectolite plastic. Some of the very best modern alternatives are known as Hokeye lures. These consist of a small luminous rubber fish-shaped body with a reflectolite tail and a luminous bead mounted on the trace at the head. These are devastatingly effective. Once again, Mustad produce a heavy-duty range suitable for cod fishing, the Hokeye Tempter Rig, which consists of three lures tied using 4/0 hooks to 60lb BS line. Feathering is an excellent technique for novice and junior anglers.

MUPPETS

Muppets are rubber squid imitators, and are available in a large variety of different sizes and colours. Whether or not cod actually strike a muppet because they think it is a real squid, or simply out of a combination of aggression and curiosity, it matters little. The simple fact remains that muppets are a very successful cod lure.

Muppets are normally fished in conjunction with other lures, usually pirks. The pirk provides the weight to send the terminal rig down to the sea bed as well as, no doubt, providing additional attraction. Two or three muppets are then rigged paternoster style above the pirk.

Most muppets are bought singly, the angler supplying the hook. My own choice of hook when tying a muppet rig is a Mustad Uptide Viking No79515BR, usually either size 4/0 or 6/0. It is important that decent-quality mono with a breaking strain of not less than 60lb is used when tying multiple-hook rigs. Lighter breaking strains are too easily smashed if several sizeable fish are hooked together.

Selection of rubber muppets, artificial squid imitators that are very effective, either fished on their own or in conjunction with another lure, with or without the addition of natural bait.

John Wilson with a plump Danish codling, caught on a combined pirk and muppet rig.

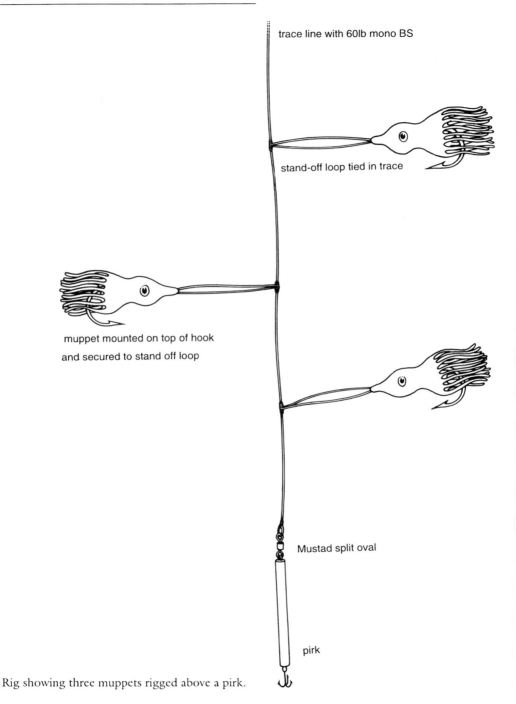

trace line with 60lb mono BS

stand-off loop tied in trace

muppet mounted on top of hook
and secured to stand off loop

Mustad split oval

pirk

Rig showing three muppets rigged above a pirk.

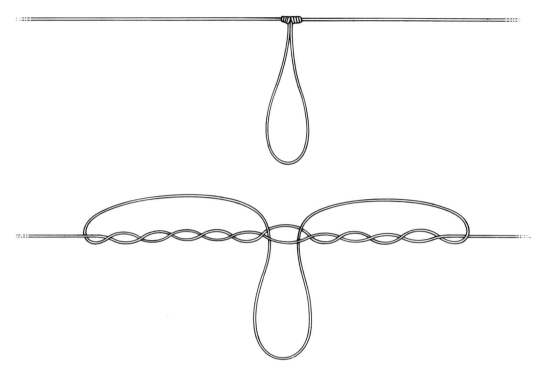

Method of tying a stand-off loop, a quick and simple knot for attaching muppets and other similar lures to a trace.

The hooks are attached to the trace either via short stand-off loops tied directly into the mono or by using short paternoster booms. The muppet is then threaded on to the hook so that the tip of the muppet passes over the hook eye. Try to keep the hole in the tip of the muppet as small as possible as this will help to prevent the muppet from getting ripped off the hook. A split oval is then tied at the bottom of the trace to attach either the pirk or the weight, and a quality swivel at the other end to which the main line can be tied.

Muppets work very well on their own, but the addition of a strip of bait can boost their appeal. The normal bait used is a strip of mackerel. Mustad produce an excellent three-hook wrecking rig which consists of three different-coloured muppets ready rigged on size 5/0 O'Shaughnessy hooks, on a trace tied from good-quality 60lb BS mono, complete with swivel and easy link. I have used these for many years and caught a lot of cod when using them. Never have I seen one fail.

SOFT AMERICAN RUBBER LURES

A few years ago soft rubber lures imported from America started to appear in British anglers' tackle boxes. On that side of the Atlantic soft rubber lures, which come in an

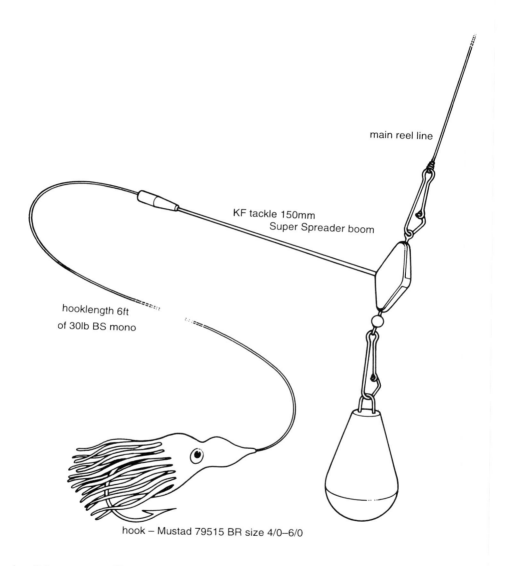

main reel line

KF tackle 150mm
Super Spreader boom

hooklength 6ft
of 30lb BS mono

hook – Mustad 79515 BR size 4/0–6/0

Rig used to fish a muppet off a long trace. The same rig can be used with other similar lures.

incredible selection of different sizes, shapes and colours, are used by anglers to catch both fresh and saltwater fish. The big advantage of this style of lure when compared to other lures, is that they are very cheap and extremely lifelike. I have caught a wide variety of species in European waters using this style of lure, including plenty of cod.

It is very easy for the angler to become totally bewildered when faced with such a large variety of lures. My own favourite style for general sea fishing are the rubber worms with a twist at the end of their tail. I use worms about 6 inches in length, and those made by Mr Twister are among the best. I have tried many different colours and I have had the best results when using either plain orange or jet black with a crimson tail.

There are two ways that these lures can be used to good effect when targeting cod. Firstly, they can be used as a substitute for muppets and fished paternoster style in twos or threes, as described above. Secondly, they can be fished singly, in a similar style to artificial sand-eels. My own favourite technique is described in the chapter on reef fishing.

SPINNING

Spinning is not a method generally associated with cod fishing, but I can assure you that spinning can be a highly productive technique in certain areas. It is possible to spin for cod both from a boat and from the shore. When I use the term 'spinner' I am referring to that

Selection of American-style rubber worm lures.

The Bridun Lance lure, a superb lure for boat and shore anglers alike. Note the single hooks, which many anglers feel are more effective than the treble hooks often seen on lures of this kind.

whole family of lures which includes all sorts of different spoons and bar spoons, plugs and mini-pirks up to about 2oz in weight, which can often be cast great distances.

Afloat, I have found that it is invariably small heavy lures, which are really mini-pirks, that work the best. There are many to choose from, some of the best being produced by Solvroken, Jensen and Bridun. Once again, it is possible to use this type of lure in conjunction with very light tackle.

I find that the best technique when using small heavy lures from a boat is to cast them in the direction in which the boat is drifting. Allow them to sink swiftly to the bottom, trying to maintain contact as the lure falls, for fish often intercept the lure as it falls. As soon as the bottom is felt, quickly retrieve the lure about half-way back, then allow it to fall to the bottom and repeat and retrieve. Takes are normally positive and hard to miss.

The best way to fish plugs afloat is in conjunction with a downrigger, or, when fishing in very shallow water, by trolling them directly from the rod. I have used many different types of plug extensively in Scandinavia, where they are incredibly effective for catching cod. Trolling and the use of downriggers are covered fully in the section on boat fishing.

Spinning works from the shore for cod, too. By and large, the most productive venues are those which have very deep water within easy casting range. These are typically found in Scotland, the west of Ireland and Scandinavia, although there is plenty of scope for experimenting from piers, harbour walls and breakwaters, indeed anywhere where cod come to within casting range.

Given the depth of water, once again it will generally be the small heavy lures which work the best, simply because they can be cast the furthest and sink quickest. The sink and draw technique described above works well, although there is obviously an increased risk of the lure snagging when fishing from the shore.

On the whole, it is always worth experimenting with spinners, whenever you know there are cod within casting range. An incident in Denmark proved this point for me perfectly. We were spinning from an open beach for sea trout; the water was on average less than 6ft deep and crystal clear. After about an hour's fishing I hooked my first fish using a 1oz ABU Toby spoon. I fully expected to see a bright silver sea trout leaping out of the water, so you can imagine my surprise when a plump codling emerged out of the surf!

MAKING YOUR OWN LURES

It is an unfortunate fact that most lures are not cheap, but luckily it is very easy to make many different types of lure. Pirks are easily made by filling suitable lengths of chrome pipe with lead, cutting the ends at an angle and then attaching your own swivels, links and hooks. You can experiment with different diameters of pipe, and with practice you will be able to gauge how heavy a given size of pirk will be. Always exercise extreme caution when pouring molten lead into steel pipes: if there is the slightest drop of moisture within the pipe, the lead will spurt back out of the top, often with explosive force. Thoroughly warm the pipe before you pour the lead, to remove all traces of moisture.

You do not need chrome or stainless pipe to make pirks. Very effective pirks can be made from ordinary copper pipe. The finished pirks can then be left copper coloured, which work really well, or painted or wrapped with different-coloured insulating tapes.

Spinners and spoons are easily cut and fabricated from ordinary household spoons. Visit a car boot sale and for a few pounds you should obtain enough old spoons to make a large selection of different lures, which often work as well as shop-bought spinners. Sand-eel lures are easily made from strips of peeled electrical insulation, cut to shape and threaded on to a hook.

Strings of feathers are very easy to make, and I know several anglers who manufacture their own rubber worms from different-coloured silicon bathroom sealants. They simply cut the end of the tube to a suitable diameter and run off whatever length lures they require on a piece of glass. If you want to be really imaginative you can add some glitter to the sealant for additional attraction, before it sets.

4 Boat Fishing for Cod

Fishing afloat undoubtedly offers the angler his very best chance of catching a really big cod nowadays. Double-figure cod are still expected and even relatively common occurrences for anglers fishing afloat, at many venues in the UK. Twenty-pound fish raise a few eyebrows at some venues, and even thirty pounders are still caught with a degree of regularity. And each year the pictures of smiling anglers holding fat forty-pound-plus cod grace the pages of the angling press. As will be seen later, the angler who is prepared to travel abroad for his cod fishing will have a realistic chance of catching fish well in excess of fifty pounds.

There are many different methods used to catch cod afloat, and the most effective usually depends on the conditions found at the venue chosen. Factors such as the water depth and temperature, the sea-bed topography, water clarity, the time of year, the strength of tide and the availability of natural food, all play a part in determining which will be the most productive method to use.

Over the years, local anglers and charter skippers have honed to perfection the methods and baits that produce the best results in their area. Whenever travelling to a new area it naturally makes good sense to contact local charter boat skippers, tackle shops or angling clubs in advance, and ask for their advice on the best techniques and baits to use in that area. Then, having sought such advice, follow it.

Time and time again, I have seen anglers who have been advised to buy a certain bait, maybe black lug or squid, turn up for a day's fishing with a box of cheaper bait, usually frozen mackerel. Or, similarly, anglers who have been advised that uptiding is the most efficient technique arrive armed for the day with a selection of meaty 50lb class wrecking rods and a bucketful of pirks. It usually follows that their catch at the end of the day – assuming that they have actually caught anything – does not come anywhere near the potential of a catch taken by anglers using more appropriate techniques and baits.

WRECK FISHING

Wrecks have a well-deserved reputation for producing big cod. Often lying among an otherwise barren sea bed, wrecks can be considered as something of an 'oasis in the desert' for marine life. Within a very short time any new wreck will become covered in marine growths and algae. This, along with plenty of cover in which to hide, soon attracts a multitude of other life forms, including small fishes. Small fish are food for large predatory species of fish such as cod, and it will not be long before these fish move in. In short, an established wreck is host to a complete marine eco-system stuffed full of life, from the bottom to the very top of the food chain.

A nice double-figure cod caught by an angler fishing a heavy pirk over an offshore wreck.

Example of a multi-lure rig.

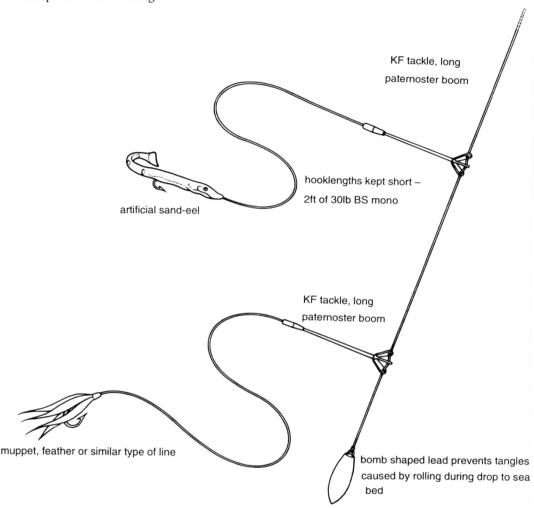

KF tackle, long
paternoster boom

hooklengths kept short –
2ft of 30lb BS mono

artificial sand-eel

KF tackle, long
paternoster boom

muppet, feather or similar type of line

bomb shaped lead prevents tangles
caused by rolling during drop to sea
bed

Cod are attracted to wrecks where they feed heavily on small fish. The North Atlantic is littered with countless numbers of wrecks, and almost all pay host to foraging shoals of cod at some time of the year. However, inshore wrecks are invariably heavily netted and consequently barren, when compared with 'virgin' wrecks further offshore. Today it is not unusual for the fastest charter boats to travel up to 70 miles offshore in search of quality sport. Expensive and time-consuming it most certainly is, but the rewards reaped by anglers fishing aboard these boats more often than not justify the expense and effort involved.

There are several ways that anglers catch cod from offshore wrecks. Occasionally fish

Anglers fishing multi-lure and single sand-eel rigs over a wreck.

are taken on natural baits but, more often than not, these fish are an accidental though welcome by-catch taken by anglers who are really fishing for other species such as conger and ling. Lure fishing is the most effective way of catching cod over wrecks; after all, most lures are simply an imitation of baitfish, and that's the reason why cod are there in the first place.

The two types of lure which are most effective for catching wreck cod are pirks and artificial sand-eels. Pirks are often fished with two or three rubber muppets or artificial sand-eels rigged above paternoster style, known as 'killer gear'. It is not hard to determine why this arrangement earned its name, as multiple catches of two or three cod are often taken per drop. The overriding emphasis of this book is on sports fishing, and I hardly think it sporting to set out deliberately to fish in this style. However, I do concede that under certain circumstances, such as when fish are scarce or when other species are being targeted as well as cod, the use of multiple-hook rigs can be acceptable.

Pirking

There is a lot more to fishing a pirk success-fully than first meets the eye. The newcomer to wreck fishing might well think that all he has to do is to tie a suitable pirk on to the end of his line, drop it down into the wreck and jig it up or down until a fish hangs itself on it. I can assure you that this is not the case. In order for a pirk to fish effectively, it is very important that it fishes in as near to a vertical line as possible. Pirks dragging horizontally many yards behind a drifting boat not only catch few cod, but they are far more prone to dragging across the wreckage and snagging than a pirk fished correctly.

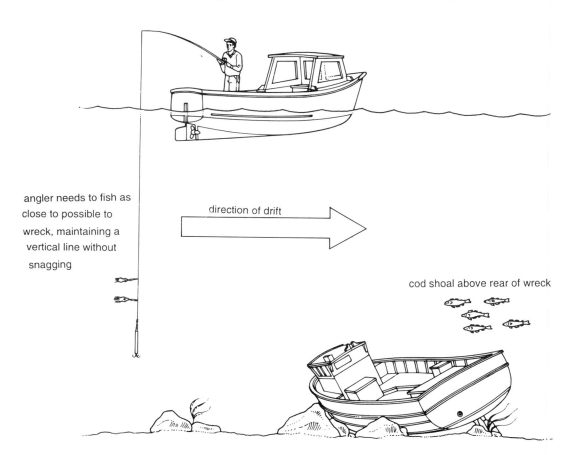

angler needs to fish as close to possible to wreck, maintaining a vertical line without snagging

direction of drift

cod shoal above rear of wreck

Angler fishing a pirk and muppet combination over a wreck.

angler lobs pirk 20–30yd down drift, where it sinks to bottom. This
helps ensure the pirk is on a vertical line for longer than if just
lowered right down

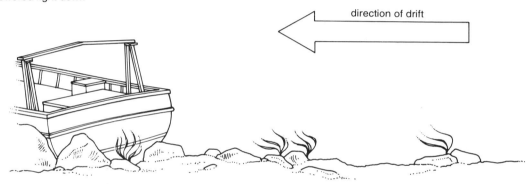

direction of drift

Pirk casting technique.

Many wrecks lie in very deep water and
when the tide, wind or both are creating a very
fast drift, a pirk simply dropped straight down
will probably already be many yards behind
the boat before it reaches the wreck. In order
to counteract this effect, anglers fishing off
north-east England, an area which can
perhaps be considered as the stronghold for
wreck fishing for cod in the UK, devised a
method of pirk casting.

Pirk casting does not involve swinging great
lumps of metal around the boat. This would
not only be highly dangerous, but more or less
impossible when using short stout rods and
large metal-spooled multiplier reels. At the
commencement of the drift, the angler simply
lobs his pirk as far as he comfortably can in the
direction that the boat will drift. Twenty or
thirty yards is more than adequate.

The pirk is allowed to fall as quickly as
possible down to the sea bed, so that it should
be on the bottom by the time the boat has
drifted over the top of the wreck. As soon as
the angler feels his lead tap bottom, he re-
engages the reel spool and starts jigging.
Depending on the speed of the drift, the
angler will now be able to fish his pirk effectively, until it once again starts to trail behind
the boat. It is normally acceptable to knock
the reel back into free spool once or twice on
each drift and drop the pirk back down to the
bottom. On particularly long drifts, which are

The Shimano TLD-2-Speed-30, a fantastic reel with a huge line capacity, ideal for deep water cod fishing, especially when using pirks. The high speed retrieve is perfect for swiftly retrieving lures from deep water between drifts, while the low speed comes into its own when playing large fish.

rare when wreck fishing, it might be more effective to retrieve the pirk swiftly and cast a second time to prevent it trailing too far behind the boat.

Pirks come in all shapes and sizes, but it is generally the larger pirks, between 12oz and 1½lb, that are of most use when fishing for cod on wrecks. In order to fish with such heavy lures, a strong set of fishing tackle is essential. The angler really needs a good-quality 50lb class boat rod with plenty of backbone, and a reel to match. A reel with a strong frame and sound gearing is absolutely essential, and a fast rate of retrieve is preferable to retrieve the pirk quickly from deep water.

When I first tried this style of fishing I thought that I would be able to fish with 30lb or 40lb line, and I thought that the 70lb line the locals were using was ridiculously over the top. When after several drifts I remained fishless while all around me the fish boxes were steadily filling with cod, I realized that I was clearly either doing something wrong or different from everyone else. We were all using the same pirks and similar rods and reels, so what else could it be?

Luckily, the skipper had been observing my plight and, taking a length of my line in his gnarled and weather-beaten hands, gave an impressive demonstration of just how much stretch there was in my relatively light line. He went on to explain that with such a high amount of stretch no amount of vigorous jigging with a rod and reel was going to be transmitted down through the depths to my pirk. All of my effort was being absorbed in the elasticity of the line. Thankfully, I had a second reel in my tackle box loaded with 60lb line so I changed reels between drifts, and for the rest of the day my catch rate was on a par with that of everyone else.

An increasing number of anglers are using many of the modern braided lines for this style of fishing. Braided lines offer the advantage of an incredibly high strength to diameter ratio and virtually no stretch, which results in more action being imparted into the pirk by the angler's jigging technique. When pirking, this equates to a far higher level of sensitivity and control over the pirk, and in turn results in more hooked fish and far fewer snag-ups on the wreck.

A large percentage of fish caught when pirking are actually caught on the drop; that is, they take the pirk as it falls to the sea bed. On other occasions I have had fish hook themselves when I have been quickly retrieving the pirk at the end of the drift. In most cases the fish will hook themselves.

When a fish is hooked it is vital that the angler maintains as tight a line as possible. Obviously, the reel clutch should be set, but set at as tight a setting as is practical given the breaking strain of the line used. When drifting over a wreck it is imperative that hooked fish are wound well above the wreckage and into clear water as soon as possible, or else they will be lost by diving among the wreckage.

Anglers in the north-east still regularly use the traditional Nottingham and Scarborough wooden centrepin reels for pirking. These reels offer the advantage of a direct drive with plenty of cranking power, plus the fact that they are cheap and virtually maintenance free. I know they are not everyone's preference,

It is important to keep a tight line whenever playing a fish hooked on a pirk. An inch of slack will often allow the fish to shake free of the hook hold.

but I have fished with many competent anglers who will use no other type of reel.

Artificial Sand-Eels

Sand-eels form a major part of the diet of most predatory species of fish, and they are one of the most important links in the marine food chain. Anglers have used artificial sand-eels to catch fish for many years, and at times when fish are feeding on sand-eels, artificials can be used with devastating success.

An old-fashioned wooden Scarborough reel, still very popular with many anglers who fish in the north-east of England.

A cod that fell for a pirk/muppet combination.

In order to maximize fully the sporting potential of any fish, it is important to use fishing tackle that is as light as practical. Artificial sand-eels allow the angler to use incredibly light and sporting tackle when fishing for cod over deep-water wrecks. The classic way of fishing an artificial sand-eel is in conjunction with a rig known as the 'Flying Collar Rig', which utilizes a French Boom. Today most anglers dispense with the traditional wire French Boom in favour of a long plastic tubi-type running leger boom. It is important that for the rubber eel to work efficiently it is fished off a long hooklength, and the tubi-boom helps to prevent the hooklength from tangling around the main line.

Artificial sand-eels are manufactured in all shapes, colours and sizes. When wrecking and specifically targeting cod, I normally use the larger eels, those in excess of four inches long. There has been a great amount of debate among anglers regarding which are the best colours of eels to use, with scientists telling us that beyond a certain depth fish cannot distinguish between different colours. The most popular colours of sand-eels used by most wrecking regulars are nearly always red, orange and black. When fishing in deep water I, too, tend to alternate between these three colours, but I favour the more natural-coloured eels whenever I am fishing in shallow clear water.

The actual rig to use for fishing an artificial sand-eel over a deep-water wreck is simplicity in itself. The tubi-boom is threaded on to the main reel line, followed by a small bead; a

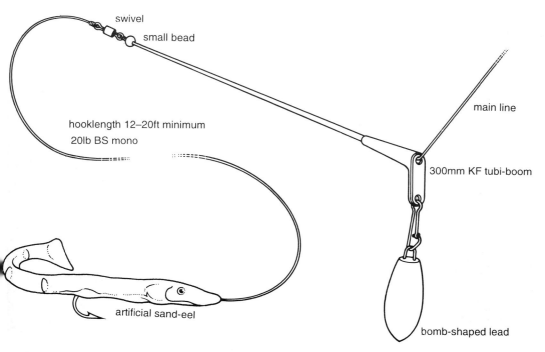

swivel
small bead
main line
hooklength 12–20ft minimum
20lb BS mono
300mm KF tubi-boom
artificial sand-eel
bomb-shaped lead

Method of fishing an artificial sand-eel in conjunction with a 300mm KF Tubi-boom.

Alternative method of fishing an artificial sand-eel in conjunction with a fixed boom – a 200mm KF Super Spreader.

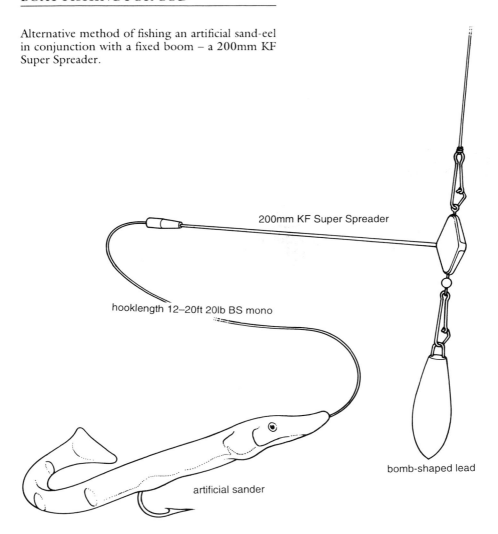

200mm KF Super Spreader

hooklength 12–20ft 20lb BS mono

bomb-shaped lead

artificial sander

small high-quality swivel is then tied on the end of the line. The bead protects the knot from abrasion caused by contact with the end of the boom. The lead weight is attached to the clip on the boom. It is important to use a bomb-shaped weight which will fall through the water smoothly, and not have a tendency to roll and twist thus causing tangles, as can happen when using leads of other shapes.

As I have mentioned, artificial sand-eels work best when fished in conjunction with a long hooklength. Consider a 12ft hooklength as being a minimum, although specialists regularly use a hooklength in excess of 20ft. I use clear nylon with a breaking strain of around 20lb for my hooklengths for this style of fishing. Heavier line will seriously impair the action of the eel and lighter lines tend to be too weak, as they are too easily damaged by abrasion. When using a very long hooklength, it is important to use at least one swivel tied approximately midway in the hooklength, to prevent line twist. The eel is tied directly on to the end of the hooklength.

Many anglers experience problems with tangles when fishing artificial sand-eels. The biggest mistake that most make is simply dropping the rig into the water and allowing it to fall quickly to the sea bed. This will nearly always result in a horrendous tangle which will render the lure useless. The correct way is to hold on to the boom in one hand and drop the eel into the water. Always try to position yourself on the side of the boat away from the direction that the boat is drifting, to prevent your line dragging under the boat. On a charter boat this will usually mean the skipper will have to alter the angle of the boat on each drift, with anglers on either side of the boat fishing alternate drifts. This is a far more sensible tactic than everybody attempting to fish on one side on every drift, as too many lines in the water will almost certainly cause continual tangles.

Allow the drift of the boat to straighten the hooklength out fully, and only then drop the boom with lead attached into the water. Do not let the rig fall too quickly to the bottom, as this will result in the eel spinning back and tangling around the main line. The correct technique is to steady and control the rate of descent using your thumb on the reel spool. When the bottom is felt re-engage the reel spool and start retrieving the lure. Do not try to jig the eel up and down, as once again this will not only cause tangles but catch few, if any fish.

Retrieve the eel with a slow and steady rate of retrieve, which will work the lure to its greatest effect. Bites will be felt either as a series of taps and jerks as the fish plucks and pulls at the lure tail or, more usually when fishing for cod, as a solid lunge as the fish engulfs the lure and attempts to dive to the bottom. If a fish is felt playing with the lure, it is important to maintain a steady rate of retrieve and nearly always the fish will eventually be induced into taking the lure, often well off the bottom. Speeding up, slowing down, or any other method of attempting to set the hook will nearly always result in a missed and spooked fish.

The ideal outfit to use when fishing with artificial sand-eels over wrecks is either a 20lb or a 12lb class boat rod matched with a small multiplier reel loaded with about 15lb BS line. Many anglers use uptide rods. It is always important to ensure that the reel clutch is correctly set, as almost always the fish's first reaction on taking the eel and feeling the hook and resistance of the line is to turn and dive for cover.

When using artificial sand-eels over wrecks you will almost always catch far more pollack than cod, but when a wreck with a sizeable population of cod is located the sport is tremendous. It is important to remember that the cod will not feed for 24 hours a day, and often the feeding times can be quite short. The best times of the tide to fish with artificial eels for cod vary considerably, but results will nearly always be at their best when the tide is running hard.

REEF FISHING

Offshore reefs are excellent places to fish for cod as they provide a rich and varied source of food, including countless types of crustacean and small fish. Many cod actually take up residence over reefs, and these fish are easily distinguished from migratory fish by their colouring. Reef cod, or rock cod as they are locally known in some areas, are a beautiful rich mix of dark red and gold, the perfect camouflage when living among the fronds of kelp and rock. Cod living more over open

A 'red cod', caught from a reef off the west coast of Ireland.

The author with a double-figure cod caught from an inshore reef.

ground tend to be various shades of light green and brown in colour.

By and large, cod caught over reefs tend to be of a smaller average size than cod caught over wrecks. Typical reef cod tend to average less than 10lb in weight, with fish weighing between 3lb and 7lb probably being classed as typical reef fish. That said, I have both seen and personally caught some very large cod when fishing over reefs, though such fish tend to be individual captures.

Fishing on the drift is the usual way of fishing over a reef. By drifting, it is possible to cover a much larger area of the sea bed than would be possible were the boat anchored. This allows the anglers to locate any isolated pockets of fish, which often have a tendency to hole up in a particular area.

Feathering

Both lures and baits or a combination of both, are used when drifting a reef for cod. I suppose a string of feathers is the most widely used type of lure among anglers for this type of fishing. The best type to use, when you can get hold of them, are those which are tied specifically for cod fishing. These are available in traces of between three and six feathers, in either plain white or a selection of different colours. Cod feathers are tied using stronger line and larger hooks than the more readily available mackerel feathers. I prefer using plain white feathers when cod fishing.

I have already mentioned that I do not generally favour using multiple-lure rigs for fishing, much preferring to catch fish on an individual basis. However, I have found that the action of a set of up to six feathers working together is, on occasion, more likely to produce a take from a single cod than a feather or similar lure fished singly. I suppose it is more natural for the cod to see several bait fish swimming together?

The feathers are weighted using either a plain lead or a pirk. The trouble with using a pirk over some reefs is that it is far more prone to snagging on the sea bed than a plain lead. That said, I am convinced that it is far more effective to use a pirk with either the hooks removed or the standard treble replaced with a single hook, as the flashing and added action of the pirk undoubtedly helps to attract fish.

Many anglers use baited feathers, typically long thin strips of fish or squid, peeler crab, ragworm or mussel. The addition of bait can make a big difference when fishing a reef, and also increases the likelihood of catching other species such as wrasse, coalfish, pollack, bream, gurnards, etc. But I am convinced that plain feathers are just as effective for cod as baited feathers, with the possible exception of small codling which are more likely to take a bait than a lure.

Feathers are really very easy to fish. All the angler has to do is to drop them to the sea bed and bounce them around, but there are a few tips and subtle adjustments which will improve the overall efficiency of the basic technique. Whenever fishing over a very snaggy area it is wise to attach the weight via a short length of weak line known as a rotten bottom, to help minimize tackle losses should the lead become snagged. Another useful trick

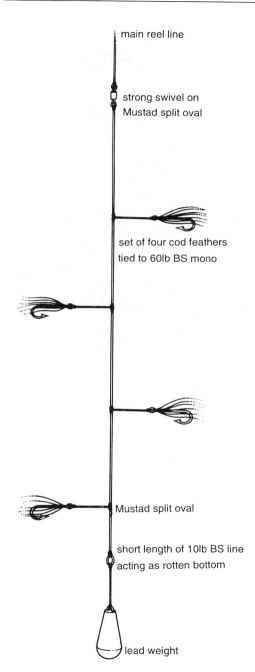

main reel line

strong swivel on Mustad split oval

set of four cod feathers tied to 60lb BS mono

Mustad split oval

short length of 10lb BS line acting as rotten bottom

lead weight

Set of cod feathers with the lead attached via a rotten bottom.

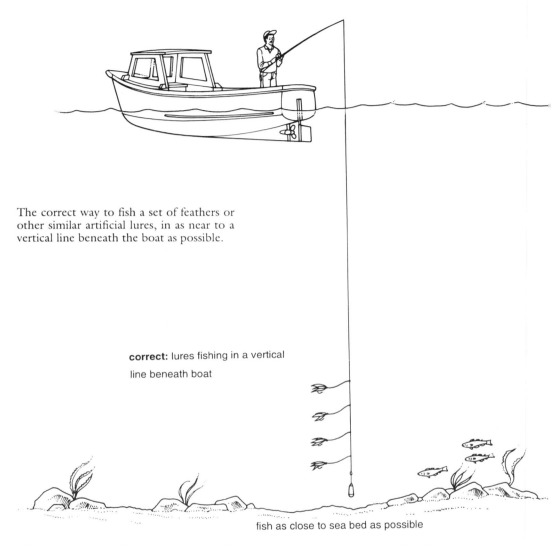

The correct way to fish a set of feathers or other similar artificial lures, in as near to a vertical line beneath the boat as possible.

correct: lures fishing in a vertical line beneath boat

fish as close to sea bed as possible

which reduces tackle losses, especially when there is a lot of kelp on the bottom, is to cut a standard string of six feathers into two separate sets of three. Obviously, this halves the likelihood of a hook getting snagged.

It is important that the feathers are fished in as near to a vertical line as possible. Not only are they more effective when fished vertically beneath the boat, but they are far less prone to snagging than if they are trailing many yards astern of the boat. For the best results when specifically targeting cod over a reef, keep the feathers working on or very near to the sea bed, even at the risk of getting snagged up sometimes, as this is where most cod will be feeding.

In recent years, a wide variety of modern alternatives have arrived in the tackle shops, all but replacing the traditional hen hackle feather. I have tried many of these and most are really no better than natural feathers when fishing for cod, only considerably more expensive. There are, however, a few exceptions to the rule. I particularly like rubber squids or muppets as they are called, which can often sort out the better-quality fish.

The other really effective lure is the Hokeye, and its many variations. These are very effective – too effective in fact – and when used over a reef the angler who is specifically targeting cod should be prepared to catch just about everything else that is swimming near the bottom as well!

Pirking

There are many deep-water reefs where the angler can use heavy pirks to catch cod in exactly the same way as he would over a wreck. Over shallower reefs and when it is desirable to use lighter tackle, it can be far more productive to use small mini-pirks, by which I mean pirks of less than 6oz in weight.

The first thing I do whenever I am going to fish a mini-pirk over a reef is to replace the treble hook with a single. This not only greatly reduces the risk of the lure snagging, but a single hook will almost always produce a more reliable hookhold than a treble hook when fished in the following style. A mini-pirk should ideally be fished vertically beneath the boat, just the same as the larger pirks. This works fine in shallow water but not so well in deep water, when it becomes hard to maintain contact with the lure and the sea bed as it takes so long for a small lure to fall to the sea bed. Alternatively, my own favourite way to fish a small pirk over a reef in shallow water is by casting it away from the boat.

The ideal outfit for this style of fishing is a light uptider matched with a small multiplier reel, loaded with about 12lb to 15lb BS line. I use a shockleader of about 30lb BS nylon to help prevent crack-offs when casting. The lure is cast in the direction in which the boat is drifting, and given time to sink swiftly down to the sea bed. Then it is quickly retrieved with a sink and draw technique, so that the lure is continually working close to the reef. Tackle losses are inevitable, but with a little practice these can be kept at a minimum. The results, on the other hand, more than make the loss of a few lures worth while.

American Soft Rubber Worms

At first I was somewhat sceptical about the effectiveness of this type of lure for our species, but I am now convinced that soft rubber worms are one of the biggest breakthroughs in European sea angling for many decades. I have used rubber worms extensively and in many different situations over the past few years, and the list of species which I have caught on them is impressive, and still growing. When used over a reef, American soft rubber worm baits are one of the very best lures available for cod.

There are several ways that these lures can be fished, one of which is in exactly the same way and using exactly the same technique as that described for artificial sand-eels in the section on wreck fishing. My own favourite technique is described below; it allows the angler to fish for cod over the roughest ground using very light tackle. In order to get the most out of this technique it is important to use a light rod and reel. A spinning rod rated for use with lures up to about 1oz and matched with either a small multiplier or a fixed-spool reel, loaded with 8lb BS line, is ideal. Either a 1oz or 2oz barrel lead or drilled bullet is threaded directly on to the main reel line followed by a bead and a small high-quality swivel. The hooklength is attached to the other end of the swivel; I use about 6ft of

Playing a good cod caught from an inshore reef on light tackle.

20lb BS clear nylon. An Aberdeen hook (between size 4/0 and 6/0 is ideal for cod) is tied to the other end of the hooklength.

The worm is lightly threaded on to the hook, starting at the head, threading about 1 inch of the worm on to the hook. When fishing over very rough ground, particularly when there is a lot of weed about, the point of the hook can be buried into the worm, which prevents it from getting snagged but in no way reduces its hooking potential.

To fish this rig, slowly lower the lure down to the sea bed, then steadily retrieve it, just as you would an artificial sand-eel. Fish can very often be felt plucking at the worm and it will be a great temptation to speed up or slow down the retrieve, or attempt to strike. You must resist, and maintain exactly the same rate of retrieve. In most cases, the fish will eventually decide enough is enough and take the worm. I have seen cod to 20lb plus caught from a reef off Ireland by an angler using exactly this technique.

There are several advantages to using soft rubber worms instead of artificial sand-eels, the first being cost – rubber worms are available at a fraction of the price of rubber sand-eels. The second big advantage is that worms work well when there is little or no tide and fished at a very slow rate of retrieve, whereas artificial sand-eels really need a good run of tide in order to get the most efficient action out of the lure's tail.

The last big advantage is that the rubber worms are incredibly soft to touch, and shy fish are definitely less inclined to reject them.

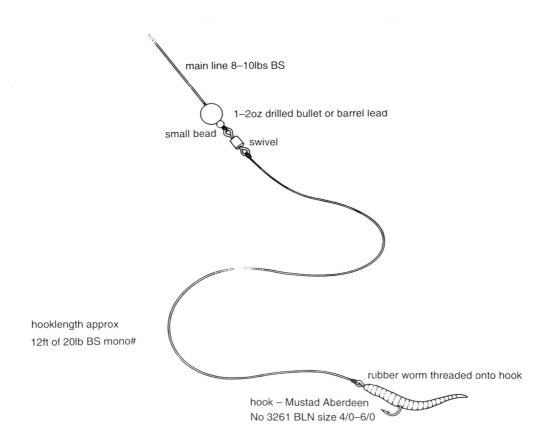

main line 8–10lbs BS

1–2oz drilled bullet or barrel lead

small bead

swivel

hooklength approx
12ft of 20lb BS mono#

rubber worm threaded onto hook

hook – Mustad Aberdeen
No 3261 BLN size 4/0–6/0

Rig for fishing artificial rubber worms in conjunction with light tackle.

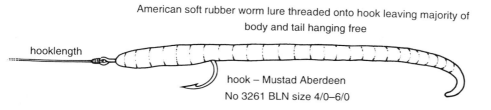

American soft rubber worm lure threaded onto hook leaving majority of
body and tail hanging free

hooklength

hook – Mustad Aberdeen
No 3261 BLN size 4/0–6/0

Method of mounting American soft rubber worm lure onto hook.

Some of the newest worms coming into the country from America are even impregnated with fish oil and other attractors, which can only help to increase the overall effectiveness of these wonderful little lures.

It is hard to determine just how much difference the colour of the worm makes to results. From my own experiments I would suggest that red, black and orange tend to be the most productive, but this has probably got a lot to do with the fact that these are the colours which I tend to use the most. There is still a lot of research waiting to be carried out on the effectiveness of different-coloured lures, and until such time it will always pay to experiment.

DOWNTIDING

In many ways downtiding, or 'up and down' fishing as it is known in some areas, can be considered as the forgotten art of boat angling. With the advent of uptiding many anglers have switched almost exclusively to this modern method, to the exclusion of all others. However, downtiding still has its place in the modern boat-angling scene, indeed in many areas where cod are caught it is by far the most efficient method to use.

Downtiding is most certainly an art: the art is in maintaining bottom contact with your terminal rig and bait. When fishing for cod using natural baits from an anchored boat, the angler will be targeting fish which are primarily hunting for food on or very near the bottom. Naturally, therefore, it is very important for the angler to ensure his bait is fishing in close proximity to the sea bed.

The time when most anglers elect to downtide for cod in preference to uptiding, is when fishing in deep water with a strong run of tide. Uptiding remains effective to a maximum depth of around 100ft, often less when the tide is running really hard. However, many productive boat marks for cod are found with depths well in excess of 100ft, where maintaining bottom contact with even a modest run of tide is at best difficult.

There are several ways for the angler to combat these conditions. The most obvious and probably the most widely adopted is simply to attach sufficient lead to hold the terminal rig firmly on the sea bed. This technique does work, but often leads well in excess of 2lb will be required, and these obviously restrict the fighting capabilities of all but the largest fish. Most anglers like to experience and enjoy the fight from their fish, and fishing with enormous great lumps of lead not only spoils the fight, but makes extremely hard and tedious work out of what should be a pleasurable pastime.

Alternatives to Large Leads

Thankfully, there are several alternatives to using excessively large weights. The first is to use a smaller lead and steadily trot it back in the tide, in order to maintain bottom contact. For example, it might be necessary to use, say, 1½lb of lead in order to keep a bait nailed on the bottom directly beneath the boat, but by allowing the tide to trot the baited terminal rig steadily downtide an angler might be able to fish effectively with just 8oz of lead.

The basic technique is to lower the terminal rig slowly down to the seabed; you should distinctly feel the lead tap on the bottom. Initially, you should keep the reel in free spool, checking the flow of line with your thumb. The tide will form a bow in your line between the rod tip and the terminal rig. After a few minutes, gently raise the rod tip and lower it again, feeling for the lead tapping on the bottom. If you feel the lead bounce on the

boat anchored uptide of reef and fish

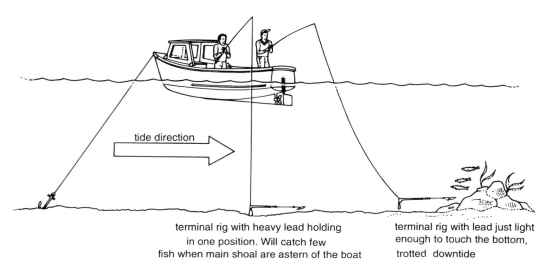

tide direction

terminal rig with heavy lead holding
in one position. Will catch few
fish when main shoal are astern of the boat

terminal rig with lead just light
enough to touch the bottom,
trotted downtide

Downtiding technique.

bottom you will know you are fishing effectively; if you do not, release extra line until you do confirm the rig is on the sea bed.

When downtiding it is very important to hold your rod at all times, and continually confirm the position of your bait by using the technique described above. Gradually, your terminal rig will work its way downtide of the boat, until eventually it will come to rest on the sea bed when sufficient line has been released; the distance will depend on the depth of water and the strength of the tide. The other big advantage when using this technique is that all the time you are steadily trotting your bait downtide your terminal rig will be covering new ground, and possibly locating isolated pockets of fish well astern of the boat.

Another alternative to excessively large leads is to use wire line. Size for size, wire is much thinner then standard mono lines with a similar breaking strain. This allows the angler to use a wire line with the same breaking strain as suitable mono, but which is much thinner in diameter. The thinner diameter has a vastly reduced surface area on which the tide can exert pressure, and this allows the angler to use a much smaller lead when using 40lb BS wire rather than 40lb BS mono. The other big advantage with wire line is that it has minimal stretch, whereas mono lines have a fairly considerable amount of stretch. This provides the angler, using wire line, with far greater sensitivity, vastly improved bite detection and much greater hooking power.

However, wire line is not without its problems. Firstly, wire is very expensive to buy, when compared with mono lines. Wire lines cannot be used on a standard rod as they will very quickly cut into the rings. A rod with roller rings is therefore essential. A reel with a very strong spool, preferably a metal spool, must be used to withstand the crushing pressure exerted on it when using wire lines. The ideal way to load a reel with wire is firstly to half fill it with old mono to absorb most of the strain, then top up with the wire. Lastly, using wire successfully does take a fair bit of practice. Standard wire lines are very prone to kinking and very easily overrun, causing a horrendous tangle on the spool.

In recent years, braided lines have become very popular with European anglers. The big advantages with braided lines are once again a low diameter and minimal stretch, but unlike wire they can be used in conjunction with standard fishing tackle. In fact, it is advisable not to use braided lines with roller rings, as the diameter is so thin is easily slips off the roller and jams between the side of the roller and the frame. Shimano have started fitting roller rings specifically designed for use with thin braided lines to some of their downtide rods, and undoubtedly more of these will appear in tackle shops as the popularity of braided lines grows. Unfortunately, braided lines are also very expensive, though the price is falling as more appear.

New-style ring as fitted to certain Shimano Beastmaster boat rods. This type of ring, made by AFTCO, has been specifically designed for use with low-diameter braided lines.

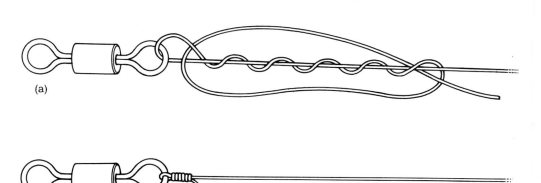

(a)

(b)

The tucked-half-blood knot: a good all-round knot for tying hooks, swivels and so on.

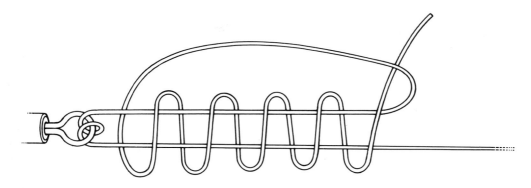

A uni-knot incorporating a double turn around the swivel or hook eye. This is a secure knot for use with modern braided lines, particularly when given a drop of super glue on the knot.

Many anglers also experience difficulties tying strong knots in braided lines. A few specialist knots have been devised for use with braided lines, but many of the standard knots, such as the uni-knot and half-blood knot, work well if they are tied with an extra tuck or two. A lot of anglers use a dab of super glue such as Stren Lok Knot, which is designed specifically for use with modern fishing lines, to improve knot security.

Tackle and Rigs

The ideal outfit for fishing downtide is a standard 6ft to 7ft boat rod. A 30lb class rod is a perfect all-round downtiding rod for cod, which will cope comfortably with the vast majority of situations. A lighter 20lb class rod might be more suited when fishing certain marks, and a 50lb class rod when it is necessary to use very large weights for fishing in very deep water. As mentioned above, roller rings throughout or a rod with a roller tip and butt ring are a must when fishing with wire lines.

A reel with sound gearing, a steady rate of retrieve and a smooth reliable clutch are a must when downtiding for cod. Shimano offer an extensive range of reels which meet the angler's requirements when fishing downtide. The Shimano Charter Special offers a reel with a silky-smooth lever drag and a level wind, an ideal reel for most mid-range downtiding situations. My own favourite downtiding reels are the Shimano TLDs, ranging from the TLD 15 right up to the TLD 30 2 Speed, which can be changed from low- to high-speed retrieve. The low speed is ideal for pumping large fish to the boat in deep water. All reels within the TLD range feature superb lever drags and a high standard gearing, which is all too rarely seen in fishing reels today.

The standard downtiding rig is the simple running leger. I favour the excellent Knotless Fishing Tackle range of booms for my downtide fishing. These are an extremely simple and functional range of booms specifically designed for downtide fishing. A big advantage with the Knotless sliding booms is that they can be easily removed and re-attached to the reel line without needing to break the entire terminal rig down.

The boom is first threaded on to the main line, followed by a small bead and a high-

An angler playing a sizeable fish on a 9½ft uptide rod.

quality swivel. The bead protects the knot between the line and the swivel. The hook-length is then tied to the opposite end of the swivel. When downtiding specifically for cod, I use a length of standard monofilament line about 50lb BS, between 4ft and 6ft in length. Do not use excessively long hooklengths for this style of fishing, as these can allow the tide to raise the bait well off the sea bed, and out of reach of any fish feeding on the bottom.

Choice of hook is very important. Bearing in mind that we are fishing for a strong species of fish in deep water and often with a strongly flowing tide, the last thing any angler would want is for an inferior quality hook to straighten out under pressure, resulting in the loss of a fish. My own favourite hooks are the excellent Mustad Uptide Viking range, No. 79515 BR, usually either size 4/0 or 6/0.

However, when I fish downtide for cod I am often targeting big fish, using big baits. Whenever you use big baits it is very important to match the size of the hook to the bait, and a 6/0 Viking can be too small when using two whole calamari squid or a large cuttlefish. Whenever this is the case, I use a larger 7/0 or 8/0 Mustad O'Shaughnessy No. 3406, an extremely powerful hook which is capable of holding the largest cod you are ever likely to hook.

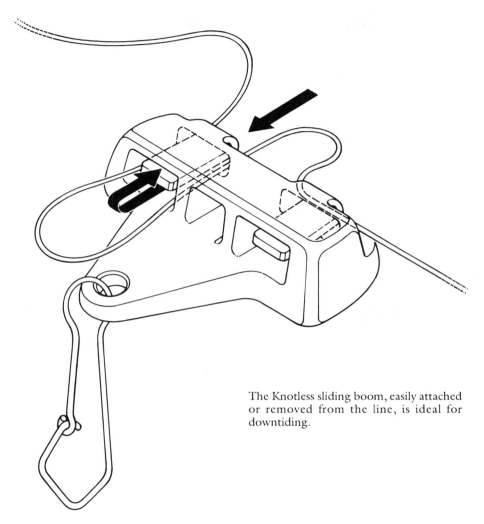

The Knotless sliding boom, easily attached or removed from the line, is ideal for downtiding.

Whenever I use wire line I always attach a 30ft length of mono line to the end of the wire, via a very small high-quality swivel, on to which the terminal rig is attached. This length of lines serves effectively as a rotten bottom. For example, if I am using wire with a breaking strain of 60lb I will use 30lb BS mono. In the event of the terminal rig snagging on the sea bed, the mono line will give way well before the wire, saving an expensive loss of wire line. Also, a terminal rig fishes far more efficiently and in a more natural manner off mono line than off wire. I adopt a similar approach when using braided lines. In this case, the mono once again acts as a rotten bottom and prevents wear to the expensive braided line, caused by the boom sliding up and down the braided line.

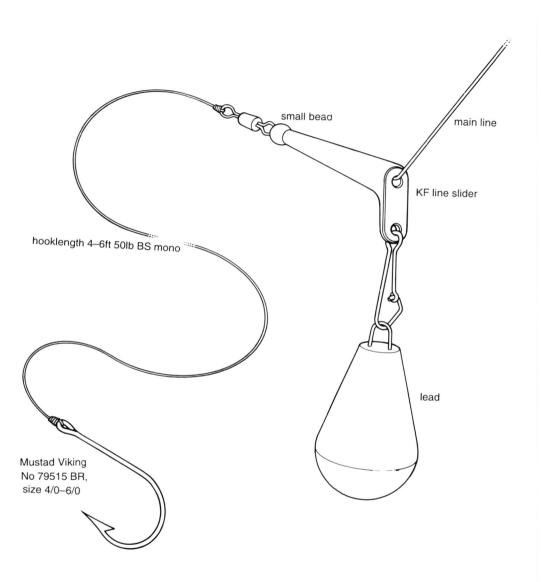

small bead

main line

KF line slider

hooklength 4–6ft 50lb BS mono

lead

Mustad Viking
No 79515 BR,
size 4/0–6/0

Simple downtiding running leger rig.

Bite Detection

We have already determined that part of the art of downtiding is in maintaining bottom contact when using light and sporting tackle; the other part is in bite detection. There is no place for a rod rest when fishing downtide, other than in acting as a convenient support for your rod when either unhooking fish or baiting up. At all other times it is vital that you hold your rod, feeling for bites. When cod fishing, the first indication the angler will have that a fish has located his bait will often be a nod on the rod tip. It must be stressed that the size of the bite should in no way be used to determine the size of the fish. Indeed, it is often the biggest fish which cause the most delicate of bites.

The reel should still be in free spool, with the angler checking the flow of line from the spool with his thumb. As soon as the first indication of a bite is felt the angler should respond by giving the fish a few yards of slack line. This in effect feeds the bait to the fish, allowing the fish to feel minimal resistance as it takes the bait into its mouth. For a sizeable predatory species of fish cod often bite very cautiously, and it is important to give the fish sufficient time to take the bait fully into its mouth before you make any attempt to strike. A lot of very good cod have been lost to impatience on the part of the angler.

After you have given the fish a few yards of slack line, re-check the flow of line and wait until you feel a more confident nodding on the rod tip. If at first you feel nothing do not be in too much of a rush to reel in and put a fresh bait on, as I have often had cod play with a bait for several minutes before they have finally taken it.

When you feel the time is right – and really only experience will let you know just when – re-engage the reel spool and swiftly retrieve all slack line. Only when you have achieved a straight line of contact between the rod tip and the hook, attempt to set the hook by lifting into the fish. Aggressive jerky strikes should be avoided especially when using wire or braided line, as it is all too easy to literally rip the hook from out of the fish's mouth.

UPTIDING

Wherever cod are caught over relatively clean ground, in depths of less than about 100ft, and with a strong run of tide, uptiding will almost always be the most effective method for catching them. Uptiding started to evolve into its present-day format in the Thames Estuary, back in the 1970s. There a group of anglers realized that when a boat is anchored in relatively shallow water certain species of fish, including cod, were deterred from swimming directly beneath the boat by noise caused by the boat, the anchor warp, and the anglers stamping around on deck. They realized that as a shoal of fish approached a boat, a high percentage of them would swim away from the area of greatest disturbance. In those days downtiding was the most popular method among boat anglers fishing at anchor, so most anglers were actually fishing in the area with the least fish, i.e. directly below and immediately astern of the boat.

It was discovered that if baits were cast away from the boat and held in place with a grip lead, much the same as when beach fishing, the anglers would be presenting their baits away from this area of disturbance, and in an area with a high concentration of fish. Catch rates began to soar and as the news spread, the popularity of uptiding grew across the country. Anglers fishing in areas with similar conditions to the Thames Estuary, such as the Bristol Channel and the Solent, were quick to recognize the tremendous advantages of the new technique, and before too long anglers all

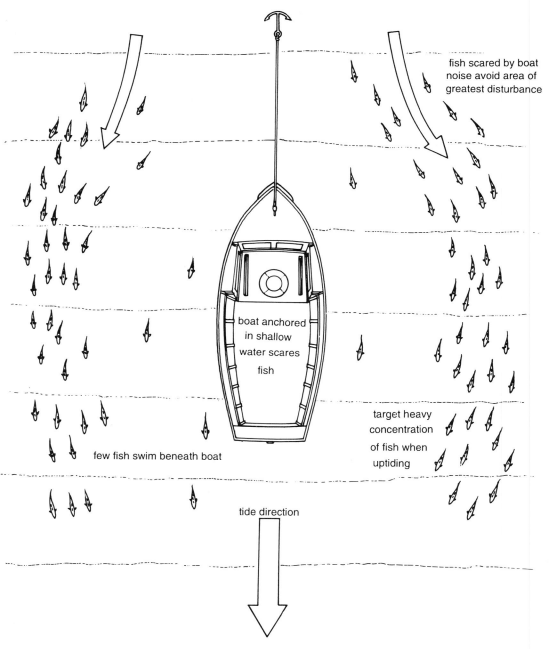

fish scared by boat
noise avoid area of
greatest disturbance

boat anchored
in shallow
water scares
fish

few fish swim beneath boat

target heavy
concentration
of fish when
uptiding

tide direction

The theory of uptiding. Plan view of a boat anchored in shallow water
showing how the majority of fish avoid swimming close to the area of
greatest disturbance.

over northern Europe were enjoying increased catch rates wherever uptiding could be applied.

Today the basic theory of uptiding remains much the same, but the technique has been polished to perfection. We now have rods designed specifically for uptiding, and reels which are far more suited to the technique. Anglers have a larger selection of different items of specialist terminal tackle from which to choose, and end rigs are far more effective. It needs to be said, however, that the most efficient terminal rigs for uptiding are almost always those that are the most simple.

Rigs

The basic uptiding rod should be between 9ft and 10ft in length, and capable, on average, of casting leads between 4oz and 6oz. Lighter and heavier uptide rods are suited to more specialist situations, but a rod which can comfortably handle a decent-sized bait and leads in the 5oz range should be considered as a good all-round uptider.

A good uptide rod should possess three important characteristics. The top third of the rod should have a fine and reasonably flexible tip for maximum bite detection, and to prevent the action of a boat rocking at anchor from prematurely breaking the grip lead out. The middle third of the rod should have sufficient give in it to facilitate comfortable and smooth casting, yet enough inherent power to play fish. The lower third of the rod should have the power to handle the biggest fish in a strong run of tide, and the guts to release snagged terminal rigs.

There are many excellent uptide blanks available in tackle shops today; the trouble is that too many of them are spoilt by inferior and inadequate fixtures and fittings. Fishing in a strong run of tide exerts a lot of pressure

The Shimano TLD 15 reel, an excellent choice for downtide fishing for cod.

on all items of the angler's tackle, and reel seats, rod rings and spigots which are not up to the job will take little of this treatment before they eventually fail. The various ranges of uptiders produced by Shimano, such as the Beastmaster, are among my favourites.

Likewise, there are a glut of reels on the market today. Most look as if they are good enough on a shelf in the local tackle shop, but inadequate gearing, weak frames and reel seats, a poor clutch and other inferior features are very quickly exposed. My own favourite uptide reels are ABU's timeless 7000 range and the revolutionary new Shimano 700 and 700S. Both are incredibly well-engineered reels which will provide a lifetime of use given a little care and attention. The retrieve on some modern multipliers is very fast, and care has to be taken not to wind too fast when playing a fish, as it is easy to exert too much pressure.

One of the fundamental items of terminal tackle essential for successful uptide fishing is a good grip lead, a weight capable of keeping the terminal rig nailed hard to the bottom, until either a fish takes the bait, or the angler wishes to wind in. My own choice of lead is the Gemini Breakout lead. These are available in a full range of sizes and can be moulded at home. Gemini leads are available with a selec-

tion of different-sized and shaped grip and tail wires, plus extension inserts to help increase grip under the varying conditions encountered by anglers. With the complete Gemini System, available in a convenient plastic box, the angler will be able to create the perfect lead weight for the conditions on the day.

I personally advise the use of a shockleader for most uptiding situations. A shockleader is a length of approx 50lb BS mono which is tied to the end of the main line on the reel. Its primary functions are to absorb the initial power surge of the cast and prevent the lead from cracking off, which can easily happen when using lighter breaking strains of line; lines of between 12lb and 18lb BS are standard when uptiding. A lead which cracks off during the cast will travel a considerable distance and can easily cause an injury aboard other boats fishing in the same area, not to mention aboard your own boat.

A shockleader has two other very important advantages. As will be seen, the uptiding technique involves releasing a large bow of slack line in order to assist the lead in holding in the tide. This results in the last section of the line lying in close contact with the sea bed. Were a leader not used, this would be the light main line which can be very easily damaged through abrasion with stones, mussels, etc. on the sea

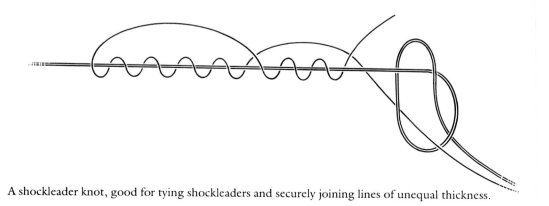

A shockleader knot, good for tying shockleaders and securely joining lines of unequal thickness.

A shockleader greatly assists when landing a cod in a strong run of tide.

bed. A shockleader very effectively prevents this from happening.

A leader can also help when landing fish. Playing a sizeable fish, such as a cod, to within landing range against a fast-running tide exerts an incredible amount of strain on the tackle. If you are using a leader you will have the insurance of a few turns of heavy line on the reel spool, which can provide that little bit of extra strength and security often required to guide your fish into the net. I have seen a lot of good fish lost over the years when the strain has simply been too much for light lines. On no account should the leader be used as an excuse to 'bully' fish into the net, and in no way should the leader be used to compensate for an incorrectly set clutch. A leader just adds that little bit of security which

can make all the difference between success and failure when landing a large fish.

On the negative side, a shockleader can cause problems when there is a lot of weed or other debris in the water. This can collect on the leader knot and jam in the tip ring, causing obvious problems when attempting to land fish. When conditions are really bad you have two options, the first being to dispense with the leader and take extra care casting. However, this option should never be considered if there is even a remote chance of a cracked-off lead hitting anyone or anything. Secondly, you can change to a reel loaded with about 25lb BS line, which provides a degree of protection when casting and is not too thick to cause problems in the run of tide. As you increase the breaking strain of line you use,

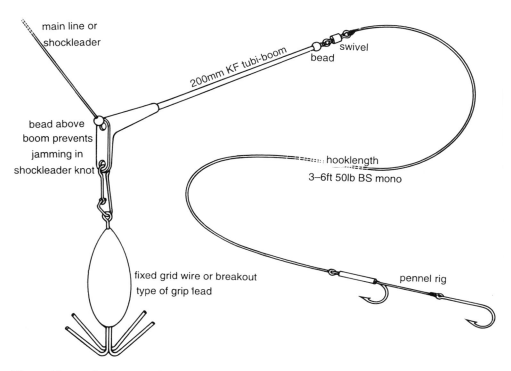

The uptide running leger rig. The 200mm KF Tubi-boom helps to prevent the hooklength from tangling around the lead grip wires during the cast.

you increase the diameter and surface area of line on which the tide can act. This can cause problems in holding bottom, unless you resort to ridiculously (and unnecessary) heavy weights.

I nearly always use a simple running leger rig when fishing uptide. The running leger is one of the easiest rigs of all to tie, it is more or less tangle free and presents baits as naturally as possible; what else could an angler ask from a rig?

I use a tubi-type boom to attach the lead; the extra length of the boom, over say a simple swivel snap link, helps to prevent the hooklength from becoming tangled around the

leader during casting. I first thread a small bead on to the leader, followed by the boom, a second bead and a small high-quality swivel. The purpose of the top bead is to prevent the shockleader knot from jamming in the top of the boom, which can happen if a good fish takes the bait and swims off, pulling the leader through the boom until the knot is reached. The second bead helps to prevent abrasion between the end of the boom and the knot which is attached to the swivel.

The length of hooklength you use is very important. Cod are a bottom-feeding species of fish, and the whole essence of uptiding is to be able to present a bait nailed hard to the sea bed. If you use a long hooklength in a very fast run of tide, the force of water can lift the bait clear of the bottom. Whenever uptiding in a very strong run of tide I keep my hooklengths to between 3ft and 5ft in length. On the other hand, when fishing in a moderate to weak flow of tide, it can be desirable to allow the tide to wave the bait gently around on the bottom, which can add to the attraction of that bait. When this is the case I will tie a hooklength of between 6ft and 8ft.

Too many anglers use line which is of far too light a breaking strain when tying hooklengths for cod. I always use good-quality 50lb BS mono which is strong enough to hold fish even if it has been subjected to the inevitable abrasion caused by the teeth of previous fish and contact with the bottom. In many areas, crabs play havoc with baits and these, too, can all too easily damage weak line with their pincers.

The pennel rig is probably the best all-round rig for uptide cod fishing, with the possible exception of when you intend fishing a livebait off a single hook. The pennel rig consists of two hooks tied in tandem, i.e. one above the other, as shown in the diagram. The top hook is held tightly in position by either thin rubber tubing – my own preference – or thin wire (it is better to be able to adjust the

A codling hooked on the top hook of a pennel rig.

distance between the hooks, to help compensate for different-sized baits).

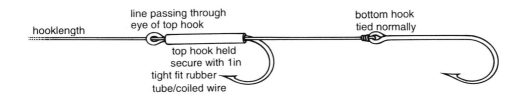

The pennel rig – ideal for mounting large baits for cod.

The pennel rig offers several advantages over a single hook rig. It is normal when cod fishing to use large baits. I regularly use worm and squid baits consisting of up to half a dozen large black lug, tipped with squid. The overall length of such a bait often exceeds 8 inches. Having a hook at either end of such a long thin bait is an obvious advantage, providing extra hooking potential regardless of which end of the bait the cod takes first. It is surprising just how many cod are landed, which are held only by the top hook.

An advantage of the pennel rig is that it greatly helps to improve bait presentation. The force of the cast when uptiding exerts a lot of pressure on what are often very soft baits. If these baits are not held securely with a combination of hooks and fine knitting elastic, then in all probability the whole lot will explode in mid-flight.

Baits

The correct way to mount worms on to a pennel rig is to thread them very carefully on to the hook. It does not matter whether or not you start at the head or the tail. The sand tail on blow lug is of no use as bait so it is best to pinch it off with your fingers. You will now have a convenient hole into which you can insert the point of the hook and start threading the worm.

The first worm should be threaded all the way around the bend of the hook, up the shank, over the eye, and up on to the hooklength between the two hooks in the pennel. Now very carefully thread the top end of the worm on to the point of the top hook, followed by a further one inch of worm, before nicking the point of the hook back out of the worm. The top hook will now hold the worm securely. Next, thread extra worms on to the pennel until you have completely filled

the trace between the two hooks, and finally tip the hook points with strips of squid. I would suggest that any cod bait should have a minimum size of about 4 inches, and much bigger baits are the norm with most specialists.

Threading worms on to a pennel without bursting them takes time, but it is important to get it right. If you burst the body of the worm many of the vital fish-attracting body juices will very quickly flow out, rendering the bait next to useless in no time at all. If the worms are not mounted neatly small fish and crabs will very quickly strip your hooks clean. If the bait is too loosely mounted, it will probably explode with the force of the cast, much to the delight of the seagulls!

Other baits such as squid and crab, etc. should be mounted on to the pennel rig in a similar way. Always take time to ensure that the hook points are well exposed and not masked by the bait. Bait is often very expensive, and hard work to obtain yourself. It obviously makes sense to take a minute or two to ensure that you present it correctly. On occasion, I substitute the swivel joining the hooklength to the shockleader with a strong spring slip. This I use to attach the swivel on the end of the hooklength, allowing hooklengths to be quickly attached or removed. This, in turn, allows me to prepare baits at my leisure between casts, helping to maximize the time I have a bait in the water, and to ensure that each and every bait is perfectly presented.

Casting

As I have mentioned above, the uptiding technique involves casting the bait uptide and away from the boat. The end rig is then allowed to sink swiftly to the sea bed, and the angler releases extra line to create a bow in the tide to assist the lead in gripping. As a rule of thumb you should aim to cast at an angle of approximately 45 degrees to a line drawn through the anchor warp and the centre of the boat. There is no need to try to cast a bait beyond the horizon, a smooth lob of about 50 yards will be more than adequate in most cases.

Casting a baited end rig and spiked grip lead aboard a boat is not without its risks. Before you cast, make sure that all anglers aboard the boat are fully aware that you are about to cast. Simply muttering 'casting' under your breath is not sufficient. Wherever possible try to hang the terminal tackle outboard prior to the cast, and keep it outboard during the cast. This will not always be possible, but if it is safer to walk to the back of the boat to cast, then that is what you must do.

A good tip is to hang the bottom hook of the pennel rig on to one of the lead grip wires prior to casting. This will give you a much improved casting angle, by preventing the bait from dangling in the water. It will also help to keep the bait intact during the cast, in much the same way as a bait clip assists the beach angler. Provided that you have used a tubi-boom there will be minimum risk of the hooklength tangling during the cast. As well as other anglers, before you cast make sure that you will not catch any other fishing lines, and pay particular attention to radar scanners and radio masts.

In a moderate flow of tide, casting at 45 degrees is about right. However, as the tide increases in flow it will be easier to maintain a grip on the bottom if you reduce the angle, until you are more or less casting parallel to the anchor warp when the tide is pulling at its strongest. Conversely, as the tide starts to slacken off towards low water increase the angle, so that you are casting about 90 degrees or straight across the tide at slack water.

Only experience will show you exactly how much slack line to let out. The factors to take into consideration are water depth and tidal

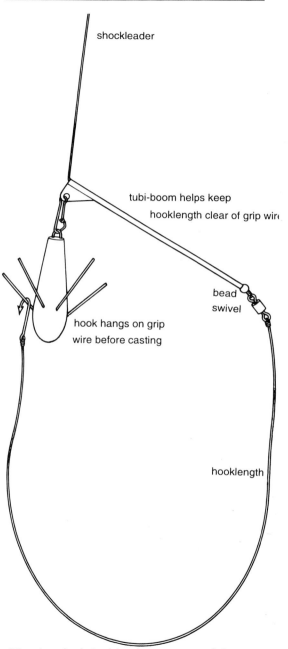

shockleader

tubi-boom helps keep
hooklength clear of grip wire

bead
swivel

hook hangs on grip
wire before casting

hooklength

Hanging the baited hooks onto one of the grip wires prior to casting is a wise safety precaution, and greatly assists casting within confined situations.

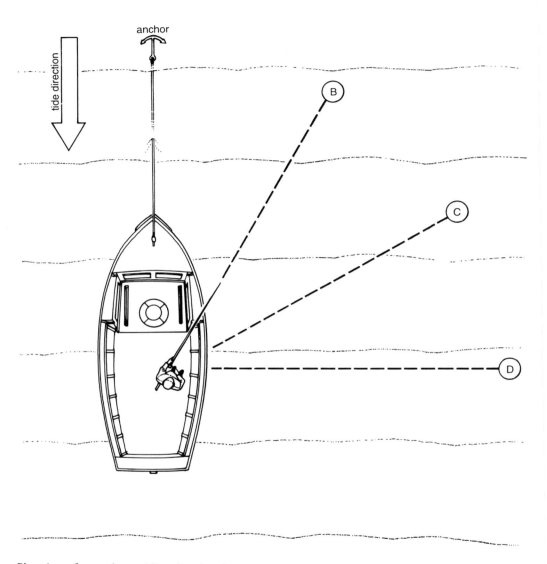

Plan view of an angler uptiding showing the varying casting angles depending on different strengths of tide. The angler casts to position B when the tide is running hardest. He then increases the casting angle to C as the flow moderates and then increases further to D just before slack water.

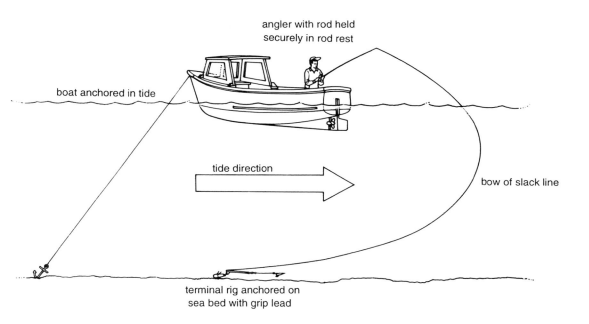

angler with rod held
securely in rod rest

boat anchored in tide

tide direction

bow of slack line

terminal rig anchored on
sea bed with grip lead

Cross-section of an angler uptiding aboad a boat showing how the bow line should lie in the tide. When the tide is running hard the angler releases a large bow of slack line. As the tide eases off he gradually reduces the amount of slack line released and the size of the bow.

flow; as these increase you will have to release extra line, and vice versa. By and large, if you are experiencing problems with your lead prematurely breaking out, your first course of action should be to cast at a tighter angle to the anchor warp and/or release extra line. Increasing the size of lead is not always the answer.

When fishing at slack tide or when there is little tide running, it is sometimes possible, and productive, to fish uptide with plain lead weights and allow the tide steadily to drag the baited terminal rig across the bottom, hoping to locate and attract fish. This can be a very

productive method during the slack-water period when the boat starts swinging at anchor. Try to calculate which way the boat is going to swing (this will depend on the wind direction and direction of the next tide), and cast your bait more or less straight out of the back of the boat. Slack line should be avoided. Not only will bites be difficult to spot if you have too much slack line out, but there will be a danger that the slack line will drift beneath the boat and snag either the propeller or rudder, or risk damaging your line on the boat's hull.

Uptiding is one form of angling where it is

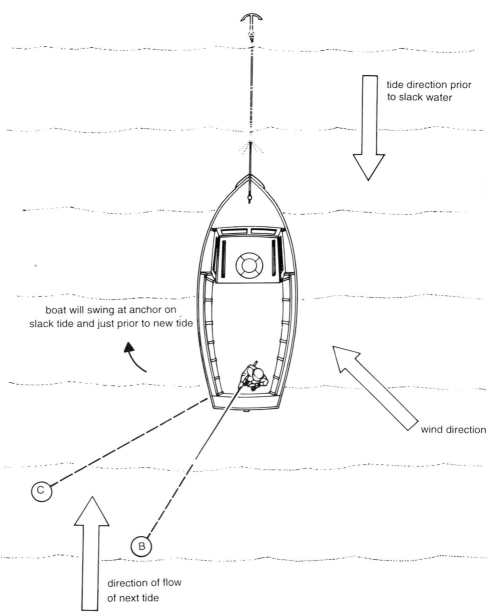

tide direction prior to slack water

boat will swing at anchor on slack tide and just prior to new tide

wind direction

C

B

direction of flow of next tide

Diagram showing the best angle to cast at slack tide, just before the boat starts to swing at anchor. The angler casts to B as slack tide approaches and then to C as the boat starts to swing. He then has to retrieve the slack line in order to maintain a tight line. Using a plain lead at such times is useful when fishing over clean ground.

Bite Detection

There are two different types of bite detection which you are likely to see when uptiding. The first I call the 'classic uptide bite'. When the rod is held in its rest the tip of the rod bends over with the force of tide on the line. If a good fish takes the bait and tries to swim off it can break the lead free from the sea bed, usually hooking itself in the process. When this happens, the first indication the angler will have that a fish has taken his bait will be when the tip of his rod springs smartly upright, with the sudden reduction in pressure on it.

The second type of bite is a nodding on the rod tip. There is a saying, 'two nods for a cod', which refers to the typical cod bite, i.e. a double nod on the rod tip, which often precedes the lead getting broken out. By and large, when you see the bite it will be time to reel in, bearing in mind that you have a bow of slack line to retrieve before you can attempt to set the hook. Cod in particular are not cautious feeders: if they want a bait they generally try to engulf it in one.

Playing the Fish

The biggest problem with leaving fish for too long before winding them in is that they can quickly swim a long way downtide, which will result in the angler having to pump the fish back to within landing range against the tide. A lot of good fish have been lost as a result of this, especially when they have broken the lead free and swum all the way downtide before the angler has noticed what has happened.

When the angler sees a bite he should swiftly try to retrieve the bow of slack line, and if the lead has not broken free, break it out by a combination of winding and pumping as soon as he can. Only when he has a straight line of

Playing a fish on an uptide rod in a strong run of tide. It is important that the angler does not attempt to set the hook until he is sure he has a straight line of contact between the rod and the fish.

advantageous to place a rod in a secure rod rest, and then sit back and wait for something to happen. Note that I say 'a secure' rod rest. When fishing in a strong run of tide, rods which are not held securely can all too easily be lost over the side, especially if a fish takes off downtide or a large raft of seaweed snags the line. Unless the boat has pod-mounted rod rests I strongly advise that you tie your rod in place against the railings.

Andrew Leaves holds a fit a 14lb cod caught uptiding aboard the author's boat in shallow water.

contact between the tip of his rod and the fish should he attempt to set the hooks. Trying to set a hook with a large bow of line in the tide is totally futile, regardless of how hard the angler strikes. When it's time to strike, the angler should wind the rod tip down and set the hooks to be firmly lifting into the fish. Sharp jerky strikes should be avoided.

When uptiding for cod, the correct way to play a fish is by steadily winding, and keeping firm but not excessive pressure on the fish at all times. The trick is to keep the rod bent at all times. If the rod is bent there is pressure holding the hook in the fish; give the fish an inch of slack and all but the deepest-hooked fish will probably get free.

Occasionally when uptiding you will find that you drop several fish off before they can be netted, which is obviously very frustrating. Assuming that your hook points are sharp and not masked by the bait, I have found that slightly reducing the size of the bait and making sure that the hook points stand really proud can result in a more secure hookhold. This problem is usually more evident when fishing in little run of tide; I suppose that when the tide is running hard the extra pressure helps to set the hook on the fish, which will have less time to mouth a bait before taking it.

TROLLING

Until a few years ago I would never really have considered trolling as being a recognized technique for fishing for cod. Then I visited a small town in Denmark called Ebeltoft, to fish for sea trout in the sea. We would be fishing aboard small 16ft and 17ft dinghies which were fully equipped for trolling with down-riggers, the favoured technique for catching sea trout in that part of the world.

The sea off Ebeltoft is extremely shallow and for much of the time we were fishing in less than 30ft of water, often less than 10ft. The water was also crystal clear, not, you would imagine, ideal conditions for cod fishing. We had only been fishing for about 10 minutes when we had the first strike on one of the lures, a Rapala J13, which was fishing just below the surface. Fully expecting a sea trout to leap clear of the water at any moment, I was surprised to find that the fish stayed deep in the water. By the time I had played the fish to within reach of the landing-net I had correctly guessed its identity as a codling, a beautifully marked fish of around 4lb in weight. Initially I put this first cod capture down to a one-off fluke, but by the end of the day when I had

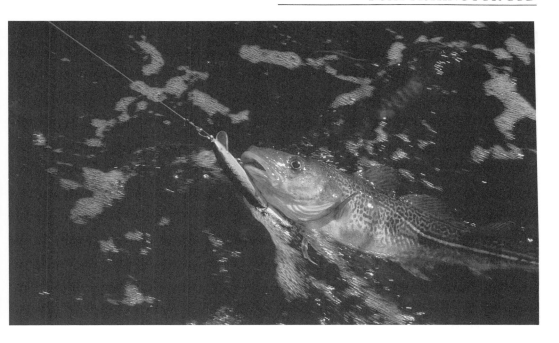

A Danish codling caught trolling a jointed plug.

Two rods fishing in conjunction with a downrigger.

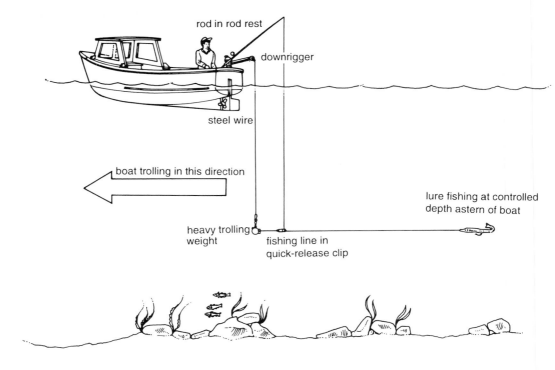

rod in rod rest

downrigger

steel wire

boat trolling in this direction

lure fishing at controlled
depth astern of boat

heavy trolling
weight

fishing line in
quick-release clip

A downrigger in use.

personally caught somewhere in excess of 30 similar fish, I began to look upon trolling as a useful method for catching cod!

Now I am not suggesting that trolling will work everywhere for cod, but I remain convinced that there is plenty of scope for experimentation in certain areas. The fish in Denmark were caught over a mix of open sandy ground and rock. Elsewhere, I think that trolling over the rockier marks will be most likely to produce cod.

In Denmark I found that the excellent range of plugs made by Rapala, the largest manufacturer of fishing lures in the world, were by far the most productive. I used the Rapala J11 and 13 lures, jointed plugs, in a wide assortment of different colours. The Rapala Silver and Magnum range, which have

been specifically designed for saltwater fishing, would almost certainly also catch cod.

The advantage of using a downrigger for trolling is that the depth at which the lures work can be very accurately set. By working the downrigger in conjunction with a good fishfinder, the angler will be able to fish his lures to within a few feet of the top of a reef, or wreck, increasing and decreasing the depth of the lure accordingly as the bottom contours change. Downriggers are becoming more and more popular among European anglers; the Cannon downriggers marketed by Normark are the best I have seen and are ideal for use aboard small boats. This is one area of boat-fishing where there is certainly plenty of scope for anglers to experiment, for cod and many other species.

5 Shore Fishing For Cod

At certain times of the year, generally following onshore gales during the autumn and winter months, cod swim to within casting range on many beaches. And when the angler finds himself on the right beach at the right time, he can experience some exceptional sport. Around the UK anglers fish for cod off many different types of beach, ranging from the rugged, snag-ridden, rock marks so typical of the north, to the open expanses of sand and shingle often associated with cod fishing in the south. Cod are caught from other locations, too, including many tidal estuaries, piers and breakwaters.

Naturally, the techniques adopted by anglers fishing these wide-ranging venues vary considerably. On one mark the angler will find it necessary to fine-tune and polish his casting style and the aerodynamics of his terminal rig, in order to present a tempting bait at long range. On other venues distance is not such a prerequisite to success, as cod are more commonly caught within comfortable casting range for most anglers. More often than not, these close-range venues will be those which give access to deep water and there will probably be a price to pay; for instance, often the angler will now be fishing over rock and weed where tackle losses can be high.

Over the years, anglers have cunningly devised many little items of terminal tackle, techniques and dodges which help to adapt when fishing different venues. Tackle manu-facturers have been quick to provide a full selection of injection-moulded plastic 'gizmos', some of which have been a tremendous asset on the beach, but many others will catch little more than gullible anglers looking for easy results.

In this section, I offer advice on how to fish different types of shore venue and give suggestions on those techniques, rigs and tackle accessories which over the years I have found to be useful. Sadly, there is no fast road to success, and my advice to any angler – and especially the shore angler – would always be to maximize your effort towards using the right bait, in the right place and at the right time. Only then will you stand a chance of catching cod from the shore on a regular basis.

FISHING OVER CLEAN GROUND

Many of the most productive beaches for cod are those which are steepest, and often consist of shingle and pebbles; Dungeness in Kent and Chesil Beach in Dorset are two good examples. However, it is not only those beaches with deep water close in which produce fish, anglers fishing very flat beaches can also catch a lot of fish but, by and large, they have to be able to cast baits a long way on this type of beach in order to reach the fish. Many of the beaches in East Anglia fall within this category.

Beach fishing for cod following a strong onshore blow. Cod will often move inshore following such conditions to mop up shellfish and worms that the heavy wave action will have ripped out of the sand.

As mentioned above, the best results when fishing open beaches are generally achieved by those anglers fishing either during or just after a good onshore blow. Many of the items of food upon which inshore cod feed live buried in the sand and shingle, and include all sorts of marine worms and shellfish. During rough weather the wave action rips these out of the sanctuary and security of their burrows, providing easy pickings for hungry fish. When the gale is still blowing the majority of fish will probably remain outside of most anglers' casting range, but as the waves start to subside they move inshore to gorge themselves. This is often the best time to fish. At other times, few cod venture to within casting range, other than under the cover of darkness.

The exception is when it is possible to fish in a deep gulley or other feature, which cod swim past at certain stages of the tide.

In shallow, clear water most cod will only venture inshore to within casting range under cover of darkness.

Always try to study a beach at low water before you fish when the tide has covered all important features. Not only will this help prevent tackle losses, but it will help you to locate the best spots to catch cod.

Wherever the beach forms a natural headland deflecting the run of tide there will almost always be an area of fast, deep water at the very tip of the headland, which has been scoured out by the tide over the years. Often such a feature will form a vast eddy, and will invariably be an excellent place to fish for cod.

One of the best pieces of advice I can give to anyone planning on fishing a beach for cod, or indeed any other species of fish, is to study the beach thoroughly first at low water. Try to pick out those features which might attract cod when the tide has come in, especially areas where the fish might concentrate and feed. These might include such features as small areas of rough ground, mussel beds, deep gullies which act as natural food traps, or small

sand or gravel banks. Few beaches are totally featureless, even though they might appear to be so at first glance. The best time to view any beach is at low water on a big tide, as this is when the largest area of the beach will be exposed.

Rigs and Baits

The angler who intends fishing open beaches should gear up to fishing at long range, but should never overlook the fact that even over open beaches cod will, on occasion, feed very close to the surf line. Fishing successfully at range involves taking the time to develop a suitable casting style along with tailoring terminal rigs for maximum-range fishing, by making sure they are as aerodynamic as possible.

A good beachcaster balanced for casting leads of between 5oz and 6oz matched with either a fixed spool or a multiplier reel will be needed. Do not be tempted to rush out and but a high-performance beachcaster capable of casting great distances if your casting technique is not yet fully developed. Such rods will only cast long distances if they are made to work, and in order to make them work you will first need a sound casting technique. If you do not have the technique then in all probability you will cast a considerably shorter distance when using a high-performance rod than if using a more forgiving blank, suited to a more general style of casting.

Any good tackle shop should be able to advise you accordingly, provided you give them an honest and not exaggerated appraisal of your casting ability. Most tackle shops should also be able to put you in touch with a casting instructor who, for a nominal fee, will be able more or less instantly to improve your casting ability.

Too many anglers attempt to over-complicate their end rigs, when in reality the most efficient rigs will almost always be those which are of the simplest design. For long-range fishing over open beaches for cod my own choice and the choice of many other cod specialists, is a straightforward single-clipped paternoster rig incorporating either a single hook or, more often than not when targeting cod, a pennel rig.

When deliberately fishing cod it is almost always advisable to use a decent-sized bait, and obviously large baits will seriously impair casting performance. For this reason, it is generally best to fish a single bait. The most efficient rig from both a fishing and a casting point of view, will have a bait clip incorporated into the rig just above the lead weight. This

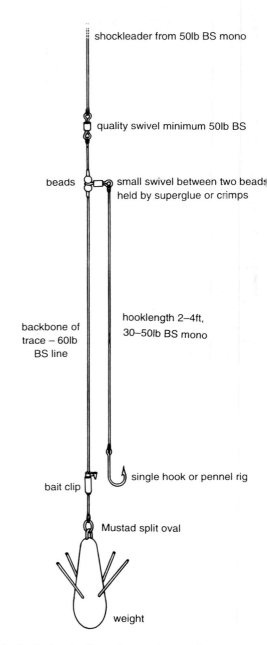

A single hook clipped paternoster rig: a good basic all-round rig for beach cod fishing.

Rig incorporating a bait clip, which prevents the bait from getting damaged during the cast, then releases the hook on contact with the water.

Blow lug mounted onto a pennel rig and clipped behind the lead weight, a standard technique used by shore anglers targetting cod.

holds the bait against the backbone of the rig during casting.

If the bait were allowed to flap wildly about during the cast, not only would the distance of the cast be greatly reduced but the bait presentation would almost certainly be damaged. When using soft baits such as lugworms or mussel, baits which are not clipped down can be ripped completely off the hooks. Also, by clipping the bait just above the lead weight it will ride within the slipstream of the lead during the cast, again helping to maximize on distance.

Beach anglers use a wide variety of baits

when cod fishing from open beaches. In most areas, good-quality black lugworm take a lot of beating, either used fresh or salted. Blow lug are also very good, as are ragworm. Many types of shellfish, notably razorfish, also make excellent baits when used over clean beaches, especially following rough weather.

A whole squid is another very good bait when used by anglers targeting big fish, but nothing can beat a livebait whenever the angler wants to catch a double-figure fish or bigger. Many of the biggest cod ever caught from the beach have been caught on live whiting and pouting, though in most cases

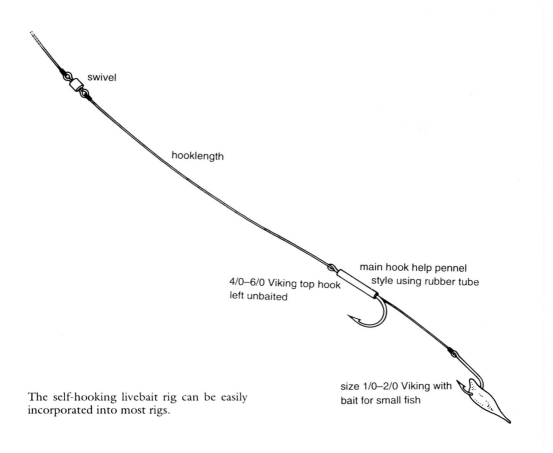

swivel

hooklength

4/0–6/0 Viking top hook
left unbaited

main hook help pennel
style using rubber tube

size 1/0–2/0 Viking with
bait for small fish

The self-hooking livebait rig can be easily
incorporated into most rigs.

they have taken a fish which has hung itself on
a larger bait and gone unnoticed. Then a large
cod has seized the hooked fish, and somehow
managed to hook itself in the process.

There is, however, a technique beach
anglers can use which is designed to fish a livebait at long range. There is still a great element
of chance when tactic to fish on a second rod.
The rig is known as the self-hooking livebait
rig. The actual hooklength (shown in the
diagram) used for this style of fishing can be
used as an element of most designs of rig.
Basically the angler baits the smaller hook, and

leaves the larger hook free. The rig is then cast
out and left. In theory a small fish, such as a
whiting, pouting, poor cod or rockling, finds
the bait on the smaller hook, takes it and
hooks itself. It is now tethered below the
larger hook. Eventually the bait fish's frantic
struggling attracts a large cod, which engulfs
it and hooks itself on the larger unbaited hook
in the process.

FISHING OVER ROUGH GROUND

Some of the most productive marks for catching cod from the shore are found in the vicinity of rough ground. Patches of rough ground, which include either extensive systems of reefs or smaller isolated areas, invariably hold a wealth of food, and many species of fish, including cod, either become resident or visit them at certain times of the tide to feed. Naturally these marks can be very productive for the shore angler, though fishing successfully over rough ground is generally far more difficult than fishing over clean ground.

The single biggest problem facing the angler when fishing a rough-ground mark is the ever-present risk of his terminal rig becoming snagged, which can result in heavy tackle losses and/or the loss of hooked fish. Thankfully, there are several techniques the angler can adopt which will greatly help to reduce the risk of such losses. The ideal choice of outfit will depend on whether it is necessary to fish at close or long range. Long-range fishing over rough ground requires a far higher level of skill and experience than does short-range fishing.

Rigs and Baits

The first point to note is that rough ground and light tackle rarely go well together so the first requirement when fishing any rough-ground venue is a strong rod and reel. A rod with the necessary backbone to pull out of snags and prevent hooked fish from swimming into snags is a must. Similarly, a reel with a strong one-piece frame and reliable, well-engineered internal gearing is a must.

Many anglers make the mistake of using small multiplier reels when fishing rough ground. Many of these reels, which include the ABU 6500c and other similar models, are, essentially, designed for salmon spinning using 1oz and 2oz lures, though with care they can be used with great effect for long-range fishing over clean ground. However, they do not have the inherent strength to handle rough-ground fishing and when overloaded their frames very quickly distort, their spools burst and the internal gearing all but collapses.

Thankfully, there are many reels ideally suited to fishing over rough ground available on the market. In my opinion the best of the bunch is the Shimano Speedmaster TSM IIC. This particular model has an excellent line capacity, a very strong one-piece frame, and the best internal gearing I have seen on any reel in its class. The Speedmaster casts very well and is a particularly smooth reel to use, but best of all it has a very fast rate of retrieve which is ideal for keeping terminal rigs and hooked fish well up in the water, and away from the worst of the snags.

Some form of rotten bottom incorporated into the terminal rig is a must when tying all rigs intended for use over rough ground. By attaching the lead with a rotten bottom (a length of line with a breaking strain below that of the main reel line, shockleader and all other components of the terminal rig), it will be possible to break the terminal rig free in the event of the lead becoming snagged, resulting in the loss of just the lead. In most cases, it is the lead which becomes snagged by getting wedged between rocks. If other items of tackle, such as the hooks, become snagged, it will often be possible to pull free by applying steady pressure.

There are several different ways by which a lead can be attached with a rotten bottom. The single biggest problem when tying a rotten bottom is in ensuring that the lead does not snap off prematurely during casting, which will almost certainly happen if it is

101

The Shimano Speedmaster TSM II, one of the best long-range, rough-ground beach reels ever made.

attached to the terminal rig directly with a length of weak line. Over the years I have experimented with several different methods of attaching leads for rough-ground fishing and the method described below is by far the most efficient I have found when fishing rough ground from the shore.

A short loop is tied into the bottom of the terminal rig, which should be constructed from line with a minimum breaking strain of 60lb. The weak line, usually line with about 10lb BS, is tied to the bottom of this loop. A length of about three inches is a good average. The other end of this weak line is tied to the lead. Prior to casting, the loop is passed through the eye of the lead weight and held in place with a stainless-steel panel pin, which as first been pushed through a small block of foam rubber or polystyrene. The pin keeps the

lead securely attached to the loop during casting, but floats free on contact with the water, leaving the lead tethered to the terminal rig by the weak line.

Now if the lead becomes snagged, the remainder of the terminal rig can be broken free easily, resulting in just the loss of the lead. This technique is particularly important when retrieving a hooked fish. The last thing any angler would want is to lose a fish simply because the rig was snagged with a lead which could not be broken free.

A shockleader is an essential safety element when beachcasting, but there is nothing worse than having to continually re-tie shockleaders lost in snags. Unfortunately, whenever it is necessary to fish at long range the angler will have no option other than using a leader in conjunction with a relatively light main line, which will generally be around 18lb BS. However, when it is possible to fish at short range and the angler does not have to put so much effort into casting, a 25lb BS main line straight through from the reel to the terminal rig should suffice, as long as the angler exercises caution prior to every cast. Whenever there is the slightest doubt about casting safety, a shockleader must be used.

This heavier main line has the disadvantage that it will reduce the total line capacity of the reel and restrict maximum casting performance. But when fishing at short range these two factors are more than offset by the increased breaking strain, which makes it possible to break free from most snags with only the loss of the lead.

When fishing over rough ground the choice of terminal rig is important. Complicated multi-hook rigs are far more prone to snagging than single-hook rigs tied using a minimum of tackle components. This is true

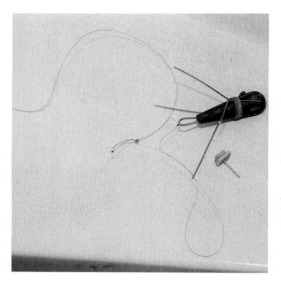

Rotten bottom rig that incorporates a loop tied in the end of the trace, a short length of weak line, and a pin.

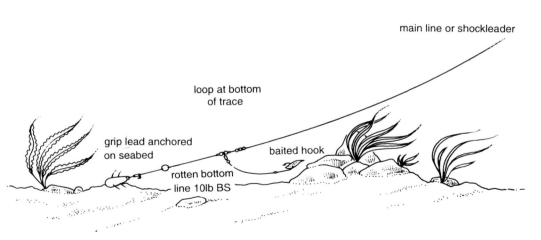

Diagram showing a rotten bottom rig in use. If the lead becomes snagged, firm pressure from the angler should easily snap the weak line resulting in just the loss of the lead.

Fishing a rough-ground mark for cod.

Diagram showing a lead lift in use. The lead lift is attached just above the lead weight and causes the terminal rig to plane upwards and clear the worst snags during retrieval.

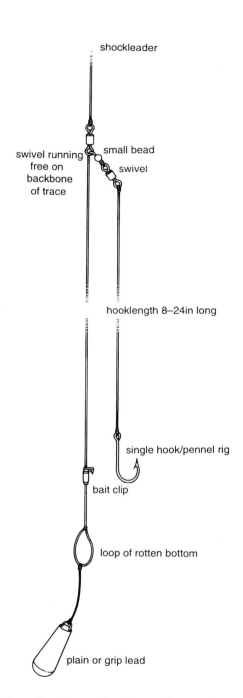

shockleader

swivel running free on backbone of trace

small bead

swivel

hooklength 8–24in long

single hook/pennel rig

bait clip

loop of rotten bottom

plain or grip lead

The pulley rig, excellent for rough ground.

when fishing both at short and long range. When fishing at short range there will rarely be any advantage in using anything more complicated than a single paternoster rig, either tied with a single hook or a pennel rig.

One useful item of terminal tackle which is worth using, more so when fishing at long range, is a lead lift. Several tackle manufacturers produce lead lifts which are very similar to plastic dart flights and are attached to the bottom of the terminal rig. The lead is invariably attached to the bottom end of the lead lift. When the baited terminal rig is cast out the lead lift serves little use; it is when the rig is retrieved that its usefulness will be appreciated. As the angler starts to retrieve his rig, the shape of the lead lift automatically causes the rig to plane upwards through the water, raising the entire terminal rig high above the worst of the snags and greatly reducing the probability of the rig snagging on the way in.

The pulley rig is by far the most efficient all-round terminal rig to use when fishing at long range over rough ground. The action of this rig ensures that when retrieving a hooked fish the lead, if it has not already broken free, rides high in the water this minimizes the chance of it becoming snagged, which would almost certainly result in the loss of that fish.

The best baits to use over rough ground for cod vary considerably from area to area but, as is almost always the case in angling, the most efficient bait will be the bait which the fish are actively searching for. Peeler crab easily tops the list of baits for rough-ground cod in most areas, as crabs make up a very large part of the diet of inshore cod. In some areas, local anglers use mussel to great effect, along with other types of shellfish. Worms are not generally the most efficient rough-ground cod baits, but in reality no hungry cod is likely to turn its nose up and swim past a juicy worm bait. Whole squid and livebait frequently sort out the better fish.

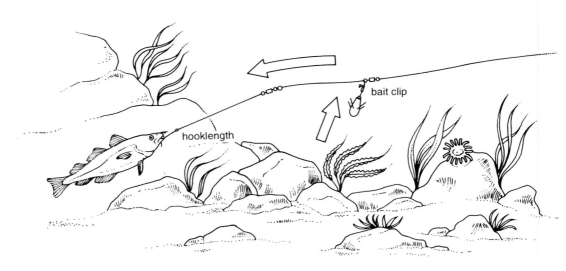

bait clip

hooklength

The pulley rig in use. The pulley action of the rig has ensured that the weight of the hooked fish has pulled the weight high in the water and clear of snags, preventing it from becoming snagged on the way in.

FISHING FROM PIERS AND BREAKWATERS

Piers and breakwaters are among the most productive of fishing marks for the shore-bound angler. These man-made structures provide shore anglers with easy access to deep water, without having to resort to boats, and they attract many species of fish in exactly the same way as a wrecked ship lying on the sea bed quickly becomes inhabited by a multitude of marine life, which in turn attracts larger species of fish. The base and underwater section of piers and breakwaters very quickly become encrusted with a rich variety of life, attracting thousands of small fish and their predators. On occasion, cod move among the pier pilings and along the base of breakwaters to feed and can be caught by dropping a bait straight down from the vantage point above;

however, more often than not the best cod fishing will be had by those anglers casting well away from the actual structure.

Breakwaters – and to a far lesser extent elevated piers – deflect the flow of tide, which over the years scours out a deep-water channel off the end of the structure. The exact position of this deep-water channel will depend upon many factors such as the direction and rate of flow of the main tidal current, in relation to the length and angle of the breakwater. Often one side of the pier will be flushed with a very strong flow of water, while the water on the other side, generally the inner side, will be comparatively slack. Often the best place to catch cod will be wherever the water is at its deepest and fastest.

One of the biggest problems which many anglers encounter when fishing off piers and breakwaters is holding bottom with their

Piers and breakwaters often offer the shore angler easy access to deep water.

grip on the sea bed by reducing the angle of pull. The reel spool is now re-engaged and the rod placed securely in its rest, with its tip bending over in the tide.

When a fish locates the bait, the bite will be registered in one of two ways. Firstly, the angler will see the tip of his rod nodding, and secondly, which is generally the case with larger fish, the next indication he will see will be when the rod tip suddenly springs upright as the fish breaks the lead out of the sea bed. In either case, the fish invariably hook themselves against the resistance of the anchored grip lead.

Different anglers use a wide range of end rigs when fishing from piers and breakwaters, the final choice often being dictated by the range at which the angler intends to fish, the depth of water and the exact nature of the sea bed, i.e. rough ground or clean. My own favourite pier rig when targeting cod is the simple running-leger rig, which apart from being very easy to tie casts well and presents what are often large baits in a very natural way. Occasionally I adapt the hooklength to a wishbone rig, which gives me the best option for catching both large and small fish. Piers and breakwaters are excellent venues from which to fish a livebait, especially in conjunction with the self-hooking livebait rig described in the section on clean ground.

Landing fish, especially large fish, from piers and breakwaters can be difficult. The answer is to ensure you have a drop-net ready to hand should you need one. Many tackle shops now sell purpose-made drop-nets, though equally functional nets are very easily made. Climbing down to land fish by hand can be very dangerous, especially in rough seas, and is therefore best avoided.

terminal rig in the strong run of water. Naturally, grip leads will almost always be required, but even then the flow of water off many of these locations is such that even the largest leads are ripped straight out of the sea bed, unless the angler adopts the correct approach.

The answer when faced with such testing conditions is to treat fishing fast water off piers and breakwaters in exactly the same way as when fishing off a boat, i.e. by uptiding. The angler casts his bait well uptide of the spot which he intends fishing, and allows it to sink swiftly to the sea bed. When the angler feels his lead touch bottom he releases a bow of slack line, which helps the lead to maintain its

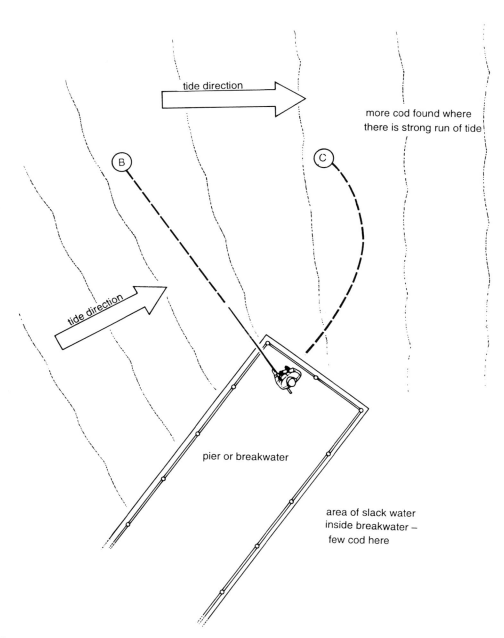

The correct angle to cast when fishing off a pier or breakwater with a strong run of the tide. The angler casts to B and the lead touches the bottom at C and grips. The angler then releases a bow of slack line into the tide to help the lead maintain its grip.

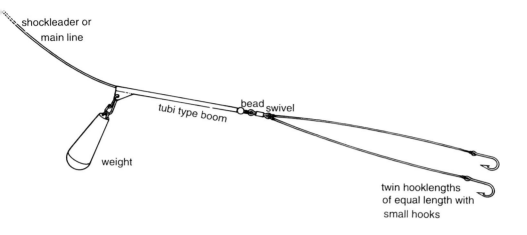

shockleader or
main line

tubi type boom

bead swivel

weight

twin hooklengths
of equal length with
small hooks

Running leger rig incorporating a wishbone rig. In use this offers the best chance of catching large and small fish. The combined scent trail from two small baits is equivalent to one large one, and attracts fish of all sizes. Small fish can take just one bait while larger ones often take both. The rig can also be fished as two pennel rigs for maximum hooking power.

FISHING WITHIN ESTUARIES

At certain times of the year cod can be caught in many of the estuaries of northern Europe. It is not too difficult to fathom out just why these fish, which are more often associated with the open sea, migrate so far inland and into waters which are often extremely shallow and coloured to the point of zero visibility, and with high volumes of fresh water diluting the salt content: food. Compared with many areas of coastline, most estuaries are heavily populated with a rich assortment of life, ranging from the tiniest sand-fleas to various species of shellfish and massive populations of crabs, shrimps and prawns. Often there will be vast populations of small fish resident within an estuary, which are either the fry or at the juvenile stage of larger species, or fish which are species in their own right such as sand-eels. Together, all of these help to provide a well-stocked larder and food aplenty for hungry cod.

In most cases, cod start to move inshore and into estuaries in the autumn, though in some cases the first fish arrive in late summer. The actual time that these fish stay varies considerably and is dependent upon many factors. These include the continuation of the availability of food, water temperature, and, probably the most important consideration of all, the amounts of fresh water flooding into the estuary.

In a normal year most rainfall occurs throughout the autumn and winter months, and as this fresh water enters the upper reaches of the estuary it rapidly starts to dilute the salt content, as it works its way into the lower reaches and the open sea. Cod display a reasonable tolerance towards brackish conditions, but once certain levels of salinity are approached they quickly start to drop back towards the mouth of the estuary and more favourable conditions. The estuaries of the Thames, Humber and Mersey and the upper reaches of the Bristol Channel are among the most productive for autumn and winter cod fishing, within the British Isles.

By and large it is mainly smaller codling which are caught within estuaries, with fish weighing between 1lb and 4lb being the average. However, much larger fish are often caught, and the chances of a double-figure specimen should never be totally ruled out. For example, from September until the end of December large numbers of codling are caught by anglers fishing at Redwick, Magor and Goldcliff in the Severn Estuary. On occasion, double-figure fish are taken and fish to over 20lb have been caught here in recent years. The water is heavily coloured, several major rivers continuously pump millions of gallons of fresh water into the system just a few miles upstream, and the water depth is often less than six feet, yet these mature fish thrive under these conditions.

One of the real beauties of cod fishing within an estuary is that long-range casting is not always necessary; indeed, at times it can be a positive disadvantage. A well-defined deep-water channel along which the tide floods before spilling out over the neighbouring mudflats or sand banks is a central feature within most estuaries. Initially, when fishing around low water or when the tide is just starting to flood, most fish will be concentrated within this channel so it will be the optimum area in which to present a bait. As the height of the tide increases and starts to flood out of this channel, it will not be too long before the first fish start to follow, eager to get among new feeding grounds. In the Severn Estuary, where much of my own shore cod fishing has taken place, I have frequently seen anglers catching codling in less than three feet of water.

A study of the estuary at low water will often pay dividends when you return at a later date to fish. Many estuaries all but dry up at and around low water, especially on spring tides, allowing the angler to visit the precise areas he will later return to fish. Try to note the location of any isolated patches of rocks, rough ground or weed, or any depressions or deeper gullies, or ledges. You should try to note any feature which will be attractive to food items, and will consequently hold the greatest concentrations of feeding fish when covered by the tide.

Baits and Rigs

Many anglers take full advantage of low water within estuaries in order to obtain their bait.

A happy angler holding a plump codling, caught in a muddy estuary.

Many estuaries have large populations of ragworm and lugworm which are among the most productive baits an angler can use here. There is no more satisfying way of catching fish than by first collecting your own bait at low water, and then using that bait to catch fish a few hours later. Peeler crab is a tremendous bait for winter cod, but unfortunately peeler crabs are not generally available to most anglers at the time of year when most cod are caught within an estuary. Frozen peeler crabs make an excellent alternative to live crab, when these are not available. Squid, mussel, razorfish and, of course, live baits, are all effective when used in an estuary for cod.

The optimum type of end rig to use will vary considerably from estuary to estuary and, as is always the case, will be dictated by the prevailing fishing conditions. Detailed descriptions of different types of rig used for both long- and short-range fishing over rough and clean ground have already been given in the earlier sections of this chapter and, depending on the fishing conditions found, these will be equally effective when used within an estuary.

Casting

One of the biggest problems anglers experience when fishing within an estuary is holding bottom in the incredibly strong tides that are often experienced. During the flood the tide often moves at a more sedate pace as it works against the contours of the land and the flow of water running out of the estuary. However, as the tide peaks and turns, the flow of water rapidly accelerates, creating very difficult fishing conditions, particularly when there is a lot of floating debris about following spring tides and/or heavy rain inland.

Thankfully, the angler will often be fishing in relatively shallow water, or else holding bottom might be more or less impossible. The trick is to tackle these conditions just as the boat angler would, i.e. by uptide fishing. Instead of casting straight out or slightly uptide, walk several yards uptide of your fishing position and cast well uptide. Do not re-engage the reel spool straight away, but walk back to your fishing position with the reel in free spool, using your thumb to release slack line out gradually. When you have estimated that you have released a sizeable bow of slack line into the tide – the exact amount being dependent on and gradually increasing with the strength of the tide, the range at which you are fishing and the depth of water – re-engage the spool and place the rod into its rest.

By walking and casting uptide of your fishing position you will ensure that by the time the lead has sunk to the bottom it will either be anchored in front of or slightly uptide of your actual fishing position when it finally grips. The bow of slack line released into the tide lowers the angle of pull on the lead and the terminal rig, greatly assisting its ability to hold bottom. Just as when uptiding, bites will take one of two forms: either you will see a delicate nodding on the rod tip, or a couple of more powerful nods before the rod tip springs upright as the fish breaks the lead free of the bottom. In both cases, the fish will usually hook itself.

LURE FISHING FROM THE SHORE

A brief mention has already been made, in the chapter on artificial lures, on the merits of using lures from the shore for cod. I personally feel that in many areas spinning is a technique which is greatly underused by shore anglers fishing for cod. It needs to be pointed out that not all venues where cod are caught are ideal for spinning. The sort of marks which offer the most potential will invariably be those which have very deep water within casting range. Within the UK, the north and west coast of Scotland and certain areas of west Wales and the West Country are most likely to produce fish. Much of the west coast of Ireland and Scandinavia, too, have excellent possibilities for catching cod on artificial lures.

The best types of lure to use in these areas are short heavy lures, such as the Bridun Lance and the smaller pirks, 2oz and 4oz in weight, made by Solvroken and Jensen. The advantages which these lures have to offer over other designs are: firstly, they cast very

well and, secondly, they sink swiftly to the bottom. In inshore waters cod feed primarily on or very near the bottom, and lures intended to catch them must be fished in this area. Few cod will be caught on lures fishing in mid-water.

The best technique is to cast the lure as far as possible, and then allow it to sink swiftly to the bottom. Retrieve the lure with a sink and draw technique, as shown in the diagram, making sure that you keep it working as close to the bottom as possible. Yes, you will lose a few lures which get snagged amongst the rock

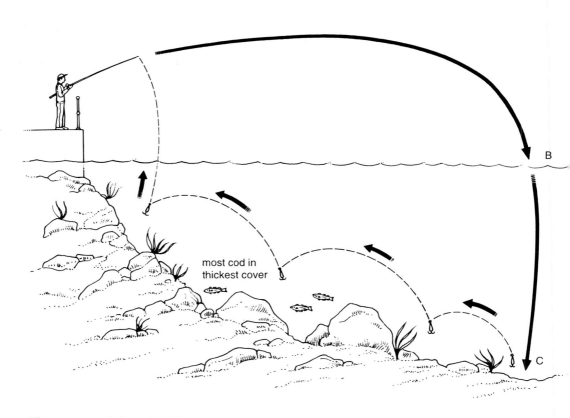

most cod in thickest cover

The correct technique for fishing a spinner in deep water from the shore. The angler casts to B and lets the lure sink to C. He then retrieves via the sink and draw as shown, trying to fish the lure as close to the seabed as possible. Most cod will be among the thickest cover.

The author with a codling that took a spinner fished from the shore.

and weed, that is inevitable, but if you want to catch cod with this technique such losses will be a fact of life.

With a bit of practice, lure losses can be kept to an absolute minimum; experience will help you to gauge when the lures are working within the correct zone. Another useful dodge is to substitute the standard treble hook with a single, which will greatly reduce any risk of snagging and will not, as many anglers wrongly assume, affect the hooking power of the lure. Indeed, Bridun supply a range of their lures with single hooks as standard, and from my experience I am convinced that the hooking power of lures with a single hook is actually higher than lures fitted with treble hooks.

NIGHT FISHING

In many areas, fishing from the shore for cod during the hours of darkness is far more productive than fishing during daylight. This is especially true when fishing in clear shallow water, into which cod will rarely venture outside of the hours of darkness, except during or immediately following a spell of rough weather. (Other times when fishing from the shore in daylight can produce fish are when it is possible to cast into deep water or when the water is coloured, as found in many estuaries.)

On the face of things it might appear that the only significant difference when fishing at night will be the need for a good light source. Naturally this is true, but I can assure you that,

113

in general, fishing in darkness is far more difficult than fishing at other times of the day.

Lights

Today anglers have a huge choice of different
lights from which to choose. You will need
both a lantern and a headlamp. The lantern is
used to provide a large pool of light around
your chosen pitch on the beach. This will be
required for tasks such as baiting up,
unhooking fish, etc., tasks which are taken for
granted when fishing in daylight. The headlamp provides a directional light source essential
when you move outside of the field of illumination provided by the larger lantern. It will
also be an invaluable aid when attempting to
pick out and land fish in the surf.

The traditional beach lanterns were always
powered by paraffin, but in more recent years
lamps which run on unleaded petrol have
become very much in vogue with beach
anglers. The big advantage with petrol
lanterns is they are very easy to light, and the
fuel is both cheap and readily available.
However, petrol is an extremely volatile fuel,
and even though I have not heard of any
accidents resulting from petrol-powered
lanterns, I am much happier using lamps that
run on paraffin.

For several years I have successfully used the
Magnalux pressure lantern, distributed in the
UK by Relum. This is probably the brightest
lantern currently available, and with its rapid
pre-heating facility is as easy to light from cold
as a more expensive petrol-powered lamp.
Few gas lights have sufficient illumination to
be of much use to the beach angler, and they
are expensive to run in comparison.

There are a wide range of headlamps from
which to choose, though be warned: the
market is saturated with cheap low-cost lamps
which are next to useless. The current market

The brightest paraffin lamp available, the
Relum Magnalux.

leader is the Petzl, which is available as both
a standard and a high-powered model with a
halogen bulb. Powered by a decent long-life
battery and relatively inexpensive at around
£25 for the standard lamp, the Petzl is the
ideal night fisherman's headlamp. A few firms
market more expensive and far more powerful
headlamps fitted with rechargeable batteries.
For the serious beach angler these will be a
sound investment.

Clothing

For most anglers, shore fishing for cod, particularly at night, coincides with the coldest

months of the year. Adequate clothing to keep you warm and dry is a must, both from a comfort and a safety point of view. The days when anglers used to wear traditional oilskins over copious layers of clothing to keep warm are, thankfully, long gone. Modern fabrics have allowed manufacturers to produce an excellent range of all-weather angling clothing, which is far more comfortable and practical to wear.

For both boat and beach fishing I always advise anglers to invest in a one-piece thermal/flotation suit. Several manufacturers now produce these excellent suits, which in addition to keeping you warm and dry have built-in buoyancy to keep you afloat should you fall in. Each year shore anglers, who are often fishing specifically for cod, either fall in or are swept into the sea and drown. I have met several shore anglers who undoubtedly owe their lives to the flotation suits which, fortunately, they were wearing when they fell into the sea. A good pair of thermal boots, thermal socks, neoprene gloves, and a warm hat – all available through good tackle shops – complete the outfit.

Chris Martin with a brace of fat cod caught after dark. Note the latern, headlamp and one-piece flotation suit. All help greatly when fishing after dark in cold weather.

Preparation

When it comes to actually fishing from any particular beach at night, my first piece of advice would be never to attempt to fish any mark in darkness which you have never visited, or preferably fished, at least once before in daylight. Many beaches are most productive when fished on a flooding tide from low water up to high water. In certain areas the tide does not flood evenly up the beach but back fills into gullies, all too easily cutting off the retreat of any unwary angler. By fishing a new mark in daylight you will be able to pick out and note any areas that do get cut off at certain states of the tide.

The other major advantage with visiting a mark at low water on a few occasions in daylight before you fish in darkness, is that you will be able to note certain features. Apart from features that will possibly attract the fish, such as gullies, mussel beds, ledges, etc., you will be able to see if there are any areas which are best avoided due to snags. I remember once fishing a section of a beach which I had never actually fished before, even though I had fished other areas of the beach on many occasions. During the course of a five-hour session I lost count of end rigs I lost to snags; in fact, throughout the entire session I only managed to retrieve a handful of casts.

By chance, I was in the same area a few days later, my visit coinciding with low water. I decided to investigate why I lost so much tackle, and it did not take long to discover the reason. I had been fishing directly on top of several boat moorings. The boats had been removed for the winter, but the moorings had been left. Not only did I manage to recover most of my own end rigs along with a few lost by other anglers, but I found the remains of what was obviously once a very good cod still attached to one of my traces!

Preparation is definitely the key to successful night fishing. Having done your groundwork and located a suitable mark, the next step is to prepare fully for the planned session. The most successful night anglers are invariably those who are the most organized. Attention to fine detail will ensure that the session runs as smoothly as possible, and you spend the most time with a bait actually in the water. There is nothing worse than messing about on the beach in darkness tying on shockleaders or assembling traces. Not only is this infuriatingly difficult and a total waste of valuable fishing time, but tying important knots efficiently can be next to impossible with cold fingers.

I always try to ensure that I carry an adequate stock of pre-tied traces, and at least three reels loaded with line and with shockleaders already attached. By having plenty of traces, replacing lost rigs takes a minimum of time, and I can always have a second ready-baited trace standing by, which I can instantly attach and cast out whenever I retrieve a fish or wind in to replace my bait. This technique is frequently used by competition anglers and is known as double-patting.

Bird's nests are a fact of life for all anglers, and believe me there is nothing more frustrating than frantically trying to untangle a bad bird's nest or tie on a replacement shockleader, when all around are catching fish! It is far easier simply to replace the reel with another, attach a new trace, and get straight back into the fishing. The duff reel can then either be sorted out while you have a bait in the water, or better still left until you get home.

On some beaches anglers will be able to enjoy the luxury of setting up a beach camp, either using a large angling brolly or a purpose-made beach fishing shelter. This will only be possible when fishing an area with a minimal tidal range. The shelter provides the ideal refuge from the elements, and a central point where the bait and all other items of equipment can be stored.

On many beaches anglers will not be able to enjoy the luxury of fishing from within a fixed camp as the distance between high and low water is too great, making it necessary to keep on the move constantly in order to keep ahead of the advancing water line. When fishing on the move there will always be a risk of losing small items of tackle so it is important not only to carry the absolute minimum of gear, but to fish in a methodical way. As individual items are used they should be replaced in their correct place in the tackle box or pocket straight away, otherwise I can guarantee that they will be lost to the darkness and the tide.

Casting and Bite Detection

Actually fishing in darkness is much harder than fishing during daylight. Many anglers find casting in darkness a lot harder than casting during daylight, certainly when it comes to casting accurately. The best advice I can offer to the novice night angler is to avoid the temptation, which all anglers instinctively have, to blast baits as far as possible. In many instances, and especially when fishing at night, baits fishing at long range will actually be beyond the fish. Concentrate on casting accurately, and the distance, when required, will steadily increase with experience.

Given that long-range casting will not often be possible or even desirable when night fishing, it makes sense to 'detune' your reels accordingly. Many anglers insist on fishing with their reels running at peak performance, again driven by that overpowering urge to be able always to cast as far as possible. I rarely have my reels running at such a level, not only because I am not a tournament caster, but because I much prefer to spend my time fishing rather than sorting out tangles.

Bite detection at night causes problems for many anglers. Provided that you have an adequate light source, as described above, and you keep an eye on the rod tip, detecting bites should not pose too many problems. Wrapping the top six inches or so of the rod tip with reflective tape or painting it white (ordinary household emulsion paint is ideal) will greatly improve bite detection. Tackle shops sell a variety of light sources designed to fit to the tip of the rod and improve bite detection, ranging from luminous diodes to battery-powered lights. In my experience, these are not only far more expensive than tape or paint, but they are not as efficient.

6 Where and When to Fish for Cod

ENGLAND

The thousands of miles of English coastline offer the cod angler a rich variety of cod fishing. Although the species remains the same, the type and style of cod fishing in different areas vary considerably, and the need for the angler always to endeavour to obtain up-to-date local advice cannot be over-emphasized. Even though those cod caught in the Thames Estuary are identical in every biological way to those caught off the north-east of England, the tactics and techniques employed to catch them vary considerably.

The North-East

The stretch of coast between Berwick-upon-Tweed on the Scottish border and Grimsby offers some of the best cod fishing in the UK; indeed, in this area few other species are deliberately fished for. Offshore, there are two distinct approaches used by anglers targeting cod. Almost all boat fishing in the north-east is done on the drift. The majority of boats fish within close proximity to the shore, certainly less than 10 miles offshore. These boats target the inshore reefs and wrecks with a selection of pirks and other artificial lures along with natural baits, which typically include mussels and lugworm.

The second, and by far the most productive type of fishing as far as the serious cod angler is concerned, involves fishing aboard faster charter boats over wrecks and occasionally reefs many miles offshore. Often these boats do not start fishing until they are at least 30 miles out. Pirking is more or less the only method practised.

The main ports where charter boats are based are Berwick-upon-Tweed, Amble, Hartlepool, Whitby (home of one of the largest charter fleets in the UK and the port from where the current UK record cod of 58lb. 6oz. was caught in 1992), Scarborough, Bridlington and Grimsby. The main cod season runs from Easter through until the weather breaks in the autumn, though a few boats now fish all year round, weather permitting.

The shore fishing for cod within this area can be equally productive. There are many marks along the entire coast which regularly produce cod, the main season being through the autumn and winter months, and often lasting well into the spring. Some of the most popular marks fished by shore anglers in Northumbria include Newbiggin promenade, the rocks and beaches between Holy Island and Amble, Warworth and Druridge beaches. Seaton Point, Sugar Sands and Haukley are all local hot spots where a double figure fish is always possible. The best results are often made after dark, and top baits in this area include worm baits, crab, squid razorfish and mussel. Further south, Whitley Bay, Collywell Bay and Cullercoats harbour can be equally productive.

The Tyne Estuary can be very good for codling, provided there is not too much freshwater flowing out of the river. The beaches, rock marks and cliffs between South Shields and Sunderland can produce good bags of codling, especially when fishing in rough weather and after dark. The beaches between Seaham and Hartlepool, including Hawthorn, Chemical, Easington Horden and Seaham Hall are equally productive.

In Yorkshire, some of the top cod venues are found on the stretch of coastline between Ravenscar and Boulby, including Robin Hood's Bay, South and North Hawsker, the piers at Whitby, Saithes and Runswick Bay. The Filey Brig area, south of Scarborough, is another cod hotspot. The south landing at Flamborough, the North Pier at Bridlington, and the Barmston area on the Holderness beaches, Ulrome, Hornsea, and Mappleton are also noted cod venues.

The South-East

South of Grimsby from the Wash around East Anglia and into the Thames Estuary, the style of cod fishing starts to change. Offshore, although a few boats still target wrecks, most boats fish at anchor using bait, generally uptiding. The beaches start to consist of sand with fewer rock outcrops and much shallower water, so now long-range casting starts to become a requirement. The main cod season starts in October and runs through until March, though those boats which fish further offshore catch cod throughout the year.

Main charter ports in the area include Great Yarmouth, Lowestoft, Felixstowe, Walton-on-the-Naze, Brightlingsea, West Mersea, Bradwell, Burnham-on Couch and Southend.

The top shore marks are Yarmouth North Beach, which like many beaches in the area is best fished immediately after a good onshore blow when the cod move into the shallow water to mop up the easy food pickings ripped out of the sea bed. The beaches at Corton, Kessingland, Orford, Bacton, Pakefield, and Southwold all produce codling, given the right conditions.

The general standard of cod fishing improves dramatically in Essex. The beaches and piers at both Walton and Clacton, and Frinton Wall and Holland beaches are all noted for cod throughout the winter. Best results are often made when fishing at night and after a good onshore blow. Further south, Southend pier is one of the most consistent shore cod venues in the area.

The Kent coast has long been associated with good cod fishing, often for fish with a higher average size than those caught in East Anglia. Boat anglers fish both at anchor, when uptiding is the main method, and on the drift with various types of lures. The main charter ports include Ramsgate and Deal (the closest port for anglers wishing to fish the famous Goodwin Sands, one of the area's top cod venues), Dover, Folkestone – from where boats fish the Varne Bank and The Road – and Dungeness.

Some of the area's most productive cod beaches include Thanet chalk ledges at Broadstairs, Deal, Kingsdown, Walmer, Seabrook Princess Parade, Sandgate Castle Promenade and the many piers in the area, such as the Prince of Wales and Admiralty at Dover, and Folkestone Pier. Dungeness is considered by many as being the all-time classic cod beach. Sadly, catches made here in recent years are just a shadow of the famous catches made throughout the 1970s and early 1980s, when huge hauls of what were often very large fish were commonplace. Today you will stand your best chance of a cod from

Dungeness if you get to the beach as soon as you can following a good onshore blow.

The South Coast and Channel Islands

From Sussex to Cornwall the overall standard of shore cod fishing is poor. In some years reasonable numbers of fish occasionally show off certain beach marks, but by and large these are very inconsistent. The best time to catch cod along the south coast is throughout the autumn and winter months, and following a spell of rough weather. Night fishing will almost always be far more productive than fishing during daylight. Some of the most consistent shore cod venues along the south coast include Selsey Point in Sussex, Hurst Shingle bank in Hampshire and Chesil Beach in Dorset.

Boats fishing this area are far more successful. On the whole, the best of the cod fishing is had by anglers fishing mid-channel wrecks. Pirks are not so widely used along the south coast of England as most anglers tend to use artificial sand-eels fished on light tackle, a far more enjoyable and sporting method of catching cod, I think.

The exception is the area around the Isle of Wight. Here anglers tend to fish with great success at anchor. On the shallower marks in the Eastern Solent uptiding is popular, but in the deeper water where the tide runs very hard downtiding with either wire or braided line is necessary, in order to present baits on the bottom. The Needles area has a well-deserved reputation for producing big cod; fish over 40lb are caught most winters. These big cod want big baits: two or three whole calamari squid, cuttlefish and, of course, live baits are the most productive.

The major charter ports along the south coast include Hastings, where charter boats are launched from the beach, Eastbourne, Newhaven, Brighton, Shoreham, Little-hampton, Hayling Island, Lymington, Keyhaven, Mudeford, Poole, Swanage, Weymouth, Exmouth, Teignmouth, Torquay, Brixham, Dartmouth, Salcombe and Plymouth. Most cod are caught throughout the summer months from mid-channel wrecks; bad weather invariably restricts offshore activity throughout the winter.

The Channel Islands are more or less the most southerly point where cod are caught on a regular basis. I have fished from Jersey, Guernsey and Alderney on several occasions, and caught cod on most trips. A few cod are caught on the various inshore reefs off the Channel Islands, but for the most consistent sport it is normally necessary for the charter boats to head north and fish wrecks in the approaches to the English Channel. Pirks and artificial sand-eels tend to be the most effective lures.

The South-West

The English side of the Bristol Channel offers some excellent cod fishing, the season running from October through until late March. The first run of fish tend to be codling in the 2lb to 6lb range, but as the season develops both the numbers and average size of fish caught increase. The biggest fish are usually caught during the first few months of the year, and include plenty of specimens over 20lb, with occasionally much larger fish. The standard technique used is uptiding using large worm baits, usually tipped with squid. The main charter ports on this coast include Minehead and Watchet, though boats occasionally run out of Ilfracombe, Porlock, Weston-Super-Mare and Clevedon.

The shore fishing along this entire stretch of coastline from Ilfracombe up to the Severn Bridge, is very good, though the best of the

A double-figure cod caught by Phil Hine. This fish is typical of the stamp of winter fish caught by anglers fishing at Minehead.

The North-West

The final stretch of English coastline runs from the Mersey up to the Scottish border. Shore-fishing activity for cod is restricted in this entire area due to the very flat and often featureless beaches which are predominant, though one or two venues do produce fish. The Mersey itself, Blackpool pier, the rock marks at Harrington and Lowca, Walney Island at Barrow-in-Furness, St Bees North Heads and Whithaven Pier are useful places to try. The main cod season in the area runs from October until February, and worm baits tend to be the most consistent.

The main ports from where charter boats can be hired are at Fleetwood, Barrow-in-Furness and Maryport. Dinghy fishing is very popular in this area; indeed, far more anglers fish aboard their own trailerable dinghies than aboard charter boats. The main area fished by dinghy anglers is between the Mersey and Rossall Point near Fleetwood. The average size of cod caught is between 2lb and 6lb, but much bigger fish are caught on occasion. In the past, fish weighing well over 30lb have been caught by dinghy anglers in this area.

WALES

As far as inshore cod fishing is concerned, south Wales must rank, in my opinion, as one of the top venues within the UK for both the boat and the shore cod angler.

South Wales

The main area where cod are caught is the Bristol Channel coast between Swansea in the west and the Severn Bridge in the East. The season here starts in the extreme east of the region, normally around the middle of

cod fishing is generally to the east of Minehead. At Minehead the Gasworks beach and the harbour walls are both productive marks, along with a few of the more remote areas between Minehead and Porlock. The low-water reef marks at St Audries are noted for big cod: fish to over 20lb have been caught here in the past. The sea wall at Burnham, Brean Down, the beaches at Sand Bay and Weston, Sand Point, Lady Bay at Clevedon, Battery Point at Portishead, and Aust Rocks, beneath the Severn Bridge, will all produce fish.

121

September, but a few fish are often caught as early as August.

The eastern end of the Bristol Channel consists of tidal mud and peat beds, separated from the adjoining farmland by a sea wall which runs for many miles along the coast. From the start of the season until Christmas, the entire area can be considered as something of a cod mecca for the shore angler. The top marks are Sudbrook, Magor, Redwick, Goldcliff and St Brides.

Anglers fish either from the sea wall or off the mud flats. It needs to be pointed out that fishing off the mud flats is potentially very dangerous, with an ever-present risk of getting stuck in the mud or having your retreat cut off by the flooding tide. I would certainly not advise any angler to venture out onto the flats alone, and never until they know how the tide floods across any given area.

In general, the fishing in this region is best over the smaller tides, the run of tide tending to be too fierce on larger tides. In certain places, such as Redwick, it is possible to fish for a full 24 hours on the smallest neap tides, from the top of the peat ledges in front of the sea wall. At others, anglers generally fish for about three hours either side of high water.

The most productive baits tend to be black or blow lugworm, ragworm and peeler crab. Livebaits, fished in conjunction with the self-hooking livebait rig as described in the section on shore fishing, consistently sort out the biggest fish. The average size of fish, though, tends to be small with fish ranging from around 1lb to 3lb. However, many much

Anglers fishing the peat ledger for cod at Redwick.

Terry Thomas holds a double figure cod caught off Penarth in south-east Wales.

larger fish, which often include specimens weighing well into double figures, are caught during most seasons. The fishing throughout most of this area is over clean and snag-free ground, where basic paternoster rigs fitted with a 5oz breakout-type lead work well.

Further west, Cardiff foreshore and Penarth beach are also very productive venues through-out the autumn. As the season progresses towards the Christmas period and then on into the New Year, the main population of fish start to drop back down the channel. Sully Island, the various points and headlands in the Barry area, Rhoose Point, Aberthaw and Stout Point are all noted for producing big fish. By and large, these are all rough-ground venues which are most productive when fished over low water and on the larger tides, especially

following a period of rough weather and when fishing during darkness. The current and long-standing British shore-caught cod record, a stunning fish of 44lb 8oz caught by local angler Brandon Jones, was landed at Tom's Point at Barry back in 1966. Tom's Point is a small and unimpressive-looking rock venue behind Cold Knap Point; the successful bait was herring.

Witches Point and Ogmore Deeps, located a few miles to the east of Porthcawl, are two very popular big cod venues, which peak during the first few months of the year. Several 20lb fish and a few over 30lb are caught by shore anglers fishing here most seasons. Once again, these are very dangerous marks which should never be fished during rough weather. In recent years, anglers have ignored this advice

123

and taken a chance, losing their lives as a consequence.

Penarth marina is the focal point for most boat-fishing activity in the area, with a fleet of around ten fully equipped and registered charter boats. Between September and the end of February it is no exaggeration to describe the cod fishing in this area as outstanding, certainly when compared with other venues. Penarth-based charter boats regularly return with over fifty fish per boat per day. These will mostly be fish in the 2lb to 6lb range but double-figure fish are common and many over twenty pounds are caught every season. Fish to over 40lb have been caught by anglers fishing aboard Penarth-based charter boats.

This area of the Bristol Channel is pure uptiding country. Anglers typically use rods rated for casting leads between 4oz and 8oz, which are necessary when using leads of around 5oz or 6oz and the very large baits which work best here. The most efficient bait in the area is good-quality fresh black lug tipped with squid though most other baits do work well, notably livebaits, used by anglers targeting the bigger fish. The main fishing areas for the Penarth fleet are off the Cardiff foreshore and Penarth beach, mid-channel marks around the English and Welsh buoy, Sully Bay and Aberthaw.

Swansea Bay and the surrounding area has a long association with cod fishing. The first codling are caught in Swansea Bay towards the end of September and early October, the average size of fish gradually increasing as the season develops towards its peak in January on February. A large modern charter fleet is based in Swansea marina, which boasts excellent facilities for anglers, including several tackle shops where fresh bait can be bought.

Once again, this is uptiding country, though many anglers adopt downtiding tech-

Swansea is noted for producing 40lb plus cod such as this one.

niques when fishing some of the deeper marks further offshore. The most productive baits are invariably various types of worm tipped with squid. Whole squid and livebaits nearly always account for the biggest fish of the season. Swansea has a well-deserved reputation for producing very big cod. In recent years several 40lb-plus fish have been caught by anglers, and fish weighing over 50lb have been netted in the same area. Swansea is one venue which really is capable of producing the next British record cod.

The most productive shore-fishing venues in the Swansea area are Sker Rocks to the west of Porthcawl, fished over low water, Port Talbot and Swansea Breakwaters (permits required), Mumbles Pier and the various rock headlands off the beautiful Gower Peninsula.

West and North Wales

Heading further west, Milford Haven is the next major angling area where cod are caught. In comparison with Penarth and Swansea the standard of cod fishing in and around south-west Wales, including Milford Haven, is poor. Each autumn large numbers of codling enter the Haven and at times the fishing can be very good, though few large fish are caught. At other times of the year there will always be a chance of catching an occasional fish, but the serious cod angler would do far better concentrating on the more productive areas to the east.

The same is true for much of west and North Wales. At certain times of the year, generally the autumn, codling can be caught offshore and from many of the beaches in the area, but results are at best sporadic. The best cod fishing is invariably found by anglers fishing wrecks well out into the Irish Sea. Often these are big fish but unfortunately, as far as cod anglers are concerned, catches are unreliable with the greater emphasis being on pollack fishing. Those fish which do get caught from the inshore grounds in West Wales are usually red rock cod which occasionally take up residence on inshore reefs, and due to a combination of diet and habitat turn a wonderful rich colour of deep red and gold.

It is not until you reach the Menai Strait and start heading east along the North Wales coast and towards the estuaries of the Dee and the Mersey, that more substantial numbers of codling once again start to show. In recent years, the numbers of codling caught in this area has definitely been on the increase, probably due to vast improvements of the water

clarity in the area. Hopefully, this welcome upward trend in catch rates will continue and, who knows, maybe the fishing in North Wales will one day mirror that of the more productive south?

SCOTLAND

There is excellent cod fishing all around the Scottish coast which, for the most part, is available all year round. The west coast of Scotland is for the most part broken and rugged, consisting of deep inlets of the sea and countless islands. The east coast is more or less the exact opposite.

Western Scotland

On the west coast, Kirkcudbright is the first port of major interest to anglers, with a small fleet of charter boats. Cod are caught throughout the year though the best fishing is generally available from the autumn to winter. Bad weather generally restricts boat fishing through the winter months, both here and at most other Scottish ports.

The area around Glasgow used to be famous for cod fishing, notably the Gantocks, where back in the 1960s and 1970s some huge record-breaking cod were caught. Unfortunately, these fish exist now only in the record books, commercial pressure all but wiping the population out. However, in recent years there have been signs that numbers are once again on the increase, though the average size of fish caught still tends to be small. The main charter port in the area is Ayr.

There is excellent cod fishing from many of the Western Isles of Scotland, though once again the average size of fish caught is not large, with most fish weighing less than 10lb.

This is more a reflection upon the type of angling which is typically practised in Scotland, rather than any indication of the area's true potential. Most charter boats tend to concentrate on the inshore reefs where these small fish are predominant. There is little doubt that were there more serious effort to locate and fish wrecks and reefs further offshore, much bigger fish would be caught. Tobermory on the Isle of Mull, Ullapool in mainland Scotland and Stornoway on the Isle of Lewis, Outer Hebrides, are three of the main angling centres.

The shore-fishing potential for cod is excellent all around Scotland. The Clyde area sees the most angling activity, notably around the Saltcoats and Gourock area. The most productive baits include peeler crab, lugworm and mussel. The most famous shore-fishing venue in Scotland in undoubtedly Balcary Point, in southern Galloway. This is a venue which consistently produces huge cod: in the past, fish to over 40lb have been caught from the shore here. The best fishing is throughout the autumn and winter months. Never fish this exposed venue in rough or unsettled weather, as anglers have been swept to their deaths here. Big cod like big baits, and Balcary cod are no exception, the most consistent baits being whole squid, large worm and crab baits and, of course, livebaits.

Almost all shore marks which give access to deep water along the western coast of Scotland will produce cod. The best of the cod fishing is generally throughout the autumn and winter, and baits such as lug and ragworm, peeler crab and squid will be the most consistent fish catchers. There is plenty of scope for experimentation from the shore with artificial lures. Small pirks and heavy spinners fished close to the bottom catch plenty of codling, and when used on light spinning tackle there is no more sporting way of catching cod.

The North

Scrabster, more or less on the very tip of Scotland, is a thriving fishing village with a sizeable charter fleet. I have fished at Scrabster on several occasions, and I have always caught plenty of good cod there. Again, the average size of fish is not big, but the inshore reefs where most fish are caught are well stocked with a healthy population of fish in the 4lb to 12lb range. As in most of Scotland, these fish are typically caught using a wide variation of pirks and other artificials, or natural baits which include mussels, lugworm, and freshly caught mackerel. Unlike many other northern ports, Scrabster boats often fish throughout the winter, weather permitting, not so much for cod, but for the huge porbeagle shark which frequently rip-hook cod and other fish off anglers' lines!

The northern islands of Orkney and Shetland are even more productive for small- to medium-sized cod, though once again the true fishing potential remains virtually untouched by rod and line.

Eastern Scotland

The main ports on the eastern side of Scotland include Peterhead, Stonehaven, Arbroath, Pittenweem and Anstruther, and Eyemouth, just above the English border. Much of the angling activity here consists of fishing the inshore reefs and wrecks for small fish, although there are a few faster and more modern boats which are starting to venture further offshore, with some encouraging results.

The beaches and estuaries along the eastern coast of Scotland produce good shore fishing for cod, as do the many harbour walls, piers and breakwaters, where fish to double figures are frequently caught. Some of the most productive cod venues include Carnoustie beach, Soutars Head to the south of Nigg Bay, and Arbroath Esplanade where it is possible to fish when rough weather prevents fishing most other marks. Rumness, to the north of Auchmithie, is an excellent low-water venue, though it is unsafe to fish this mark in bad weather. The rough ground at The Usan, to the south of Montrose, is an excellent mark for codling. Inverbervie beach is yet another good venue, especially when fished during darkness and following a spell of bad weather.

Further south, the rocks at Coldingham Bay and the cliff marks in front of St Abbs lighthouse can be good for cod and codling. The Grips rocks behind Dunbar Harbour, Belhaven beach, the marks near the golf course south of North Berwick, the west breakwater inside Leith docks, Crail Harbour and lighthouse, and the rocks at Anstruther are all noted cod venues.

IRELAND

Ireland is one of the great sea-angling centres of Europe, with a wealth of different species of fish, including cod, swimming in the rich seas around her coast. Geographically speaking, the coast around Ireland is equally varied, and this often has a considerable effect on the distribution of cod.

East Coast

The east coast consists mainly of steep shingle beaches, which are very popular with shore anglers, especially match anglers. By and large, the cod caught off these beaches tend to be small codling, though on occasion bigger fish are caught. The stretch of coastline between Dublin and Wicklow tends to hold the highest concentration of fish, with Greystones, Kilcool, Newcastle and Wicklow beach being the main centres of activity.

The cod fishing in this area is at its best between November and February, peaking over the Christmas and New Year period. One of the main attractions of this area is that long casting is not always necessary to catch fish; indeed the fish are often caught within thirty yards of the shoreline. The average size of fish caught does, however, tend to be small, between 1lb and 3lb, but what these fish lack in quality, they more than make up for in quantity. The best baits are lugworm, mussel and peeler crab. Night fishing is often far more productive than fishing during daylight.

There is limited boat fishing on the east coast of Ireland. Hardly any charter boats operate through the winter months, and anglers wishing to fish offshore will generally have to use their own boats, which can be launched off the beach at Greystones. There are a few charter boats based at Rosslare and Kilmore Quay, which tend to restrict operations to fishing from the spring through to autumn. The Tusker Rock area is one offshore mark noted for cod fishing.

South Coast

Cod are caught throughout the year off the south coast of Ireland, though the best of the shore fishing is generally found throughout the winter months. Offshore, the best fishing is generally from wrecks and reefs. Most anglers use various types of lure for catching cod off the Irish coast; these include feathers, pirks and artificial sand-eels. However, baits do work well when fishing over many of the inshore marks, especially over the reefs and within the estuaries. Lugworm and mussel tend to be the most consistent baits.

Anglers fish for cod within the river estuary at Dunmore East; Cheek Point, on the Water-ford side of the river, is the local hotspot. The next main cod fishing centre is Dungarven, where cod are caught from the local pier, and at Helvick Head during the winter months. There are several good charter boats based at Dungarven. The Blackwater Estuary at Youghal is another mark where the cod fishing tends to be consistent during the winter. The most productive marks are usually located when fishing in the deeper water, such as from the road bridge and the harbour quays. Offshore, the area around Capel Island is very productive. Mussel is an excellent and widely used bait here.

Cork Harbour is a huge natural inlet of the sea, with plenty of deep and sheltered water offering excellent fishing for both the boat and shore angler. The most notable areas for cod are found at Cobh and Monkstown. The next angling centre along the coast is Kinsale, situated at the mouth of the Bandon Estuary. Here cod fishing is mainly restricted to boats, but anglers fishing into deep water off the road bridge often catch codling, once again mainly throughout the winter months.

West Coast

Cod fishing along the west coast of Ireland tends to be sporadic. Certainly, big fish are caught, but unfortunately it is often very much a case of here today, gone tomorrow. One of the biggest cod I have seen caught in Ireland was caught off Ballydavid Head in Co. Kerry. The fish weighed almost 20lb, and was caught by an angler fishing a soft rubber worm for pollack. We fished in more or less the same area for three full days, yet that single big fish and three smaller ones weighing about 5lb were the only cod we saw.

There is, however, some evidence to suggest that the fishing within the huge Shannon Estuary for cod throughout the

winter months might be more productive, were more anglers to try fishing at this time of year. Certainly, in recent years those anglers who have taken the trouble to fish here have caught respectable catches of codling. The Foynes area tends to be the most consistent.

North of Co. Clare and Galway Bay, the overall standard of cod fishing starts to improve again dramatically. There is little or no shore fishing in north-west Ireland during the peak months for cod, i.e. through the winter, with Donegal Bay being the single exception. Here, anglers who make the effort catch reasonable amounts of codling, along with whiting, coalfish and dabs. Most cod fishing here takes place from the boats.

The main boat-fishing centres in the north-west include Clifden, Westport and Killybegs. Good numbers of cod are caught off Clare Island, and there is every indication that the rod and line cod-fishing potential in this area is untapped. Throughout the winter months most angling boats are hauled out of the water, though commercial boats fishing the area regularly catch huge cod in the 50lb to 60lb region. The continental shelf runs very close to the shore here, and it is felt that this area could be one of the main migration routes for cod *en route* to the spawning grounds.

The cod fishing of Killybegs is well established in May, with plenty of cod weighing well into double figures getting caught. Heading further north still, Tory Island and Sheephaven Bay offer Irish anglers their best chance of catching a 20lb-plus fish. Port-Na-Blagh is one of the key angling centres in Co. Donegal, with sport peaking during September and October. Once again, anglers generally use a multitude of different lures when fishing for cod.

An Irish angler holds a beautiful cod caught off Rosses Pt, Co. Sligo, North-West Ireland.

DENMARK

I have been fortunate enough to have fished for cod off Denmark on many occasions, catching what probably amounts in total to many hundreds of cod. I have caught some of my biggest cod while fishing aboard Danish boats and have personally witnessed the capture of several fish in excess of 40lb. This might sound somewhat impressive, but I assure you by Danish standards it is not. Fifty-pound cod are regularly caught off the Danish coast, 60lb fish are caught most years, and the current Danish record for cod is held with an enormous great cod of over 70lb.

There are two distinct sides to Danish cod

fishing: the inshore fishing in which I include shore fishing, and offshore fishing over the reefs and wrecks which are plentiful off the coast. The inshore waters around the Danish coast are heavily populated with cod and codling up to around 10lb. Offshore, and in much deeper water, is where the biggest fish are located.

Denmark is a small country which forms a peninsula running more or less north–south, with the brackish waters of the southern Baltic Sea to the east, and the North Sea to the west. Sea angling is a very popular sport in Denmark, as it is in most Scandinavian countries, where fresh fish is highly prized for food. There are many angling facilities in the country, with charter boats operating from most ports.

Ebeltoft is a small town situated in the Kattegat, the narrow seaway which separates Denmark from Sweden. Here, the inshore waters consist of tidal sand flats intersected with deeper channels, with the water depth increasing as you move progressively further offshore. Many of the local anglers troll for sea trout in the sea here, and cod are an abundant by-catch.

Fishing in crystal-clear and often very shallow water with various types of lure, invariably fished in conjunction with light tackle and a downrigger, the cod fishing in this area is nothing short of outstanding. The fish average around 5lb, but when they are caught using little more than trout spinning rods and light lines, I can assure you they fight exceptionally well. In my experience, it is rare to be able to target cod consistently using such incredibly light tackle.

The most effective types of lure are either floating jointed-plugs or very light spoons. These are trolled at around 5 to 7 knots, the trick being to try to work the very edges of the deep channels. Fully equipped self-hire boats are available at some harbours in Denmark; the best places to enquire about the

Top distance caster Bradley Riseborough with a fine brace of cod, caught fishing the 'windfarm breakwater' at Ebeltoft in Denmark.

availability of these are local tackle shops. In addition to dinghy fishing, there are several charter boats which will take you further offshore to fish over wrecks and reefs. Pirks and other artificial lures are generally used by local anglers.

The shore fishing in Denmark is equally productive, and at times some very impressive catches of fish can be made from the beaches, rock marks, piers and breakwaters. The best and most consistent baits are lugworm, peeler crab, mussel and razor fish. The better marks tend to be those which give access to the deeper water.

The Yellow Reef

If you want to catch some of the biggest cod in Europe, if not the world, then the Yellow Reef off the north-western tip of Denmark is the place to head for. Charter boats operate out of most ports in the area, and usually these are huge converted commercial fishing boats which take up to 50 anglers. Hanstholm and Hirtshals are two of the main ports from where charter boats sail, taking anglers to fish the Yellow Reef. Just why the Yellow Reef remains consistently productive for exceptionally large cod is no great secret: the Danes have a ban on commercial fishing on the inshore reefs.

The Yellow Reef is situated many miles offshore, and most of the charter boats are very slow. This results in a long steaming time to reach the fishing grounds and the charter fleet sails at around 3 o'clock in the morning, arriving at the reef around dawn. Anglers can then fish for up to eight hours, before making the long trek back to port. This is not as bad as it might seem, for those of you who are used to more civilized travel times! Nearly all of the boats have had their one-time fish holds converted into large sleeping areas, with racks of bunks. This way, you can get your head down as soon as you get aboard, hopefully sleeping through until it is time to start fishing. In addition to the sleeping quarters, many boats also have a well-stocked snack bar serving hot drinks, beefburgers and so on throughout the day.

You will need substantial tackle to fish the Yellow Reef. The water is very deep, and with fish of such a high average size anything less than a good-quality 50lb class rod matched with a quality reel loaded with plenty of line will be inadequate. Pirking is the name of the game here, and I would advise against using multiple-lure rigs. The risk of losing fish if you get a multiple hook-up of big cod are just too

The author with a 25lb plus cod caught fishing over the famous Yellow Reef off the Danish coast.

great. A single chrome pirk weighing between 16oz and 22oz and armed with strong swivels, links and hooks is the most efficient lure.

In addition to cod you will catch coalfish, pollack and some very large ling. It was while fishing the Yellow Reef aboard the converted trawler *Thailand*, out from Hanstholm, that I broke the Danish ling record with a fish of 48½lb – fishing in 430 feet of water!

At this point, I must mention the way in which Scandinavian anglers look after the fish they catch. As I have already mentioned, fresh fish is a major food item for many who live in the various Nordic countries, so naturally they want to ensure that the fish they catch arrive home in the very best possible condition. At the start of the day each angler is given his own fish bucket. Fish are gutted and thoroughly washed more or less immediately, then washed at frequent intervals throughout the day. In this way the condition of the fish will be far superior at the end of the day, than if they were simply thrown in the communal fish/sweat box found aboard charter boats in many other countries.

The cost of living in Denmark is higher than in the UK, and prices do tend to be quite a bit more expensive. My advice would be to take all of the fishing tackle you are likely to need and as much food as you can carry with you. Prices for a place aboard a charter boat vary considerably, but expect to pay somewhere in the region of £35 per person per day for a place aboard one of the larger charter boats. The season in Denmark is more or less all the year round, with only adverse weather throughout the winter months preventing anglers from getting afloat.

The best way for British anglers to get to Denmark is aboard one of the ferries which regularly cross from Harwich and Newcastle to Esbjerg. There are flights to several Danish airports from most large UK airports, but obviously they have weight restrictions, which, when you consider the need for several dozen heavy pirks, are difficult for anglers to stay within. Scandinavian Seaways are the main ferry operators; phone 0990 333 111 for further information: For other information, contact the Danish Tourist Board at 55 Sloane Street, London, SW1X 9SY. Tel: 0171 259 5959.

SWEDEN

Like its southern neighbour Denmark, Sweden has fishing both within the Baltic and North Sea. As far as the Baltic coastline is concerned, there is little here to interest the serious cod angler, certainly not when you consider the quality of sport which is on offer off the western coast, facing the North Sea.

The Baltic Coast

The waters of the Baltic are very brackish and in places, particularly in the north, it is common to catch the likes of freshwater pike and perch alongside cod! The salinity level increases as you move further south, and the first area of real interest is the most southerly tip of Sweden around Malmo, then moving north into the Kattegat and on towards Göteborg.

Once again, most of the many little fishing villages in this area have their own charter boats, and the best places to enquire about boat availability are the local tackle shops. As would be expected, fishing on the drift using pirks and various different types of artificial lure, which range from muppets to rubber sand-eels, tends to be the most popular technique.

The North Sea Coast

The Bohus region of Sweden north of Göteborg has some spectacular cod fishing. The inshore waters tend to be full of codling, with the average size of the fish steadily increasing as you head further out to sea. The most consistent marks tend to be in the vicinity of deep-water wrecks and reefs.

I once spent a highly productive couple of days' fishing out from the tiny island of Astol, situated just over an hour's drive north from Göteborg and a few miles offshore from the village of Ronnang. I was fishing aboard a purpose-made angling boat called *Tuna Clipper*, with owner-skipper Arne Olsson.

Boats in this area concentrate on fishing a vast area of skerries and reefs known as Pater Noster, which is marked by its famous lighthouse. My first day's fishing aboard *Tuna Clipper* was spent almost entirely around this area, and we caught substantial numbers of cod and codling, with the biggest fish weighing well into double figures. The water is very deep and the tide runs incredibly quickly off this part of the Swedish coast, and heavy pirks are needed to stay in contact with the bottom. There are several wrecks within the Pater Noster area, and Arne kept alternating between fishing these and the actual reef.

On my second day we planned to venture much further offshore and fish some special wrecks which Arne had located. Unfortunately, the weather changed for the worse during the night, and we were prevented from getting as far out as we would have liked. Nevertheless, the wrecks we did fish produced plenty of cod, though, unfortunately, none anywhere near the size of some of the fish pictured in Arne's extensive photo collection, which included several in the 40lb to 50lb range.

Following my couple of days at Astol, I drove further north to the Swedish tourist town of Lysekil. Here I spent a few more days fishing aboard an old 65ft converted trawler called *Oberon*, owned and operated by a local man Bernt Larsson. *Oberon* is a beautiful traditionally built Swedish fishing boat around fifty years old, typical of much of the Scandinavian charter fleet. With a cruising speed of less than 10 knots these old boats are slower than their modern counterparts, but I can assure you they are far more comfortable to fish from, and absolutely perfect for fishing on the drift. In a rough sea they remain stable, and unlike lighter and smaller fibreglass boats they have hardly any tendency to spin, so consequently tangled lines are few and far between.

The fishing off Lysekil was excellent. Once

Anglers fishing aboard the Swedish charter boat Oberon. Note the individual fish baskets: Scandinavian anglers go to great lengths to ensure their fish are kept in the very best possible condition.

An angler displays a double-figure cod caught from a Swedish wreck.

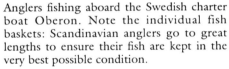

again, there were plenty of cod and codling piled up on the various reefs and wrecks Bernt took us to, with the biggest fish topping 20lb in weight, and a high average size of around 10lb.

There is no doubting that as far as Swedish boat fishing goes, the further offshore you fish, the bigger the fish. All of the skippers appreciate this, and many frequently take anglers on extended two- and three-day excursions. Given the size of many of the boats and the provision of sleeping, washing and cooking facilities, it is possible to live aboard in absolute comfort.

During these trips many of the boats call into various ports on the southern Norwegian coast overnight, such as Langesund. Deep water is found much closer to the Norwegian coast than in Sweden, and this is where the very biggest cod are invariably caught. Fishing in this area, cod of up to 30lb are taken for granted.

There is plenty of scope for the angler who wishes to catch cod from the shore in Sweden. Much of the west coast of Sweden consists of rock, with a multitude of headlands and small islands along with deeper inlets and fjords. Many of these marks give easy access to very deep water, where you will be able to catch cod. On the deeper marks, heavy spinners and small pirks can be used with tremendous effect, but bait, normally mussel or lugworm, should give more consistent results.

As in Denmark, the cost of living in Sweden is noticeably higher than in the UK. A place aboard a boat will cost somewhere in the region of £30 per person, and the cost of a long-range trip obviously rises accordingly.

Visiting anglers wishing to fish the productive west coast can either fly into Göteborg, hire a car and drive to their intended venue, or far more realistic for anglers – take the Scandinavian Seaways ferry from either Newcastle or Harwich to Göteborg and then drive the short distance north to either Astol or Lysekil. Swedish roads are very good, not to mention picturesque. Scandinavian Seaways can be booked on 0990 333111. The Swedish Travel & Tourism Council is at 11 Montagu Place, London, W1H 2AL. Tel: 0171 724 5868.

NORWAY

Of all of the Scandinavian countries, the vast coast of Norway probably offers the most potential for the specialist cod angler. The entire coastline is deeply fragmented with countless fjords, most with unbelievable depths of water within a very short distance of the rocks. The advantages of such a unique topography are many, but as far as the sports fisherman is concerned the biggest of these are minimal travel distances to the most productive fishing grounds, and always having shelter from winds from any direction. When fishing within a fjord with a mountainous backdrop climbing hundreds of feet above sea level, you will, more often than not, be fishing in flat calm conditions. To further wet your

appetite for Norwegian cod fishing, the current cod record in Norway is well in excess of 80lb!

I have fished from Bergen and Oslo, where the standard of cod fishing is exceptionally high. It is nearly all drift fishing with pirks and other artificial lures, which tends to be the most widely used technique afloat. Few anglers actually fish from the shore in Norway, and, really, the true cod-fishing potential of this beautiful country is untapped. There is, however, little doubt that there are tremendous rewards to be reaped by any angler who sets out seriously to explore the fishing potential from the shore. The single biggest problem shore anglers are likely to experience in many areas is that standard shore-fishing reels will not hold sufficient line to reach the bottom!

The southern part of Norway, around Oslo, Langesund and Kristiansand, is the area most heavily fished by rod and line anglers. The average size of fish caught here is extremely large. In Norway, anglers fish throughout the year for cod, but the biggest fish are often caught in the spring and autumn. There are undoubtedly some enormous fish waiting to be caught throughout the winter months, but you will need to be fortunate enough to get a spell of settled weather and find a skipper willing to take you to sea. The majority of Norwegian sport fishing boats are laid up through the winter.

As you start to work your way northwards up the coast of Norway, so the coastline starts to become more fractured. The main fishing towns are Stavanger, Bergen, Trondheim and Tromso, the latter situated north of the Arctic Circle. Most rod and line angling activity occurs on the weekend in these ports, when commercial fishermen offer their boats to take anglers fishing in order to earn extra money. In a few ports you might be able to hire a small boat and take yourself fishing. Considering the sheltered waters within the fjords and the minimal travel distances to the most productive marks, this is a worthwhile and probably cost-saving option.

The Lofoten Islands are a small group of islands situated off the north-west coast of Norway. In the past, this area has hosted several international cod-fishing competitions and consequently many of the local skippers here are well versed in the requirements of anglers. The sheer quantities of fish which anglers regularly catch in this area are staggering; it is more or less a case of stopping fishing when you have caught enough fish.

Of all the Scandinavian countries, the cost of living, and consequently the pricing structure, is highest in Norway. Self-catering is easily the most realistic option for most visiting anglers, and make sure you carry as much food and provisions as you can. By European standards the cost of fishing tackle in Norway is horrific, so take everything you are likely to need.

However, in addition to superb-quality angling, Norway offers visitors uncompromising beauty. The snow-capped mountains, huge coniferous forests, and seemingly endless landscapes unblighted by the human hand, are breathtaking. The air is unbelievably pure and often delicately scented with the cleansing fragrance of pine. The overall quality of life in Norway is second to none and, in my opinion, well worth any additional expense.

For more information on fishing in Norway and travel options, contact the Norwegian Tourist Board at 5–11 Regent Street, London, SW1Y 4LR. Tel: 0171 839 6255.

ICELAND

Iceland is without doubt one of the most productive venues that any cod angler could ever wish to fish. This is true both in terms of the enormous quantities of fish which are caught and the potential for catching some really large fish. There is excellent cod fishing all around the coast of Iceland, but as far as the travelling angler is concerned the area around Reykjavik, the capital city, tends to offer the best facilities for visiting anglers. There are charter boats based at Reykjavik itself and also at the idyllic little fishing town of Akranes, where I have fished, and which is reached via a short one-hour ferry crossing from the capital. Keflavik, about forty minutes' drive away and the site of the country's international airport, is another fishing town where a few charter boats are based.

When I last visited Akranes there were two fully equipped charter boats working out of the harbour. I fished aboard the *Elding II*, a locally and purpose-built charter boat, owned and skippered by Gisli B Arnason, who has several years' experience fishing these waters. Apart from the outstanding natural beauty of the Akranes area, what really surprised me was the incredibly short travel distances from the harbour to the most productive fishing grounds. Barely fifteen minutes out of port we stopped for our first drift, and literally seconds after that I caught my first Icelandic fish – a catfish! Throughout the day, we were never more than a half-hour steam from port.

Fishing on the drift is the standard technique used by the vast majority of Icelandic anglers. Around the Akranes area the average water depth was between 30m and 60m, and the speed of drift was more or less perfect for fishing. Not surprisingly, local anglers use a combination of pirks, feathers – many of which are elaborate home-tied creations – and muppets. There is no reason why artificial sand-eels or rubber worms fished on light tackle would not work well here.

For the most part, we were drifting over

Fishing in Iceland.

mixed and broken ground which, I was told, consisted mainly of lava which had erupted from various volcanoes thousands of years ago. Apart from the fishing, few visiting anglers could fail to be inspired by Iceland's rich and unique landscape and geography, which for the most part is extremely mountainous. Snow-capped glaciers carve their way down to the sea through the rough terrain. There are many volcanoes, some extinct and others which are likely to erupt at any time. Then there are the hot-water springs, which constantly spew out millions of gallons of boiling water, and supply towns such as Akranes with all of its hot water and heating requirements. It is common to see several species of whale during a day's fishing, along with thousands of different species of birds.

All of these elements help to create a truly wonderful fishing trip.

The average size of cod we caught was between 4lb and 6lb, but during the day we caught plenty of much better fish which weighed into double figures. The better fish weighed upwards of 20lb and all were in perfect condition. Apart from cod, anglers can expect to catch haddock, coalfish, catfish and the beautiful red Norway haddock. There will always be the chance of hooking the elusive halibut, a hard-fighting species which regularly top 100lb in weight. As far as tackle for Icelandic fishing is concerned, I recommend you take a good 50lb class rod matched with a suitable reel. A selection of pirks weighing between 6oz and 1lb and plenty of feathers and muppets more or less complete the outfit.

Without a doubt there is a great deal of potential for the angler who wishes to catch cod from the shore. Around Akranes, and the rest of Iceland, there are many beaches, rock marks, piers, estuaries and so on, all of which are just waiting to be fished. The few anglers to whom I have spoken, who have actually fished from the shore, report massive catches of fish, including cod.

The cost of fishing in Iceland is on a par with that found in the other Scandinavian countries. For the best deals I recommend you book well in advance. The various local tourist boards will be able to compile an attractive package for visiting anglers, with preferential accommodation rates.

For more information on travelling to and fishing in Iceland contact the Icelandic Tourist Board at Laekjaegafa 3, 101 Reykjavik, Iceland. Tel: 00 354 1 27488. Fax: 00 354 1 624749. For more specific information on fishing the Akranes area, where I have fished and recommend, contact: Tordis G Arthursdottir, Akraneskaupstadur, Skolabraut 31, 300 Akranes, Iceland. Tel: 00 354 4313327. Fax: 00 354 4314327. Icelandair, who offer an efficient daily service to Iceland from either London Heathrow or Glasgow can be contacted in the UK on 0171 388 5346.

USA

Many anglers reading this book might be surprised to learn that there is cod fishing on the east coast of the United States, but I can assure you there is – I've caught them. I have caught Atlantic cod off the coast of Massachusetts from, would you believe it, Cape Cod!

On one occasion I was fishing for striped bass aboard a small high-speed dinghy, and during the course of the day the subject of cod

Dougie Russel holds the 5lb plus cod caught by the author on a striped bass trip off Cape Cod on the north-east coast of America.

was discussed. I enquired about the probabilities of fishing for cod, and was told that the best of the fishing was available aboard long-range charter boats which fish the great systems of sandbanks many miles offshore. In America these are termed 'party boats', and are really modern versions of the huge ex-trawlers from which anglers fish in Scandinavia.

Apparently, the average size of cod aboard these boats is huge: fish in the 30lb to 40lb range are common, and much bigger fish are often caught. And when I say 'much bigger', I mean really big. The current I.G.F.A. (International Game Fishing Association)

20lb-line class record for the species is held by an enormous great fish of 98lb 12oz, caught by an angler fishing the Isle of Shoals off the New Hampshire coast, in 1969. The 50lb-class record is held with an 85lb fish caught in 1984 off New York, and the women's 80lb-class record is held with an 81lb 12oz fish caught off Massachusetts.

Towards the end of our day's bass fishing, which in itself is fantastic sport, the chap I was fishing with, having recognized my interest in cod, asked whether I'd like an hour to try for one. With a roar, the huge outboard engine fitted to the bass boat came alive, and we were soon skimming across the surface to a reef about 3 miles offshore. Rummaging through the depths of my tackle box I found a 2oz Solvroken mini-pirk, which I clipped to the end of my line and allowed to fall swiftly down to the bottom.

Within seconds, and well before the pirk touched bottom, the line went slack as something abruptly halted the little lure's descent. After a brief but spirited struggle, a 2lb mackerel came flapping aboard, another familiar face from the other side of the Atlantic! On the next drop the pirk reached the bottom, and I steadily started jigging. After about five minutes I detected a few swift taps, then all went solid as the light spinner I was using was savagely bent over at an alarming angle. Steadily I coaxed the fish clear of the reef and the worst of the snags. After a few minutes I was 100 per cent sure about the identity of the fish, the classic nodding and head-shaking fight was absolutely typical of cod. And a cod it was, not a huge fish, but a superbly coloured specimen in absolute pristine condition, which weighed somewhere in the region of 5lb.

My research has revealed that despite dramatic reductions in cod stocks off the eastern seaboard of the States, Nova Scotia and Newfoundland, there are still enough fish left to warrant rod and line fishing. Most of the party boats operate throughout the spring and summer months, and occasionally into the autumn, before laying up over winter. On my last visit the typical cost per angler was around $50 a day; that's roughly £30.

The best place to enquire about cod fishing is in any of the many tackle shops which are found in America. Incidentally, the cost of fishing tackle in the States is considerably less than at home, so much so that it is hardly worth taking any with you; just buy a complete outfit there, use it, and bring it home. Pirks and countless other suitable lures are readily available, and at approximately half the price of their UK equivalents.

Most anglers go to this part of America either on business or on a family holiday, and my advice would be to squeeze in a day or two's fishing no matter what. For further information, contact the American Tourist Board on 0171 495 4466 or 0891 136136. Alternatively, any travel agent will have a multitude of information on trips to America.

7 Looking After and Preparing Your Catch

Fresh out of the sea, with fins standing erect and eyes shining brightly, the cod is a beautiful fish. Unfortunately, such sparkling beauty is short lived, and it takes only a few hours lying sweating in a typical communal plastic fish box or, worse still, lying in bright sunshine, to transform the freshest of fish into a useless stinking heap.

The only justification for killing any living animal is if that animal is required for food, either by yourself or by others. There is no excuse for catching and killing fish which are destined to be dumped. Naturally, therefore, it is in our own best interests to ensure that those fish which we do kill are retained in the very best condition, either to be eaten fresh or frozen until a later date.

Many anglers could benefit from taking a close hard look at the shining example set by anglers fishing in Scandinavia. In the Nordic countries fish still forms a major part of the daily diet; indeed, the sole reason why many Scandinavian anglers fish in the sea is in order to stock the freezers at home. Not only do Scandinavian anglers enjoy fish, but they insist on eating only fish of the very highest quality.

Anglers fishing aboard charter boats in Denmark, Sweden, Norway and Iceland are invariably given their own fish basket at the start of the trip. In some areas traditional wooden or wicker baskets are still used, in others plastic baskets are used; both are preferable to boxes. Even on a cool day fish lying in plastic boxes will sweat and stew in their own juices, quickly discolouring and tainting the flesh. On a warm day it will only take a few hours in the fish box to spoil even the freshest fish.

The general procedure adopted by Scandinavian anglers is as follows. As fish are caught during each drift they are either loaded into each basket or left lying on the open deck. As soon as each drift is over these fish are thoroughly gutted, the angler always taking the time to ensure that all of the stomach contents are removed, including the grey lining of the body cavity. The heart and liver are also cut out which helps to bleed the fish, thus preventing bruising and staining of the otherwise snow-white flesh.

Each fish is then thoroughly washed in clean sea water to remove all traces of blood and body juices. This practice is religiously followed throughout the trip, with the entire catch receiving a regular wash-off with cool clean sea water. This is where a basket is preferable to a box, as all excess water and juices can swiftly drain away. Naturally, the catch is stored well out of the way of direct sunlight. Then, at the end of the day, the angler returns home with a catch of fish which is in the very best possible condition.

Aboard my own dinghy, I followed a similar procedure to keep my catch in good condition. I do not use a basket, as from a safety point of view it is important to keep the decks

Filleting a freshly caught cod aboard a charter boat.

The end result, a prime fillet of cod.

as dry as possible. I clean each fish as soon as possible, then either stack them in a fish box and give them a regular wash-off in the sea, or thread them on to a 'stringer' (a length of rope threaded through to gills and mouth), which is tied off with the fish suspended over the side of the boat in the sea. It should be relatively easy for shore anglers to keep their catch in pristine condition.

Filleting Cod

There is nothing worse than watching an inexperienced angler carving up and totally destroying a good fish in an attempt at filleting

it. Successfully filleting fish is an art which does take time to develop, though there are certain things which even a novice angler can do to help himself. Firstly, a razor-sharp filleting knife is essential: a really sharp knife will slice effortlessly through flesh, helping to produce cleanly cut fillets. A blunt knife will not cut cleanly, and consequently requires more physical effort on behalf of the angler. It is when the angler has to start forcing the knife through the fish that accidents are likely to occur. Far more accidents are caused from using blunt knives than from using sharp knives.

There are many good filleting knives available in shops. Tackle shops almost always stock a full range, but the very best knives are found in hardware stores or the cutlery departments of larger shops. I have several top-quality filleting knives which I keep at home, and carry a Normark filleting knife in my tackle bag for gutting fish and preparing baits. Normark produce an excellent range of filleting knives, complete with leather sheaths, to cover all budgets. When buying a filleting knife look for a knife with a narrow blade around 6in to 8in long, with a little flex and a strong backbone. Avoid knives which are too flexible: these are nearly always made of inferior steel which will not hold its edge and they will not have the necessary strength to cut cleanly through bone.

Keep the blade of your knife really sharp by regularly giving it a few strokes across a fine-grain sharpening stone. Many anglers allow their knives to become blunt before they attempt to re-sharpen them, which then becomes a long process. All knives when not in use should be safely retained in a sheath.

Attempting to make a good job of filleting fish aboard a boat at sea is not only difficult in all but the flattest conditions, but often exceedingly dangerous. For this reason, I usually only gut my fish aboard the boat, then either fillet them back in port, on the beach or, best of all, at home. Always fillet your fish on a wooden or nylon cutting board to prevent damage to the knife.

There are several ways that cod can be prepared for the table; the optimum way will be governed by the size of the fish. Very small codling are best cooked whole after first removing the head, but it would be better carefully to return them alive to grow bigger. Fish up to about 7lb in weight can be either cut into cutlets, or filleted. Larger fish are almost always best filleted.

To fillet a cod, start by placing the knife immediately behind the fish's pectoral fin, then cut down through the flesh until you reach the backbone. Carefully draw the knife – inserted at a depth of about 2in – back towards the fish's tail, keeping the knife pressed on to the backbone. When your cut has reached the fish's vent, push the knife right through the fish, then continue cutting back towards the tail.

Next, return to the head end and steadily work the knife deeper through the flesh, until the ribs are reached. Some anglers cut through the ribs and then continue back towards the tail; others, who prefer totally boneless fillets, discard this area by cutting around the rib-cage. This latter technique will result in slightly smaller fillets. The fish is then turned over and the same procedure followed on the opposite side. With practice, all that will be left will be the bare skeleton of the fish with no flesh.

Provided that the fish was retained in a fresh condition, fillets can be kept in a domestic fridge for several days before use. Fillets which are frozen should ideally be used within three months, and certainly within six months of capture. Prior to freezing, each fillet should be dried off with clean kitchen roll, tightly wrapped in cling film, placed in a plastic freezer bag and immediately stored in the 'freezing down' section of the freezer. As long as the catch was correctly cleaned at sea, there should be no need to wash each fillet in fresh water. Washing the fillets in fresh water removes a lot of the fish's natural flavour, and allows the flesh to absorb water. During the freezing process, this water expands and breaks down the otherwise firm flesh, resulting in inferior-quality fillets when they are defrosted.

Cod Recipes

My own favourite recipe for cooking and eating cod is quite simple. Take one fresh cod, fillet and wash, roll in flour, deep fry in hot oil for about 15 minutes, and serve with an enormous mountain of chips, peas and lashings of bread and butter and copious quantities of tomato sauce, salt and vinegar! Not exactly *nouvelle cuisine*, but damn tasty and satisfying, especially when you have caught the fish yourself a few hours earlier. A standard recipe is given below.

Standard Batter

Ingredients
4oz (125g) plain flour
1 egg
pinch of salt
5–6 tablespoons skimmed milk

Mix all of the ingredients thoroughly, preferably using a food processor, for about 45 seconds. The batter is best if left to settle and thicken for an hour before use.

Index

Berlitz

CUBA
POCKET GUIDE

Walking Eye
mobile app

Discover the world's best destinations with the Insight Guides Walking Eye app, available to download for free in the App Store and Google Play.

The container app provides easy access to fantastic free content on events and activities taking place in your current location or chosen destination, with the possibility of booking, as well as the regularly-updated Insight Guides travel blog: Inspire Me. In addition, you can purchase curated, premium destination guides through the app, which feature local highlights, hotel, bar, restaurant and shopping listings, an A to Z of practical information and more. Or purchase and download Insight Guides eBooks straight to your device.

TOP 10 ATTRACTIONS

MUSIC
In various traditional styles, live music can be heard all over the island. See page 45.

BARACOA
A picturesque coastal town in the far east of Cuba. See page 81.

PLAZA DE LA CATEDRAL
An impressive stage set at the heart of the Old City of Havana. See page 28.

BEACHES
Beautiful white-sand beaches abound, from Varadero to Playa Esmeralda, Playa Ancón to Cayo Largo.

CASA MUSEO DE ERNEST HEMINGWAY
Where things remain just as the author left them. See page 45.

EL MORRO
Santiago's well-preserved fort. See page 79.

CAMAGÜEY
The streets and squares of Cuba's third city have been restored to their former glory. See page 68.

THE PRADO
Grand old buildings flank the loveliest avenue in Old Havana. See page 38.

TRINIDAD
Frozen in time, this city is an enchanting colonial gem and a World Heritage Site. See page 62.

VIÑALES VALLEY
Visit tobacco fields and mogotes. See page 50.

A PERFECT DAY

8.00am

Breakfast

Fortify yourself for the day ahead with a good breakfast at your hotel or *casa particular*. Tuck into tropical fruits, such as mango, papaya or guava, sliced or juiced, followed by eggs, bread and local honey or jam.

9.00am

Parque Central and Capitolio

Start at the centre around the Parque. Admire the magnificent Gran Teatro, Hotel Inglaterra and imposing Capitolio. Visit the Museo Nacional de Bellas Artes to see Latin America's largest collection of antiquities, as well as works by Goya, Rubens and Turner.

11.30am

Plaza de Armas to Plaza Vieja

Walk to the Plaza de Armas, stroll round the second-hand book market and visit the Museo de la Ciudad. Head down Calle Oficios, taking in the car museum, to Plaza San Francisco and on to the beautifully restored Plaza Vieja.

11.00am

Cathedral

Visit the Cathedral where Columbus' bones once resided and have coffee at El Patio restaurant in the Plaza, a magnificent colonial square with street entertainers.

1.00pm

Lunch

On the southwestern corner of Plaza Vieja is a restaurant and bar, Cervecería Taberna de la Muralla, which has its own organic microbrewery. A cold beer here is very refreshing and you can sit outside in the square to enjoy the view or relax inside and admire the copper brewing tanks.

IN HAVANA

4.00pm

Casa de la Música Galiano

From the Parque Central, walk five blocks down Neptuno to Galiano, where you'll be able to catch a performance (5–10pm) at this live-music venue, with bars, a huge dance floor and a well-stocked music shop.

10.00pm

On the town

Get a taxi to Vedado for a great evening of jazz. At La Zorra y el Cuervo, Avenida 23, between N and O streets, the entrance is through a red British telephone box. If you want a table, get there before 11pm when things start to hot up. This is a popular place with top-class jazz musicians and the crowd shows its appreciation.

2.00pm

Bus tour

Return to the Parque Central to hop on the HabanaBusTour, which runs all day. One route travels from the Avenue del Puerto to Vedado, Plaza de la Revolución and Miramar (T1), while another takes you out past the fortresses to Playas del Este (T3). You can get off at any stop and rejoin another bus later.

8.00pm

Dinner

While in Centro Habana, you can get a memorable meal at one of several *paladares*, such as La Guarida (see page 108), advance booking essential. Service is leisurely, enabling you to linger until the nightlife gets going.

CONTENTS

INTRODUCTION

The largest island in the Caribbean, Cuba is blessed with pristine beaches, fascinating old cities with myriad architectural styles, Latin music with hip-swivelling rhythms, a surfeit of rum and the world's finest hand-rolled cigars.

For much of the 20th century, Cuba occupied a leading role on the world stage wholly disproportionate to its small size and lack of economic clout. From the overthrow of the dictator Fulgencio Batista at the end of 1958 to Fidel Castro's tenacious hold on power and declarations of socialism, this small Caribbean nation has assumed near-mythical status as a living laboratory of social experimentation, political defiance and a people's perseverance.

LEGACY OF THE REVOLUTION

For nearly half a century a combative Fidel Castro weathered the opposition of the US government and the hostility of Cuban exiles in Miami. His successor, his brother Raúl, continued his legacy with a few modifications (Raúl himself was succeeded as president by Miguel Díaz-Canal in 2018, although his vision and influence endure). The Cuban people have been required

⊙ THE FACE OF CUBA

Cuba's 11.3 million people have a distinctively mixed heritage that reflects the twists and turns of the island's history. Black slaves, Spanish and French immigrants and Chinese labourers have all made Cuba their home. During the last 200 years the various ethnic groups have interbred and today most Cubans are *mulatos* (mixed race).

to make repeated sacrifices in the face of the American trade embargo and the collapse of the Soviet Union with its support and trade. Despite all this, Cuba is still standing.

Cuban women in colourful outfits

As one of the last Communist hold-outs in the world, this nation is a true curiosity. With much of the rest of the planet racing ahead at a dizzying digital pace, Cuba crawls along in slow-motion. While internet access is improving, very few Cubans have it at home. Behemoth vintage American cars from the 1940s and 1950s, patched and propped up, lumber down the streets of dimly lit cities. In rural areas cars give way to oxen-led carts, horse-drawn buses, Chinese bicycles and pedicabs.

Cuba is inseparable from the international politics of the latter half of the 20th century. Children are sworn in at the age of six to become Young Communist Pioneers. Throughout the country giant billboards proclaim 'Socialismo o Muerte' ('Socialism or Death') and 'Viva la Revolución' ('Long Live the Revolution'). Portraits of Che Guevara, the 1960s revolutionary martyr, are plastered on the walls of shops, offices and homes.

CUBAN REALITY

Everything has always creaked and spluttered in hard-pressed Communist Cuba. The economy thrives or falters in line with world trends, hampered additionally by the US trade embargo

School children in Havana

(which remains in place pending further reforms by the Cuban government) and hurricane damage. Many families continue to live in overcrowded conditions in run-down housing, and the average wage for someone who works for the state is the equivalent of US$25 a month.

In the early 1990s Castro needed to reorganise the economy after the collapse of the Eastern Bloc which had formerly subsidised Cuba. In 1993 it became legal for Cubans to hold US currency. Much of the economy was given over to the almighty dollar, with many products and foodstuffs available only in dollar stores. Those with access to US currency soon had the advantage, and a decade later there was a deepening split between the haves and have-nots. Castro was forced to take action to halt the division, declaring that all foreign currency had to be exchanged for *pesos convertibles*, with a steep tax on converting US dollars. In 2013 the government issued plans to unify the two currencies, but a timescale has still not been announced.

The glaring deficiencies of the Cuban economy and needs of the Cuban people are impossible to ignore. Cubans also enjoy no real freedom of speech, press or travel outside the country, although some restrictions have been relaxed since Fidel Castro's death. Still, one doesn't see the heart-wrenching poverty in Cuba common in other parts of Latin America.

Housing is provided by the state and while Cubans don't get nearly enough with their ration books, they have something to eat. All Cubans are entitled to free health care and education. Average life expectancy rose from 57 years in 1958 to 79 years in 2017 – the 32nd highest in the world.

Cuba's dilapidation, poverty and restrictions only serve to highlight the indomitable spirit of the Cuban people. They are blessed with a remarkable resilience, forbearance and joy that no economic hardship seems capable of diminishing. Cubans are as hospitable a people as you'll find, inviting visitors into their cramped homes given half a chance.

PARADISE ISLAND

In dire need of hard currency, Cuba has embraced tourism, which is now the country's top revenue earner. It's obvious why; for many Cuba is primarily an idyllic sun-and-sea bolt-hole. The white sandy beaches are dazzling, with the long shores of Varadero the best known. Amateur sailors appreciate the countless natural harbours, anglers search for marlin off the coast, while scuba divers explore reefs and sunken wrecks.

Most travellers opt for package tours, but Cuba's diversity tempts independent travellers away from the sea and sand. In the island's eastern corner is Cuba's highest mountain range, the Sierra Maestra, site of many uprisings; to the west, in Pinar del Río province, is the verdant Viñales Valley with its huge *mogotes*; and central Cuba has the lush Sierra del Escambray mountains and the old sugar-cane plantations.

Then there are the towns and cities. Havana combines fine Spanish colonial architecture, vibrant street life and a range of cultural opportunities; Trinidad, a gorgeous colonial-era gem; and Santiago de Cuba, a colourful Cuban cocktail of Spanish, French and African cultures.

A BRIEF HISTORY

When Christopher Columbus disembarked on eastern Cuba on 27 October 1492, he penned a note exclaiming that the land was 'the most lovely that eyes have ever seen'. Indigenous groups including the Ciboney from Central and South America had lived on the island since at least 3500 BC.

In 1511 Diego Velázquez sailed from neighbouring Hispaniola with some 300 conquistadors. Baracoa became the first of seven settlements across Cuba. Velázquez and his followers enslaved the native peoples and in the process exposed them to European diseases. Entire villages committed suicide, and by the mid-1500s the native population had declined from over 150,000 to just 3,000.

PIRACY AND TRADE

Until the late 16th century, Cuba was a fairly insignificant Spanish colony. The port cities of Havana and Santiago de Cuba were heavily fortified to defend against pirate raids.

From the 17th century Havana became increasingly significant as a stopover point for treasure fleets. In 1762 British forces captured the city. They held it for only a year before returning it to Spain in exchange for Florida, but during this

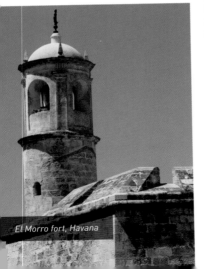

El Morro fort, Havana

period trade was opened up to additional markets. A lucrative tobacco industry had taken hold in Cuba, and after 1763 the sugar industry skyrocketed. Though settlers brought the first African slaves to Cuba in the early 1500s, hundreds of thousands of African slaves were imported in the late 18th and early 19th centuries to meet the demands of the plantation industry.

Sugar island

By the middle of the 19th century, Cuba produced a third of the world's sugar and was considered one of the most valuable colonies in the world. Half a million slaves – nearly half the population – worked the plantations.

THE ROAD TO INDEPENDENCE

Spaniards born and raised in Cuba, known as *criollos* (creoles), managed the sugar-cane plantations but were excluded from the running of the country by Spain. During the 19th century some *criollos* (particularly in Oriente, the island's poorer, eastern region) became increasingly disenchanted and desired greater autonomy. On 10 October 1868 Carlos Manuel de Céspedes, a *criollo* plantation owner, issued a call for independence and liberated the slaves from his estate, La Demajagua. During the subsequent Ten Years' War (1868–78) 50,000 Cubans – including Céspedes – and more than 200,000 Spanish lost their lives. Cuba remained a colony of Spain, but the war contributed to the abolition of slavery on the island in 1886 and cemented national consciousness.

In 1895 José Martí, Cuba's most venerated patriot, led the next and most important uprising against Spain. Born in 1853 and exiled at 18 for his political views, Martí became a journalist and poet. From exile in the United States he argued

José Martí
Memorial in Havana

for Cuban independence. Martí was killed in an ambush during the War of Independence, which began in 1895 and in which some 300,000 Cubans lost their lives.

Throughout the 19th century the United States, keenly interested in Cuba's strategic significance and its sugar market, had become increasingly involved in Cuban affairs. A US purchase of the island from Spain had long been on the agenda, even though Martí had warned of the dangers of becoming a satellite of the United States.

In February 1898 the USS Maine was sunk in Havana's harbour, killing 260 people. Although it was most likely caused by an accidental explosion, the United States used the sinking as a pretext to declare war. US victory in the Spanish-American War came swiftly, with Spain surrendering its claim to the island. A US provisional military government lasted until 1902, when Cuba became an independent republic. But the country was still subject to US military intervention which many claim crippled true independence.

FALSE INDEPENDENCE

For the next 50 years the United States, the largest importer of Cuban sugar, dominated the island's economy and largely controlled its political processes. The period was rife with political corruption, violence and terrorism. After 1933 Fulgencio Batista, though only a sergeant, controlled the strings of power through a series of puppet presidents before winning the presidency outright in 1940. He retired in 1944 but returned by staging a military coup in 1952. His dictatorship made it possible for him to invest some $300 million abroad by 1959.

Since the 1920s disillusionment with the nascent republic – with its clear dependence on the United States and its lack of political probity or social equality – had grown steadily. Although Cuba had the second-highest per capita income in Latin America, prosperity did not filter down from the upper classes. In fact, the World Bank in 1950 declared as many as 60 percent of Cubans undernourished. In Havana there was a greater concentration of millionaires than anywhere else in Central or South America, and the capital was dubbed 'an offshore Las Vegas' for its brothels, casinos and gangsters.

THE ROAD TO REVOLUTION

On 26 July 1953, rebels attacked the Moncada Barracks in Santiago de Cuba. The assault failed, but it thrust into the limelight its young leader, Fidel Castro. Castro was imprisoned and put on trial in a closed hearing; his legendary two-hour defence speech, later published as *History Will Absolve Me*, became a revolutionary manifesto. Castro was incarcerated on the Isle of Pines (now called the Isla de la Juventud) until May 1955, when Batista granted an amnesty to political prisoners.

Castro then fled to Mexico. The following year he returned to southeastern Cuba with a force of 81 guerrillas (including Che Guevara) crammed onto a small yacht, the *Granma*. Only 15 reached the Sierra Maestra mountains safely. Incredibly, from such inauspicious beginnings the so-called '26 of July Movement' grew into a serious guerrilla army, aided in no small part by local

⊘ CHE AND FIDEL: BROTHERS IN REVOLUTION

Ernesto 'Che' Guevara (*che* meaning 'mate' or 'buddy' in Argentine slang) is the official poster boy and martyr of the Cuban Revolution, idolised by Cubans. His dramatic, beret-topped visage is seen on billboards and photographs throughout Cuba. Born in 1928 in Argentina, Guevara trained as a doctor before embarking on nomadic treks through South and Central America with a pile of Marxist literature in his rucksack. He met Castro in Mexico in 1955 and for the next 10 years was Castro's right-hand man, as a guerrilla in the mountains then as director of the national bank (signing bills as, simply, 'Che'), minister of industry, and minister of the economy. In 1965, he abandoned Cuba for new causes. He was killed trying to foment revolt in Bolivia in 1967.

Fidel Castro – for 49 years the president of Cuba, secretary-general of its Communist Party and commander-in-chief of its armed forces – was born in 1926 and trained as a lawyer at the University of Havana. The world's youngest leader in 1959, Castro defied all expectations to become one of the longest-serving heads of state on the planet. Fidel, as he is known to all, was a towering but frustrating patriarchal figure to Cubans. Yet he remained, above all, El Comandante.

Fidel Castro died on 25 November 2016 in Havana, aged 90. His ashes were transported in a funeral convoy from the capital to Santiago de Cuba, retracing the route of his victory march in 1959, as hundreds of thousands of Cubans, many wearing t-shirts with the slogan 'Yo Soy Fidel' (I am Fidel), lined the streets to pay homage to their late leader.

peasants who were promised land reform.

Following a disastrous offensive by government troops on the rebels' mountain strongholds in 1958, and the capture of Santa Clara by Che Guevara and his men on 30 December, on 1 January 1959 Batista fled the country. The *barbudos* (the bearded ones) triumphantly entered Santiago, then marched into Havana one week later.

Castro by Guayasamin

FIDEL'S CUBA

Castro's fledgling government immediately ordered rents reduced, new wage levels set, and estates limited in size to 402 hectares (993 acres). A nationalisation programme followed, and the government expropriated factories, utilities and more land, including an estimated $8 billion of US assets. The foundations were set for near-universal state employment. At the same time, the government instituted programmes to eradicate illiteracy and provide free universal schooling and health care.

However, a centralised, all-powerful state didn't please all Cubans. The media were soon placed under state control, promised elections were never held and Committees for the Defence of the Revolution (CDRs) were established to keep tabs on dissenters. In the early years of the Revolution, tens of thousands of people suspected of being unsympathetic to its goals were imprisoned or sent to labour camps, along with such other 'undesirables' as homosexuals and priests.

Between 1959 and 1962 about 200,000 Cubans, primarily professionals and affluent landowners, fled the country. Expatriate Cubans settled in nearby Florida, establishing a colony that would steadily gain in political and economic power. Another 200,000 abandoned Cuba as part of the Freedom Flights Program between 1965 and 1973 and some 125,000 followed in 1980 when Castro lifted travel restrictions from the port of Mariel.

The US remained opposed to Cuba's political evolution and sought to isolate Castro in Latin America. In 1961 CIA-trained Cuban exiles attempted to overthrow Castro's regime, resulting in the Bay of Pigs fiasco. Soon after, Castro declared himself a Marxist-Leninist. Castro had not displayed any Communist inclinations in the 1950s, and some suggest that US aggression pushed him to ingratiate himself with the powerful Soviet Union and its Eastern bloc of trading partners.

In 1962 Soviet President Nikita Khrushchev installed 42 medium-range nuclear missiles in Cuba. US President John

⊘ THE BAY OF PIGS INVASION

On 17 April 1961, a force of 1,297 Cuban exiles landed at Playa Girón. The Cubans were CIA-trained and came from US ships waiting offshore; US-piloted planes had bombed Cuban airfields days before. US participation was denied at every stage. Castro's 20,000 troops, assisted by artillery and tanks, repelled the invasion within 65 hours. Some 1,180 exiles were captured and ransomed for US$53 million worth of food and medicine. The victory boosted Castro's domestic and international status. Soon after, he declared Cuba a socialist, one-party state.

F. Kennedy responded by staging a naval blockade and insisting the existing missiles be removed. After six days of eyeball-to-eyeball challenge (or the 'Cuban Missile Crisis'), Khrushchev backed down in return for the withdrawal of US nuclear missiles from Turkey. The same year saw the imposition of a trade embargo by the US (which Cubans call the *bloqueo*), which still exists today.

una estrella
quien te puso aqui
y te hizo

The ubiquitous image of Che

THE SPECIAL PERIOD

Until the end of the 1980s, Soviet trade and subsidies helped prop up Cuba's heavily centralised and often badly planned economy. But the subsequent dismantling of the Soviet Union left Cuba bereft of food, oil and hard currency. The government announced the start of a 'Special Period' in 1990, introducing new austerity measures and extending rationing.

With its economy in disarray, the government introduced a limited number of capitalist measures while maintaining a firm political grip. Foreign investment, in the form of joint ventures, was keenly encouraged.

Further measures, such as the legalisation of small enterprises in 1993 and the introduction of farmers' markets in 1994, improved the welfare of some Cubans. Life was still hard, however, and in August 1994 30,000 Cubans fled to Florida on makeshift rafts. Today, the harshest days of privation have receded.

A NEW ERA

Castro turned 80 in 2006, but had to hand power 'temporarily' to his brother, Raúl, while he underwent surgery. Poor health would continue to prevent Fidel from playing any prominent role in the country's political life. In 2008 Raúl was chosen as president of the Council of State and the Council of Ministers, and in November 2016 Fidel, Cuba's revolutionary leader, finally died at the age of 90.

Raúl Castro's first measures were to lift a range of restrictions on consumer spending for those with access to foreign currency. Cubans may now own mobile phones and DVD players, rent cars and stay in tourist hotels on the beach.

Putting public finances in order is a high priority. Agriculture has been decentralised, farmers given greater autonomy as part of a drive for greater efficiency and a plan introduced to unify Cuba's two currencies. The number of state employees is being drastically cut, while permitted categories of self employment have been widened. Rationing has been reduced with the aim of eliminating the ration system entirely.

The end of 2014 saw a thaw in US-Cuba relations as US President Barack Obama and Raúl Castro began a process of 'normalising' relations. Since then, President Donald Trump's threat to 'cancel' Obama's plans has not been an empty one: the ban on individual travel to Cuba has been reinstated, embassy personnel in Havana have been scaled back and 15 Cuban diplomats were expelled from the US in 2017 following allegations of sonic attacks on US embassy staff in Havana. Miguel Díaz-Canel, a staunch ally of Raúl Castro, became Cuban president in 2018 and will also replace Raúl as head of the party when he steps down in 2021. Though Díaz-Canel is not expected to make any drastic policy changes, the end of the Castro brothers' political hold and an unpredictable Trump in the US White House leave Cuba's path looking far from certain.

HISTORICAL LANDMARKS

1492 Christopher Columbus lands in eastern Cuba.

1511 Diego Velázquez begins Spanish settlement.

1519 Havana, founded in 1515, moved to its present site.

1868–78 Ten Years' War for Cuban independence – victory for Spanish forces.

1886 End of slavery in Cuba.

1895 War of Independence begins; José Martí killed.

1898 Sinking of the USS *Maine*; US defeats Spain, which surrenders Cuba to the US.

1902 Formation of the Republic of Cuba.

1933–58 Fulgencio Batista holds power as president.

1953 Fidel Castro launches failed attack on the Moncada Barracks.

1956–9 Cuban Revolution. Castro seizes power (1 January 1959).

1960 Castro's government nationalises all US businesses in Cuba without compensation.

1961 CIA-trained Cuban exiles defeated at the Bay of Pigs.

1962 Cuban Missile Crisis.

1990 Russian trade and subsidies disappear; new austerity measures begin.

1993 Economic reforms begin.

1994 Exodus of some 30,000 rafters to Florida; most are returned to Guantánamo Bay Naval Base.

2006 Fidel Castro undergoes surgery. Replaced temporarily by brother Raúl.

2008 Fidel Castro announces that he will not stand for president; Raúl Castro is elected.

2014 Presidents Castro and Obama trigger thaw of Cuban–US relations.

2015 US and Cuban embassies reopen.

2016 US President Obama visits Cuba. Fidel Castro dies.

2017 Trump presidency halts progress in improving relations. Hurricanes Irma and José batter Cuba, leaving a trail of devastation and 10 people dead.

2018 Miguel Díaz-Canel becomes president, and is set to replace Raúl Castro as party leader in 2021.

A street in Santiago de Cuba

WHERE TO GO

To the surprise of many first-time visitors, Cuba is no speck in the Caribbean. Nicolás Guillén, the nation's finest poet, described the island as a 'long green alligator'. Long it certainly is, at 1,250km (776 miles) from snout to tail. Nearly the size of England in terms of area, Cuba is divided into 14 provinces and incorporates some 450 offshore islands, known as cayos ('cays' or 'keys').

Given its size, you would need at least a month to explore Cuba fully. Most people begin their journeys in the capital, Havana, before heading to the prized tobacco lands further west and doubling back across the plains of sugar cane and some of the country's finest colonial towns in central Cuba. The eastern region, known as Oriente, has soaring mountains and Cuba's second and most vibrant musical city, Santiago de Cuba.

Resort hotels hug quintessential Caribbean beaches (mostly to the north) and although many package tourists stick to the coast, every region has charming, engaging towns, beguiling visitors to explore further.

HAVANA (LA HABANA)

The island's capital, **Havana ❶ (La Habana)**, with little over 2 million inhabitants, is one of the most intoxicating cities in the world. Ever since its early maritime days and through the 1950s – when gangsters who ran prostitution and gambling rackets made Havana synonymous with decadence – it has always held a slightly seedy, languorous allure. That nostalgic appeal is still evident.

Today Havana is a one-of-a-kind, fascinating study in decay and rebirth. Unrestrained ocean waves and salty sea spray have eroded elegant buildings and the seawall of the Malecón, the

Colonial buildings in Old Havana

sumptuous promenade and roadway that traces the edge of the sea. Throughout the city, crumbling houses three and four storeys tall, somehow still standing, line backstreets where children play stickball and adults survey the street from their balconies or doorways. In Old Havana, magnificently restored colonial palaces and stately Baroque churches and convents crowd pulsating squares. Once the finest colonial city in the Americas, Havana's grandeur has not been destroyed even by decades of crisis and neglect. No less defiant than Fidel Castro was himself, beneath the rubble this city is a living, breathing, vital and sensual creature.

Havana sprawls over more than 700 sq km (270 sq miles) and is divided into many districts. Those of greatest interest are Habana Vieja (Old Havana), Centro Habana (Central Havana), Vedado and – to a lesser extent – Miramar. The latter two districts are 20th-century residential and shopping barrios that extend west and south of the old city. While most areas within a neighbourhood can be covered comfortably on foot, passing from one to the other usually requires a taxi or *cocotaxi* (a buggy powered by a motorcycle engine).

OLD HAVANA (LA HABANA VIEJA)

The oldest section of Havana is the city's most spectacular, even if restoration work and gleaming coats of pastel colonial colours are leaving parts of it with a slightly more sanitised feel than the weathered working-class neighbourhoods that extend along the water and inland. As the location of the city's greatest historical sites, **Old Havana** is where you'll want to spend most of your time.

First founded in 1515 on the south coast, Havana was moved to this site along a vast natural harbour in 1519. During the 16th century a fleet of galleons laden with treasures used the port as a pit stop on the way back to Spain from the New World. By the late 16th century, pirate attacks prompted the building of extensive city defences – colossal forts, a chain across the harbour mouth, and prominent city walls – making Havana the 'Bulwark of the West Indies'.

The wealthiest residents lived with their slaves in grand mansions constructed in the *mudéjar* style, a Christian-Muslim architectural tradition dating from the Spanish medieval period. Cool courtyards bathed in penumbral light sheltered from the sun and street noise behind massive doors, slatted blinds, carved iron window bars *(rejas)* and half-moon stained-glass windows *(mediopuntos)*.

The presence of such architectural wonders, no matter how dilapidated, led Unesco to add Old Havana

Find that street

Cuban addresses usually include the street followed by a number. Helpful hints are also given: 'e/ ...' ('between the streets ...') or 'esq. ...' ('corner of ...').

(along with the city's early fortifications) to its World Heritage List in 1982. In the central tourist quarter buildings have been or are being spruced up, mainly with funds raised by the City Historian's Office, headed by Eusebio Leal Spengler. Once restored, the buildings are turned into hotels, museums and galleries, or become once more the splendid old shops they used to be. Many other buildings are propped up by wooden columns: their arcades, fluted pillars and mosaic tiles teetering on their last legs, awaiting their turn. At night, away from the main restaurant and bar areas, the darkness of the streets is punctuated only by the neon glow of television sets from tiny front rooms and the occasional headlights of gas-guzzling vintage Chevrolets and Plymouths, though much of the historical centre is now a pedestrian-only zone.

Havana's past lives on, evoked in part by legendary locations from the pages of popular novels and the lives of fiction writers. These include Graham Greene's **Hotel Sevilla**, where 'Our Man in Havana' went to meet his secret service contact, and Ernest Hemingway's favourite watering holes (El Floridita and La Bodeguita del Medio), as well as the **Hotel Ambos Mundos**, where he penned much of *For Whom the Bell Tolls*.

Old Havana is best experienced on foot, although you can also pick up a *bicitaxi* for a tour around the district with stops for photos.

Plaza de la Catedral

Havana's sumptuous **Plaza de la Catedral Ⓐ**, the focus of Habana Vieja life, could be a stage set. Tourists linger at El Patio's outdoor café, sipping coffee or mojitos and tapping their toes to Cuban *son*. The all-hours hubbub here is infectious. The glorious Baroque facade and asymmetrical belltowers of the late 18th-century **cathedral** are the square's top attraction. The church, begun by Jesuits in 1748, is a thing of beauty; one half expects its bells to erupt in triumphant song. Its interior is surprisingly plain, but it once held the remains of Christopher Columbus. Just south of the cathedral are superb colonial mansions with bright shutters and *mediopuntos*, and an attractive little cul-de-sac **(Callejón de Chorro)** where an Art Nouveau building houses the Experimental Workshop of Graphic Arts. You can watch artists at work and items are for sale.

Of particular interest in the Cathedral Square is the **Museo de Arte Colonial** (San Ignacio 61 e/ Empedrado y O'Reilly; Tue–Sun 9.30am–5pm; www.habanacultural.ohc.cu) housed in a handsome palace dating from 1622. Its most important occupant, Lieutenant Colonel Don Luís Chacón, lived there from 1726. Its little-altered architectural features are complemented by a large collection of 17th- and 18th-century

The cathedral with its Baroque facade

furniture and 18th- and 19th-century tableware, as well as a wonderful collection of historic fans.

Just round the corner, you'll find the atmospheric bar-restaurant **La Bodeguita del Medio** (Empedrado 207 e/ Cuba y San Ignacio; 8am–midnight), which according to Hemingway served Havana's finest mojito. Like pilgrims to Ernest's drinking shrine, all tourists seem required to pay their respects here and pay for an overpriced mojito. Art exhibitions are held down the street at the **Centro de Arte Contemporáneo Wifredo Lam** (San Ignacio, 22 esq. Empedrado; Mon–Sat 10am–5pm), named after Cuba's most famous 20th-century artist. Books, manuscripts and photographs of the country's best-known novelist are housed inside the **Fundación Alejo Carpentier** (Empedrado, 215 e/ Cuba y San Ignacio; Mon–Fri 8.30am–4.30pm; www.fundacioncarpentier.cult.cu; free).

Plaza de Armas

Plaza de Armas , which surrounds a statue of the patriot Céspedes and is ringed by shaded marble benches and second-hand bookstalls, is Havana's oldest square. It dates to the city's founding in 1519.

On the square's eastern side a small neoclassical temple, **El Templete**, marks the spot where the first Catholic mass was celebrated in 1519. Next door is one of the city's most luxurious hotels, Hotel Santa Isabel. To the north, the squat but angular and moated **Castillo de la Real Fuerza** (Fort of the Royal Forces; Tue–Sun 9.30am–5pm) is one

A writer's tipples

'My mojitos at La Bodeguita, my daiquiris at El Floridita'– a personal declaration of drinks and where to have them, attributed to novelist Ernest Hemingway.

of the oldest forts in the Americas, begun in 1558.

The battlements afford views over the harbour, and the bronze *La Giraldilla* weather vane on one of the fort's towers – depicting a woman scanning the seas for her lost husband, an early Cuban governor – has been adopted as the symbol of the city and of Havana Club rum.

In 1791 the seat of government and the governor's (or captain general's)

Statue on Plaza de Armas

residence were transferred from the fort to the newly built Baroque **Palacio de los Capitanes Generales** on the square's western flank. A magnificent structure that was the presidential palace and then the municipal palace until Castro seized power, it now houses the **Museo de la Ciudad de la Habana** (Museum of the City of Havana; Tue–Sun 9.30am–6.30pm; English-speaking guides). Beyond the courtyard with a statue of Columbus lies a succession of splendid marbled and chandeliered rooms, some housing old cannonballs and coaches, others decked out with gilded furnishings. The most hallowed room commemorates Cuba's 19th-century independence wars, with the first Cuban flag and venerated personal objects from generals of the day.

Calle Obispo

Running from Plaza de Armas to Parque Central, the pedestrianised **Calle Obispo** ⓓ is Old Havana's most important

Shopping in Calle Obispo

thoroughfare. Here you will find some smart shops catering to those with money to spend, and you can peer into the courtyards of Havana's oldest homes. Equally fascinating are the two parallel, partly residential streets – O'Reilly and Obrapía – where neoclassical and colonial buildings intermingle with decrepit tenements. Restored Old Havana now extends all the way to Plaza Vieja and along pretty much all of Calle Obispo.

At no. 155, Museo de la **Farmacia Taquechel** (e/ Mercaderes y San Ignacio; daily 9am–7pm) is a beautifully restored pharmacy dating back to 1896, with floor-to-ceiling mahogany shelves supporting a lovely collection of 19th-century porcelain jars containing herbal remedies and potions.

Close by, on the corner of Mercaderes and Obispo, is the refurbished 1920s-era **Hotel Ambos Mundos**; Hemingway lived on and off in room 511 for a couple of years during the 1930s. The room is kept as it was during his time here. Those not staying in the hotel can visit the room for a small fee, or go to the rooftop bar for cocktails and see the views over Old Havana.

Nearby are several museums worth visiting as much for the glorious colonial mansions that house them as for their contents. The striking lemon-yellow **Casa de la Obra Pía** (Calle Obrapía, 158 e/ Mercaderes and San Ignacio; Tue–Sat

9.30am–4.30pm; www.habanacultural.ohc.cu) is a 17th-century architectural wonder featuring a magnificent portal brought from Cadiz in 1686. There is a lovely courtyard and the rooms have been adapted to house a furniture museum. The owner, a member of one of Cuba's most important families, sponsored five orphan girls each year – an *obra pía* (work of piety) that lends its name to both the house and its street.

⊘ SANTERÍA: THE CULT OF THE GODS

Santería ('saint worship') is a syncretic religion derived from the Yoruba people in Nigeria and developed in Cuba by African slaves. Practitioners worship a complex pantheon of deities (*orishas*), each with a specific character and a parallel Catholic saint – a guise that allowed slaves to disguise the religion from their hostile owners.

Initiates are chosen by a particular *orisha*, and they will wear the specific coloured beads of that saint and maintain shrines in their homes. The saints are believed to exercise control over almost every aspect of a person's life, but to communicate with them on matters of great importance, believers need the assistance of a *babalao* (priest), who will throw shells and perform other rituals to learn of the saints' commands. Saints' days are celebrations featuring Afro-Cuban drumming and dancing.

Many Cubans have at one time practised the rituals of santería – even Castro, allegedly. While difficult to quantify, its popularity appears to be increasing. In many parts of Cuba, one can see people wearing the coloured beads of their saint – red and white for Changó, the powerful god of war, and blue and white for Yemayá, the goddess of the sea – and others dressed all in white for initiation rights 'to become sainted'.

The massive mansion opposite, nearly as impressive, houses the **Casa de África** (Obrapía 157; Tue–Sat 9am–5pm, Sun 9am–noon; www.habanacultural.ohc.cu), with pelts, drums, costumes, carved figures and furniture from some 26 African countries, as well as a collection of objects related to *santería*, the syncretic Afro-Cuban religion (see page 33) and various items related to Cuban slavery, such as manacles and traps.

On Calle Oficios at no. 16 lies the **Casa de los Árabes** (e/ Obispo y Obrapía; Tue–Fri 8.30am–4.30pm; free), a 17th-century Moorish-style building that displays carpets, robes and pottery, and contains Havana's only mosque (an ornate room upstairs). There's a lovely courtyard restaurant attached.

The streets of Havana are a living museum of chrome-finned wondercars imported during Detroit's heyday. Several that once belonged to pivotal Cuban figures – such as a 1918 Ford truck used by Fidel's father and Camilo Cienfuegos' Oldsmobile – are lined up in the **Museo del Automóvil E** (Calle Oficios, 13 e/ Justiz y Obrapía; Mon–Sun 9am–5pm).

Further south along Calle Oficios is the splendidly restored **Plaza de San Francisco F**, with upmarket restaurants and the imposing 18th-century **Convento de San Francisco de Asís** (daily 9am–6pm). The convent contains a museum of religious treasures and a beautiful cloister. Concerts are frequently held here. Nearby, you'll find several impeccable colonial-era houses with brilliantly coloured façades.

Plaza Vieja

Follow Calle Mercaderes to the fascinating **Plaza Vieja G** (Old Square), which was originally conceived in 1587. It has received a massive facelift, with assistance from Unesco, and a neoclassical marble fountain gleams incongruously in the centre. On the south side, a fine 18th-century palace, known as **La Casona**, has been

converted into an arts centre; its balcony gives a lovely view of the plaza. On the southwestern corner is the **Cervecería Taberna de la Muralla**, an organic microbrewery with café and bar, offering welcome respite. In the northeastern corner, on the roof of a yellow-and-white wedding cake of a building, is the **Cámara Oscura** (Mon–Sat 10am–5.20pm), which gives up-close views of the city as well as wider vistas. The old backstreets here are full of character. Down Calle Cuba, between Sol and Luz, stands the renovated 17th-century **Convento de Santa Clara** (Mon–Fri 8.30am–5pm) that was once renowned as a refuge for dowerless girls.

By the railway station, between Calles Picota and Egido, is **Casa Natal de José Martí** (at Calle Leonor Pérez, 314; Tue–Sat 9.30am–5pm, Sun until 1pm), the modest birthplace of poet and statesman José Martí. The numerous personal effects on display here leave no doubt about the fact that Martí is Cuba's pre-eminent national hero.

The Capitolio Nacional

Capitolio

Calle Brasil (also called Teniente Rey) leads directly west from Plaza Vieja to the monumental **Capitolio** , reopened in 2018 following an extensive eight-year renovation (work continues on the southern section, due for completion by November 2019). It is currently visitable on a 15-person tour from Tuesday to Sunday. A replica of the American capitol in Washington, DC and completed in 1929, it reflects the period when Cuba was in the thrall of the United States. Its vast bronze doors pictorially chart the island's history, and the immense main gallery inside has a replica diamond in the floor beneath the dome, that marks the spot from which all distances in the country are measured.

Directly behind the Capitolio is the **Fábrica de Tabacos Partagás** (Partagás Cigar Factory; Industria, 520 e/ Dragones y Barcelona), renowned for churning out its famously strong cigars since 1845. The building is dilapidated and although you can still buy cigars in the small shop, they are no longer rolled here. The factory is now at San Carlos 812 in Centro Habana (tours Mon–Fri 9am–1pm). Real cigar smokers should resist the temptation to buy from the *jineteros* (hustlers) gathered outside. Bear in mind that customs regulations are tight: you're allowed to take home only 20 individual cigars without official receipt, and fakes (see page 95) are likely to be confiscated.

Just east of the Capitolio, on Parque Central near the classic Hotel Inglaterra, stands the magnificent **Gran Teatro de la Habana** ❶, completed in 1837. The home of the Cuban National Ballet and Opera drips with ornate balustrades, shutters and sculpted columns. The cavernous interior is hardly less awesome but can only be visited during performances.

Those with the Hemingway bug can visit **El Floridita** ❷ (www.floridita-cuba.com), at the intersection of Calles Obispo and Montserrate, one block east of Parque Central. The writer immortalised the swanky bar in *Islands in the Stream*. A bronze statue of Papa now leans against the bar, his photos adorn the walls and his favourite daiquiri is now referred to as the 'Papa Hemingway', with double rum and no sugar (barmen claim he was diabetic). The place is a bit of a tourist trap, but is nevertheless capable of evoking the kind of hedonistic refuge expat writers adored.

On the same side of the Parque Central is the Art Deco **Museo Nacional de Bellas Artes** (www.bellasartes.co.cu; Tue–Sat 9am–5pm, Sun 10am–2pm; combined ticket available with the Arte Cubano collection). This building contains the **Arte Universal** ❸ collection, with Latin America's largest collection of antiquities, as well as works by Goya, Rubens and Velázquez, while a few blocks northeast on Trocadero is the **Arte Cubano** ❹ section, an excellent selection of works by Cuban artists such as Wifredo Lam, Carlos Enriquez and Eduard Abela, housed in the 1954 Fine Arts Palace. Many of the paintings in the Museo Nacional de Bellas Artes were left behind by ruling-class families who fled Cuba in 1959.

Opposite the Arte Cubano collection, housed in the grand presidential palace used by presidents (and dictators) between 1920 and 1959, is the **Museo de la Revolución** ❺ (daily 10am–5pm; English-speaking guides), one of Cuba's most interesting museums. Allow a couple of hours to see this exhaustive exhibition of the trajectory of the 1959 Cuban Revolution. Many of the worn exhibits feel like unashamed propaganda, but that's all part of the fascination. The most absorbing sections chart the struggle to power with countless maps, evocative photos of both torture victims and triumphal scenes, and assorted personal memorabilia from passports and worn-out shoes to Kalashnikov rifles and bloodstained clothes.

In the square outside is the *Granma*, the boat that carried Castro and his 81 rebels from Mexico to Cuba in 1956; it is now enclosed in glass, guarded by military police and surrounded by other revolutionary relics, such as a tractor converted into a tank and the delivery van used in the failed attack on the Presidential Palace in 1957.

The Prado

West of the oldest sections and intimate streets of Old Havana is an area of wide boulevards and grand palaces. The loveliest avenue, the **Paseo del Prado** (officially known as Paseo de Martí), runs from Parque Central to the sea and officially separates Old Havana from Centro. It was built in the 18th century as a promenade outside the old city walls. Grand but run-down buildings, with fading flamingo-pink and lime-green facades, and ornate columns, flank a raised promenade of laurels, gas lamps and marble

benches. In the 19th century, after the city walls collapsed, this was the most fashionable strolling ground for the city's wealthy. Now it serves as a minipark for *habaneros*, from musicians and roaming couples to children playing on homemade skateboards and go-karts, or practising baseball shots.

Havana's forts

Cuba's most impressive forts sit brooding over the capital's commercial harbour. Take a taxi through the road tunnel beneath the water to reach them. The older one, built at the end of the 16th century, is the **Castillo de los Tres Santos Reyes Magos del Morro** Ⓟ, better known as 'El Morro' (daily 10am–7pm). The views of Havana over the defiant cannons are magical.

A building on the Prado

The vast **Fortaleza de San Carlos de la Cabaña Q**, known as 'La Cabaña' (daily 10am–10.20pm), running beside the harbour, was constructed after the English capture of Havana in 1763. The largest fort ever built in the Americas, it is well-preserved, and the gardens and ramparts are romantically lit in the evening. A ceremony held at 9pm (El Cañonazo) re-enacts the firing of a cannon that marked the closing of the city gates.

NEW HAVANA

The walls surrounding Old Havana were razed during the 19th century to allow the city to expand westwards. The long, curvaceous and crumbling **Malecón** (breakwater), a six-lane highway and promenade alongside the city's north shore, links the districts of Centro and Vedado. The victim of harmful salt spray, the seafront drive is undergoing patchy renovation. Havana's youth congregate along the Malecón on fine evenings, flying kites, canoodling, swimming off the rocks and setting out to sea in giant inner tubes to fish.

Although most visitors will want to concentrate on historic Old Havana, the newer districts provide a fascinating view of the areas where most people live and work. The most interesting districts of **New Havana** are Centro and Vedado. The former is a congested, lower-middle-class *barrio* (neighbourhood) with few attractions, although a walk along its dusty streets can be an eye-opening experience. Vedado is the city's principal commercial and residential zone – the epicentre of middle-class Havana – with parks, monuments, hotels, restaurants, theatres and the University of Havana. Once the stomping ground of the elite in the 1950s, the 'suburb' of Miramar today is home to foreign companies investing in Cuba and numerous diplomatic missions of foreign governments.

Centro

Centro Habana (Central Havana) is a ramshackle residential and commercial area. The city's main shopping street, **Calle San Rafael**, traverses it from the Parque Central westwards. This might be Havana at its least guarded. You can stop to have your nails painted, or get a shave and a haircut, right there on the pavement. One of the private markets has overrun Havana's small

Eating out in Chinatown

Chinatown, at Calles Zanja and Rayo. A few Chinese restaurants selling Cuban-Oriental food are all that remain of what was once the largest Chinatown in Latin America in the 1950s.

The neighbourhood of **Cayo Hueso**, just behind the Malecón, is a rough-and-tumble *barrio* once populated by cigar-factory workers. Today the main reason to visit is to see **Callejón Hamel** ❶, where the artist Salvador González has dedicated himself to preserving the area's Afro-Cuban culture. González's studio is here, and on Sunday at noon–3pm there are performances of Afro-Cuban ritual and rumba.

Vedado

Vedado is a respectable business district as well as a leafy residential area, spacious and orderly in comparison with Habana Vieja and Centro. It had its heyday in the 1940s and 1950s, when such gangsters as Meyer Lansky held sway in the Nacional, Riviera and Capri hotels. Stars like Frank Sinatra and Ginger Rogers performed, and American tourists emptied their wallets in glittering casinos.

The Revolution put the lid on the nightlife by banning gambling and deporting the Mafiosi. Today, new or refurbished hotels of international standard welcome travellers on business or for pleasure, and this is still the place to come for nightlife.

Business is centred on **La Rampa**, the name for Calle 23 from Calle L to the sea. Opposite the tower-block Hotel Habana Libre – the Havana Hilton in pre-revolutionary days – is the **Coppelia Ice Cream Park** ❺. At this institution, locals queue for hours for the prized ice cream, ladling them into saucepans to take home. Foreigners can join the queue as well; payment is in *moneda nacional*. Coppelia was instrumental in the award-winning Cuban film *Fresa y Chocolate* ('Strawberry and Chocolate'), a daring film when it came out in 1994 which dealt with freedoms, homosexuality and revolutionary fervour in contemporary Havana (its title is a wry reference to the lack of choices of ice cream flavours – indeed, of all things – in Cuba).

A short walk up the hill brings you to the University of Havana, founded in the early 18th century, a quiet, attractive campus of neo-classical buildings.

Coppelia ice cream seller

Directly east on Calle San Miguel, 1159 between Calles Ronda and Mazón is the **Museo Napoleónico** (Tue–Sat 9.30am–5pm, Sun 9.30am–noon). The mansion holds not only Empire furniture but also a remarkable collection of Napoleonic memorabilia: portraits, busts and even his pistol, hat and a cast of his death mask from St Helena. The house and contents were appropriated by the state from a 19th-century sugar baron in 1960.

In the same year, the government acquired the **Museo de Artes Decorativas** (Calle 17, 502 e/ D y E; Tue–Sat 11am–6pm, Sun 9.30am–12.30pm), when its aristocratic owner fled the island, leaving her collection of fine art hidden in the basement. Each room in this grand 19th-century villa is furnished in a particular style: English Chippendale, Chinese, Baroque or Art Deco.

Massive marble mausoleums line the principal avenues of the **Cementerio de Cristóbal Colón** 🅣 (Columbus Cemetery; entrance on Zapata y 12; daily 8am–5pm, guided tour), which is a vast city of the dead established in the late 19th century. Cubans come here

The iron sculpture of Che on Plaza de la Revolución

to pray and place flowers at the tomb of La Milagrosa ('The Miracle Worker'), who helps people in need. It is said that she was buried with her infant at her feet, but when their bodies were exhumed, the child was cradled in her arms.

Plaza de la Revolución

The **Plaza de la Revolución** Ⓤ is a vast, stark concourse where political rallies are held; otherwise it is usually empty. The square is dominated by grim high-rise ministry buildings, erected in the 1950s by Batista, and the **José Martí Memorial** – a giant, tapering obelisk that looks like a rocket launch pad – with a pensive marble statue of Cuba's greatest hero and a **museum** about his life (Mon–Sat 9.30am–4.30pm). The obelisk's lookout gives superb panoramic views. Adorning the Ministry of the Interior building opposite is a giant iron sculpture-mural of Che, illuminated at night. South of Plaza de Revolucion at Calle 26, esq. Calle 11, is **Fábrica de Arte Cubano** Ⓥ (www.fabricadearte-cubano.com; Thu–Sun 8pm–3am, Sun until 2am), a popular venue for concerts, art exhibitions, film screenings and much more that attracts trendy crowds of habaneros as well as savvy tourists.

Miramar

To the west is the exclusive district of **Miramar**. The villas of the pre-revolutionary rich, expropriated by the state, have now been turned into apartments or offices, but embassies along Avenida 5 still imbue the area with a privileged feel.

At the corner of Calle 14, the **Museo del Ministerio del Interior** (Tue–Fri 9am–5pm, Sat 9am–4pm) has some intriguing exhibits relating to CIA espionage, including code boxes concealed in briefcases, decoding equipment, a transmitter hidden in a fake rock and a range of explosive devices. It also documents dozens of the CIA's attempts to assassinate Fidel Castro. Don't miss the Russian Embassy, between Calles 62 and 66, which looks like a giant concrete robot.

Growing as an attraction, the 22m (72ft) long and 8m (26ft) wide **Maqueta de la Habana** (Calle 28, 113 e/ Avenida 1 y 3; daily 9am–6pm) is an intricate scale model of the city in astounding 1:1,000 detail. A visit to the Maqueta can help organise the city's neighbourhoods in your mind.

Also worth a visit is beautifully restored Casa de las Tejas Verdes (Green Roof Tiles House; Calle 2 no. 318 esq. 5ta Avenida; free tours by appointment) dating from 1926 and now housing a centre for promoting modern architecture and design. It organises interesting expositions, workshops and offers guided tours.

HAVANA'S OUTSKIRTS

Havana's sprawling suburbs contain a couple of places associated with Ernest Hemingway that are magnets for those seeking to trace the author's life in Cuba. From 1939 to 1960 he lived on and off in the **Finca Vigía**, now the **Casa Museo de Ernest Hemingway**

Casa de la Música

The Casa de la Música Música in Miramar is one of the best shows in town. This is where Cubans come to dance their hearts out to salsa and other rhythms played by live bands. And foreigners join in too.

◉ ERNIE AND GRAHAM: LITERARY FOOTPRINTS

Ernest Hemingway's literary and personal footprints are as deep in Cuba as they are in Spain, and they've become part of the tourist fabric in both places. Hemingway wrote two books based in Cuba, *The Old Man and The Sea* and *Islands in the Stream*, and in large part he wrote *For Whom the Bell Tolls* (about the Spanish Civil War) from his hotel room in Havana. He was an island resident for two decades. Pilgrims can trace his life in Cuba at various sites, including Finca La Vigía, Cojímar, El Floridita, La Bodeguita del Medio and the Hotel Ambos Mundos. Despite chummy photos with Castro (they met at the annual Hemingway Fishing Tournament, which Fidel won), the writer's views on the Revolution are elusive, although all Cubans accept him as a fervent supporter. His views notwithstanding, it is certain that he identified with the Cuban people. Hemingway abandoned Cuba in 1960 and committed suicide shortly thereafter in Idaho.

Graham Greene's classic novel about Cuban intrigue, *Our Man in Havana*, was first published in 1958. Not only is it an evocative portrait of sleazy 1950s Havana, with scenes set in the Nacional and Sevilla hotels and the Tropicana nightclub, it's also eerily prescient, as the hero invents drawings of Soviet weapons hidden in the Cuban countryside, long before Castro aligned the country with the USSR. Greene was a great supporter of the Revolution, praising Castro, the war against illiteracy, the lack of racial segregation and the support of the arts. When he went to Cuba to do research for the book in 1958, he took supplies for Castro, who was secluded in the Sierra Maestra, in exchange for an interview that never took place. Greene's support wavered though when he learned of the Revolution's forced labour camps in the 1960s.

(Mon–Sat 10am–4pm, Sun 9am–1pm, closed when it rains). The house is 11km (7 miles) southeast of Havana in San Francisco de Paula, so you will have to take a taxi. The mansion looks much as Hemingway left it, but was meticulously renovated by a joint US-Cuban project to preserve the author's papers. Among the relics are 9,000 books, Hemingway's original Royal typewriter and innumerable bull-fighting posters and animal heads – mementoes from Spain and Africa. Visitors can only look in through the open doors and windows, but you get an excellent view of the large, airy rooms and their contents.

A bust of Ernest Hemingway

Hemingway kept the *Pilar* 10km (6 miles) east of Havana at **Cojímar**. Next to the little fort is a Hemingway bust, looking out over the bay. His captain and cook aboard the *Pilar* was the fisherman Gregorio Fuentes. Until his death at the age of 104 in 2002, Gregorio would regale visitors with tales of his hero. He always denied that he was Santiago, the title character in *The Old Man and the Sea*, but he did not dispute that it was in Cojímar that Hemingway found the inspiration for his famous novel. The little fishing village is now a concrete jungle and unrecognisable from Hemingway's description.

Approximately 18km (11 miles) east of Havana (20 minutes' drive), the long, sandy **Playas del Este** (Eastern Beaches) are a big draw for Cubans. They are the closest beaches to the capital and particularly lively on Sundays.

PINAR DEL RÍO PROVINCE

Due west of Havana is **Pinar del Río province**, Cuba's western-most region – a finger of land with the Gulf of Mexico to the north and the Caribbean to the south. It contains some of Cuba's most beautiful countryside among the lush Guaniguanico mountains and surrounding patchwork of verdant fields, where the world's finest tobacco is cultivated. In the beautiful Viñales Valley, tobacco fields *(vegas)* and ancient limestone formations *(mogotes)* produce spectacular scenery more reminiscent of Southeast Asia than the Caribbean. In this resolutely agricultural region, oxen pulling ploughs that till the red-earth fields and cowboy farmers *(guajiros)* on horseback are much more common than cars. Residents of Havana might think of it as a poor backwater, but the easy, almost somnolent pace and breathtaking country-side make it one of Cuba's certain highlights.

There are beaches and excellent diving further west, but for most visitors the star attractions are the irresistible little town of Viñales and its beautiful valley. Many visitors take organised daytrips to the region from Havana hotels, but an overnight stay in Viñales – overlooking the valley – is highly recommended. Start your explorations by driving west on the *autopista* (highway) linking Havana with the province's capital city of Pinar del Río. About 63km (39 miles) along the highway, a turnoff leaves the level, palm-dotted plains for **Soroa ❷**, where a richly endowed botanical garden nestles in the mountain foothills near a tourist complex. A guided tour reveals an orchid garden, lychee and mango trees, coffee plants and splendid specimens of *jagüey* and *ceiba* trees. There is a *mirador* (lookout) and a waterfall, while

Oxen ploughing the Viñales Valley

the restaurant in the newly renovated Villa Soroa-Castillo de las Nubes complex also has stunning views over the mountains.

PINAR DEL RÍO

At the end of the highway, 175km (109 miles) west of Havana, the small city of **Pinar del Río** ❸ is a busy commercial centre. Along the main street, Calle José Martí, low-rise neoclassical buildings in blues, yellows, greens and orange have a stately but dilapidated quality. You'll find a small, touristy tobacco factory, **Fábrica de Tabacos Francisco Donatien** (Maceo 157; Mon–Fri 7am–5pm, Sat 9am–noon; no photos allowed), housed in an old jail near the Plaza de la Independencia. Visitors are welcome here and at the less picturesque **Fábrica de Bebidas Casa Garay** (Isabel Rubio 189; Mon–Fri 9am–3.30pm, Sat 9am–12.30pm), where they make a local sugar cane and wild guava liqueur called *guayabita del Pinar*.

The road southwest from the city to San Juan y Martínez leads deep into tobacco's heartland – the **Vuelta Abajo** – where the world's greatest tobacco is grown. Amid fields of big green leaves ripening in the sun and plantations covered in white gauze sheets stand steep-roofed barns where leaves are hung on poles with a needle and thread and then dried, turning them from green to brown.

If you continue to the western tip of the island you come to the **Península de Guanahacabibes ❹**, a Natural Biosphere Reserve covering 1,175 sq km (730 sq miles). At La Bajada the road divides, heading west 52km (32 miles) to **Cabo de San Antonio**, where there is a small hotel and marina. Alternatively, 12km (7 miles) south of La Bajada at **María la Gorda**, on the eastern shore of the **Bahía de Corrientes**, there is a hotel offering some of the best diving in Cuba.

Some 27km (17 miles) to the north of Pinar del Río lies the most picturesque corner of Cuba. The deeply green **Viñales Valley** is spattered with *mogotes*, sheer-sided limestone masses covered in thick vegetation. These are the remnants of a collapsed cavern system that was created underwater at least 150 million years ago, in the Jurassic period. Tobacco (of slightly lesser quality than in the Vuelta Abajo) grows here in a patchwork of fields and dries in *bohíos*, constructed with shaggy thatch. Cigar-chomping *guajiros* in huge straw hats urge on their oxen, as vultures swoop overhead. At any time of day you can wander the fields and meet the farmers, who might even offer you a cigar.

VIÑALES

The little town of **Viñales ❺** is a pleasant, rural place, where colourfully painted, single-storey houses with porches line the straight streets.

Near the Cupet petrol station as you leave town heading north towards Puerto de Esperanza, is the delightful **Jardín Botánico**. The garden was first planted in the 1930s and has been maintained by the same family ever since. A guide will show you around the fruit trees and flowers and let you taste the produce (tip expected).

Nearby a couple of local tourist sights, on all the package excursions, have curiosity value but not much else. One limestone *mogote* just west of town was painted by local artists dangling on ropes in the 1960s with a **Mural de la Prehistoria** (Mural of Prehistory) – commissioned by Castro himself – that is 120m (370ft) high and 180m (550ft) long. The garish painting, an exercise in bad judgment and sloppy execution, depicts evolution from an ammonite to a dinosaur to advanced (and presumably socialist) *Homo sapiens*. All the creatures depicted were indigenous to the area. Eight kilometres (5 miles) to the north of town, the extensive **Cueva del Indio** (Indian Cave) was used as a hideout by Indians after the conquest. A tour through the cave includes a brief ride on an underground river in a boat (which would-be emigrants once stole for an unsuccessful escape attempt to Florida). Both mural and cave have tourist restaurants.

Viñales Valley and its mogotes

ISLANDS NORTH & SOUTH

Just off the province's north and south coasts are three contrasting islands. To the north, **Cayo Levisa** ❻ is a small coral cay, about 3km (2 miles) long and just several hundred metres wide at most points, which has pristine beaches, clear waters and coral reefs. The island is a half-hour ferry ride from Palma Rubia (ferries leave at 10am and 6pm). There's a well-equipped diving centre, and overnight accommodation is available in the simple Villa Cayo Levisa bungalow complex, which has a restaurant and a bar.

On the other side of Cuba, stretching eastwards from Pinar del Río's southern coast, is the Archipiélago de los Canarreos. There are two main islands. **Cayo Largo** ❼, 25km (16 miles) long and the most easterly of the archipelago, might be your Caribbean paradise – if all you're looking for is a dazzling white beach and clear blue seas. Other than the kilometres of beaches, there's not much else of consequence here except mangrove, scrub and half a dozen comfortable all-inclusive hotels with a full programme of entertainment and watersports. Turtles nest in the sand at one end of the island. At the other you can go sailing, diving and deep-sea fishing or take a boat trip to **Playa Sirena**, an incomparable strip of sand a 10-minute

Mural de la Prehistoria

boat ride away, where lobster lunches are available.

Cayo Largo, with its captive tourist audience, is considerably more expensive than the mainland. Some package tourists spend the whole of their holiday on Cayo Largo. Those with low boredom thresholds might consider coming for the day or perhaps staying overnight, taking the half-hour flights from Havana and Varadero.

Inside Cueva del Indio

By contrast, the **Isla de la Juventud** ❽ (Isle of Youth) sees few tourists except those at the rather isolated Hotel El Colony (on the Siguanea Bay, half way along the island's western shore), who come exclusively for the superb diving off the island's southwestern tip. Cuba's largest offshore island, some 50km (31 miles) in diameter, the Isle of Youth is not its prettiest. It is said to have been the location for Robert Louis Stevenson's *Treasure Island*; pirates once buried their booty here. The island received its jaunty name in the 1970s, when as many as 22,000 foreign students (mainly from politically sympathetic African countries) studied here in no fewer than 60 schools.

The island fails to live up to its colourful past. The number of foreign students has dropped to fewer than 5,000, and derelict boarding schools dot the monotonous countryside. However, there are plenty of beaches to be discovered, and in a series of caves at **Punta del Este** you can examine enigmatic symbols painted centuries ago by Ciboney Indians (restricted access).

For more accessible entertainment, **Nueva Gerona**, the island's little capital, is moderately attractive, with striped awnings along its smart, pillared main street.

MATANZAS PROVINCE

The province east of Havana – largely flat sugar-cane country – was in the 19th century Cuba's most important cane-producing region. For today's visitors, however, the focus is on the beach resort of Varadero, Cuba's biggest package tourism draw, with opportunities for side trips to atmospheric, time-warped towns and to the swamplands of the south coast.

VARADERO

Varadero ❾ has enthusiastic proponents and equally passionate detractors among its visitors. A long peninsula with many dozens of hotels and restaurants, bars, fast-food cafés and grocery shops stretching right to the tip (and more of each on the way), Varadero doesn't feel much like Cuba at all. It is a package tourist enclave, and plenty of visitors fly in and never venture further afield, so almost the only Cubans they will encounter are on the hotel staff. If you want to see and learn what makes Cuba a fascinating place, though, you'll need to escape for at least a couple of daytrips. In towns around Cuba you'll

Presidio Modelo

Just east of Nueva Gerona is the fascinating Presidio Modelo (Model Prison). The dictator Machado built this copy of a US penitentiary in 1931. Castro and 26 of his rebels were sent here after the storming of the Moncada Barracks; their ward and Castro's solitary confinement cell have been restored.

Souvenir sellers at Varadero

meet tourists who – like jailbird escapees – rejoice at having got out of Varadero.

Still, there are plenty of delighted people for whom this is heaven: a 20km (12-mile) long, virtually uninterrupted white-sand beach with shallow, clean waters. Varadero isn't a recent development by a government desperate for hard currency; it was in the 1920s that Varadero first attracted millionaires, who built palatial holiday villas. They were led by Alfred Irenée Dupont who bought up most of the peninsula and used to vacation at the opulent **Mansion Xanadú**, which he had built in 1930 and which is now an exclusive six-room hotel, and club house of the 18-hole Xanadú golf course (www.varaderogolfclub.com). Tourism proper began after World War II with the construction of hotels and casinos.

However, the beach, Varadero's best feature, can be problematic. Northern winds kick up with considerable frequency, and lifeguards put out the red flags to warn of the dangerous undertow.

There is often a strong smell from the oil pumps on the resort's outskirts. Prostitution and hassling are much less of a problem than they once were, but other pests (namely mosquitoes) can be a real annoyance. Moreover, the resort is spread out over 17km (11 miles), with no real centre, so you need transport to get around.

On the other hand, Varadero has many extremely comfortable hotels (most of them the results of international joint ventures), open bars and an excellent range of watersports. And, unlike other parts of Cuba, topless sunbathing is allowed here. If you tire of the beach, there are organised excursions to every conceivable point of interest on the island – including Havana.

Varadero occupies a long, thin insular spit of sand, with water on both sides and a bridge to the mainland. Between Calles 25 and 54 there's something of a local community of Cubans, with ancient Cadillacs parked outside rickety wooden bungalows. The liveliest area is around Calles 54 to 64, with a shopping mall, a host of restaurants and bars, and the **Retiro Josone**, a pretty park set around a palm-fringed boating lake. Spreading several kilometres further east are the newest hotel complexes.

MATANZAS AND CÁRDENAS

These quintessentially Cuban provincial towns are a world apart from Varadero. Their poorly stocked shops, dusty back-streets and primitive transport provide Varadero's package tourists with a convenient insight into Cuban life before they're whisked back to their hotels.

Matanzas ⑩, 42km (26 miles) west of Varadero, is busy and grimy. Lying alongside a deep bay, it came into its own during the 19th century as the country's sugar capital. On the leafy main square, Parque Libertad, the **Museo Farmacéutico** (Tue–Sat 10am–5pm, Sun 9am–2pm) is a wonderfully preserved chemist's shop, founded in 1882. On a street running east

On the street at Cárdenas

towards the bay is the neo-classical **Catedral de San Carlos Borromeo** (Mon–Sat 8am–noon, 3pm–5pm, Sun 9am–noon).

A little further to the east, impressive buildings on Plaza de la Vigía include the **Palacio de Junco**, which houses a second-rate provincial museum, and the **Teatro Sauto**. Constructed in 1863, the lovely theatre has tiers of wrought-iron boxes and a painted ceiling.

Las Cuevas de Bellamar (daily 9am–5pm), a short distance east, are Cuba's oldest tourist attraction. The caves were discovered by chance in 1861 by a Chinese workman. Tours (in English) take you down into a vast chamber for views of the many stalactites and stalagmites.

Fortunes have changed for the town of **Cárdenas** ⓫, 15km (9 miles) east of Varadero. Once the island's most important sugar-exporting port, it's now a somewhat ramshackle place. But the main square is elegant, and the **Museo Municipal**

Oscar María de Rojas (Plaza Echeverría e/ Avenidas 4 y 6; Tue–Sat 10am–6pm, Sun 9am–1pm), the second oldest museum in the country, houses a quirky collection of items. There is also the **Museo de la Batalla de Ideas** (Calle 12 y Plaza Eheverría; Tue–Sat 10am–6pm, Sun 9am–noon). Inaugurated by Castro in 2001, it documents the campaign for the repatriation of Elián, a local boy who was at the centre of international controversy in 1999–2000. His mother died while fleeing with him to Miami, but after months of heated controversy he was returned by the US authorities to Cuba to live with his father.

ZAPATA PENINSULA

The **Zapata Peninsula** is the largest wetland area in the Caribbean, flat as a pancake and covered in mangrove swamps and grassland plains. Its protected wildlife includes crocodiles, manatees and numerous species of birds. Frankly, though, you are unlikely to see any interesting wildlife unless you take a guided bird-watching trip from **Playa Larga**. You can see penned reptiles at the crocodile farm at **La Boca**, a popular tourist site where you can pose with a baby croc and try crocodile steak.

A more appealing prospect is picturesque **Guamá** ⑫, a half-hour boat ride from La Boca

Cabaña on stilts at Guamá

along an artificial chan-
nel and then across the
vast **Laguna del Tesoro**
(Treasure Lake). Legend has
it that the Indians dumped
their jewels into the water
rather than surrender them
to Spanish *conquistadores*.
Guamá is a group of tiny

> **Battle beach**
>
> A billboard at the Bag of
> Pigs reads: 'Playa Girón: La
> Primera Derrota del Impe-
> rialismo en América Latina'
> ('The First Defeat of Impe-
> rialism in Latin America').

islands connected by wooden bridges. A few visitors stay in
the thatched *cabañas*, but most just come to wander along the
boardwalk, greet the ducks and egrets, and have a meal.

It may be peaceful now, but the Zapata Peninsula is best
known for the violence and bloodshed that once visited its
shores. South of La Boca you soon come to Playa Girón – site
of the 1961 US-led **Bay of Pigs** invasion (see page 20), in
which more than 100 people were killed. At irregular intervals
along the often crab-infested road are a number of concrete
memorials to those who died during the invasion. There are
two simple, isolated bungalow hotel complexes on the bay, one
at quiet **Playa Larga**, the other at **Playa Girón** ⓭, where the
already scruffy beach is further spoiled by a concrete breakwater. One major attraction, however, is the excellent **Museo
Playa Girón** (daily 8am–5pm) which serves as an emotional
memorial to the three-day Bay of Pigs debacle.

CENTRAL CUBA

Tourists usually whiz through central Cuba. The only tour-
ist beacons are on or near the coasts: in the south around
Cienfuegos and in the north at Cayo Coco and Guillermo and
Playa Santa Lucía. But there is much else to see.

The Catedral de la Purísima
Concepción, Cienfuegos

Central Cuba comprises five provinces: Cienfuegos, Villa Clara,
Sancti Spíritus, Ciego de Àvila and Camagüey. Each focuses on
a provincial city of the same or similar name, typically of some
interest yet not likely to detain you for longer than a day. The west
has the best scenery, in the Sierra del Escambray mountains.
To the east of Sancti Spíritus, towns lie on flat plains. This used
to be the main sugar cane growing area in the 1970s, but the
collapse of the sugar-for-oil trade with the USSR in the 1990s
led to the closure of many sugar factories. In Camagüey, the
cattle-ranch province, watermills and *vaqueros* (cowboys) on
horseback punctuate the skyline.

CIENFUEGOS

The best feature of the port city of **Cienfuegos** ⓮ (250km/155
miles southeast of Havana) is its position, set at the back of a large
bay. Despite the industry on its periphery, the centre is attractive,

with pastel-coloured neoclassical buildings. Described as the 'Pearl of the South', it now has Unesco World Heritage Site status.

The focal point in town is **Parque José Martí**, one of the grandest squares in the country. Here you will find most of the major historical buildings, where the city was founded in 1819. The influence of 19th century French immigrants can be seen in the architecture, although there are several styles, including neoclassical and Art Deco. Take a guided tour of the town's finest colonial building, the **Teatro Tomás Terry**, on the north side of the square. Built in 1890, it was named after a rich sugar plantation owner, once a poor emigré from Venezuela. The interior, largely original, has a lovely frescoed ceiling and a semicircle of tiered boxes and wooden seats. Enrico Caruso and Sara Bernhardt once performed here, and on weekends you may be able to catch a performance by one of Cuba's top ballet companies. The **Catedral de la Purísima Concepción**, built in 1870, is on the east side of the square. It has an attractive interior with stained-glass windows depicting the 12 apostles.

The Paseo del Prado is the town's principal thoroughfare and the longest boulevard in Cuba, a palm-lined road that takes you down to the spit of land protruding into the bay past smart waterside villas. At the edge of Punta Gorda, near the end of the Malecón (Calle 37), is the spectacular **Palacio del Valle**. This kitsch, Moorish Revival-style mansion (with a few other styles

Botanical highlight

The Jardín Botánico Soledad (daily 8am–5pm), 23km (14 miles) outside Cienfuegos at Pepito Tey on the road to Trinidad, is the oldest botanical garden in Cuba (it dates from 1899) and one of the best tropical gardens in the world. Tour operators in Cienfuegos can arrange guided tours; alternatively, go straight there and join a tour at the entrance.

mixed in), was finished in 1917. It is now a restaurant with a roof-top bar and is attached to the Hotel Jagua alongside.

At the mouth of the bay, on the western side, the **Castillo de Jagua** (daily 8am–6pm) was constructed by the Spanish in 1733–45 (long before the city's founding in 1819) to ward off pirates. You reach the castle on a ferry from a terminal just south of the Parque Martí (Avenida 46 e/ Calles 23 y 25).

TRINIDAD

The scenic, undulating 80km (50-mile) road east from Cienfuegos to Trinidad skirts the foothills of the Sierra del Escambray, Cuba's second-highest mountain range. The beguiling town of **Trinidad ⑮**, the third of Diego Velázquez's original seven settlements, subsequently became rich through the smuggling, slave and sugar trades. Its sizable old town is endowed with marvellous Spanish colonial architecture and has been named by Unesco as a World Heritage Site. Cuba could package it as a time capsule: it is the island's prettiest town and one of the finest preserved colonial cities in all the Americas. Even the cobblestone streets still remain in the old centre, which restrict traffic and make things difficult for bicycles and horses. There's been a preservation order on Trinidad since the 1950s.

Within easy striking distance of Trinidad are enough attractions to make a longer stay especially rewarding, including the fine beach of Playa Ancón, the lush Valle de los Ingenios (Valley of the Sugar Mills) and waterfalls and treks in the Escambray mountains.

Restored mansions of the well-to-do have been turned into museums, while art galleries, craft shops and restaurants occupy additional lovely old buildings. The city is known for its live music venues in the centre, several of which are open air or in covered courtyards of old buildings. However, entertainment is low key,

The old town in Trinidad

and it's still a pleasant, relaxed place. If you spend a night here you can experience the town without the tour-bus hordes.

The old town clusters around the **Plaza Mayor**, a delightful square of painted railings, fanciful urns, greyhound statues and colonial buildings. The relatively plain church, Iglesia Parroquial de la Santísima Trinidad, is the largest in Cuba, with five aisles instead of three and hand-carved gothic altars. Beside it is the **Museo Romántico** (Tue–Sun 10am–6pm) with a collection of fine furniture and porcelain. The square's two other museums both have attractive courtyards and cool interiors. The **Museo de Arqueología Guamuhaya** (Sat–Thu 9am–5pm) in a beautiful mansion on the west side of the square traces pre- and post-Columbian history. The **Museo de Arquitectura Colonial** (Sat–Thu 9am–5pm) on the east side has examples of woodwork, ironwork, stained glass and other items culled from colonial houses. A block to the north of the Plaza Mayor in a former convent is the **Museo**

School children make their way home

Nacional de Lucha Contra Bandidos (National Museum of the Struggle against Counter-Revolutionaries; Tue–Sun 10am–6pm), which documents the campaign to weed out rebels who hid in the Escambray mountains in the 1960s. The 360-degree view from the yellow belltower is the big draw.

A block south of Plaza Mayor on Calle Simón Bolívar stands the grand Palacio Cantero, built in 1830. Painted pillars, scrolls, shells, pediments and drapes embellish the interior, eclipsing the historical artefacts and old furniture that now form the **Museo Municipal de Historia** (Sat–Thu 9am–5pm). It has its own fine tower, though climbing its rickety narrow stairs can be a trial if a group has arrived there first.

A block south of the Plaza Mayor are two streets completely given over to sellers of handmade lace and other crafts. Further afield, southeast along Calle José Mendoza, you'll find the evocative ruins of **Iglesia de Santa Ana**, and overlooking the town from the north is the **Ermita La Papa**, a bricked-up church, on a hill where boys fly homemade kites.

Aimless wandering is especially fruitful in Trinidad – and, since dozens of street names have changed and neither maps nor residents seem sure of what to call many of them, roaming without a plan is the only practical solution. Virtually every street has its own colonial treasure and feast for the eyes.

AROUND TRINIDAD

Trinidad's prosperity in the 19th century came from the fruits of 50 sugar mills nearby in the scenic **Valle de los Ingenios** ⑯ (Valley of the Sugar Mills). A *mirador* (lookout) with spectacular views is just 5km (3 miles) out of town. About 10km (6 miles) further east is Manaca-Iznaga, where you can explore a lovely colonial hacienda house and its startling, rocket-shaped *Torre de Manaca-Iznaga*. From the top of the tower, the Iznaga family would keep watch over their slaves toiling in the fields. Tours are available with the tour operators in Trinidad or you could arrange a taxi tour. A steam train once used in the sugar industry traverses the whole valley for tourists. It leaves from Estación Dragones, the station in the south of Trinidad, at 9.30am and returns at 2–3pm, CUC$10, but make sure you arrive at least 15 minutes before departure.

Playa Ancón ⑰, approximately 16km (10 miles) from Trinidad has an excellent strip of white sand and clear waters. Here you'll find diving at an offshore coral reef, a good choice of watersports and a scattering of mid-range hotels whose bars and sunbeds are available to all. Sunworshippers tend to congregate here, where there is a car park which serves as a transport hub. In high season there is an unreliable bus service, but there are also taxis and *cocotaxis*, or you can rent bicycles in town. Another good beach excursion is the day sail to the tiny island of **Cayo Blanco** from Playa Ancón, which should be organised through a tour operator.

SIERRA DEL ESCAMBRAY

More compact than the island's eastern and western ranges, the **Sierra del Escambray** (Escambray mountains), coated in luxuriant vegetation, are arguably Cuba's most beautiful range and easily accessible. Blessed with their own microclimate, the mountains are a wonderfully cool refuge from the heat of Trinidad.

To get to the **Topes de Collantes** ⓲ national park, take the road west of Trinidad for the steep 15km (9-mile) climb through dense forests of palms, eucalyptus and pines. You'll pass a health resort, a Stalinesque complex that has decent facilities but lacks life. Two excellent hiking trails conclude with beautiful waterfalls: Salto de Caburní, at 62m (203ft), and Salto Vega Grande. Wear sturdy shoes, as each hike is a steep trek of 4km (2.5 miles) along a narrow and often muddy trail. You can swim in the chilly natural pools underneath the falls. Jeep excursions can be hired at any tour agency in Trinidad. There's a national park charge (price dependant on the trail you intend to follow).

SANCTI SPÍRITUS

Approximately 80km (50 miles) east of Trinidad is **Sancti Spíritus** ⓳, one of Diego Velázquez's seven original townships. Although no match for Trinidad, it has some attractive colonial buildings. The **Iglesia Parroquial Mayor del Espíritu Santo** has foundations from 1522, making it the country's oldest (though the present stone church was built in 1680). Nearby is the **Puente Yayabo**, the only remaining colonial stone arched bridge in Cuba.

SANTA CLARA

A must on the itinerary of all fans of the Revolution, **Santa Clara** ⓴ is a pleasant university city famous as the last resting place of guerrilla hero, Che Guevara. It was the site of the last battle, which started on 28 December 1958 and finished when news arrived that Batista had fled the country on 1 January 1959. An armoured troop train was heading from Havana to Santiago, but Che and his men ambushed it at Santa Clara. Four of the carriages are preserved at the **Monumento a la**

Cayo Guillermo

Toma del Tren Blindado (Calle Independencia; Mon–Sat 9am–5.30pm). You can go into the carriages and see some of the items carried on the train, as well as photos. At the **Plaza de la Revolución Ernesto Guevara** is a huge statue of Che in battle dress, while underneath is the **Mausoleum** (Tue–Sat 8am–9pm, Sun 8am–8pm; free) where Che and his comrades who fell in battle in Bolivia in 1967 were interred when their remains were brought back in 1997. Next to it is the **Museo Histórico de la Revolución** (same hours as the Mausoleum), which has displays detailing Che's life and his role in the Revolution.

CAYO COCO AND CAYO GUILLERMO

These two offshore cays are reached by a causeway across the Bahía de Perros so long (28km/17 miles) that you can't see the land at the far end as you set off.

Cayo Coco ㉑ is named not for coconuts but for a bird: the ibis, as revealed in Hemingway's *Islands in the Stream*. Ibises and other wading birds, often pink flamingoes, can be seen balancing in the brackish waters around the principal causeway and a smaller causeway connecting the cay to **Cayo Guillermo**.

It's the impossibly white sandy beaches, the intensely blue waters and the excellent fishing that draw holidaymakers, and there's not much else to distract you. Both cays are covered in forest or thick undergrowth. Large, luxury, all-inclusive resorts line the 22km (14 miles) of shell-shaped beaches on Cayo Coco. A wide range of non-motorised watersports are available to hotel guests. If you hire a moped or Jeep from your hotel, there are virgin beaches to discover, though with increased development they are fast disappearing.

CAMAGÜEY

About 550km (342 miles) southeast of Havana, **Camagüey** ㉒ is an attractive colonial city; Cuba's third largest. Having been razed by Henry Morgan in 1668, it was rebuilt, with its narrow, twisting streets radiating haphazardly from the Hatibonico River as if to deter further pirate invasions. There are some half-dozen squares dotted around, each with an old church. Some, like Nuestra Señora del Carmen and Iglesia San Juan de Dios, have been nicely restored. The province's cattle-grazed plains hold little water, so the citizens fashioned huge earthenware pots to catch rainwater. Called *tinajones*, these still adorn many squares.

The city's most famous son, Ignacio Agramonte (1841–73), a general killed in battle in the Ten Years' War, was born here and his birthplace on Plaza de los Trabajadores is now a museum: **Museo Casa Natal de Ignacio Agramonte** (Avenida Agramonte 459; Tue–Sat 9am–5pm, Sun 8am– noon), a handsome, early 19th-century mansion. **Nuestra Señora de la Merced** church opposite has benefited from thoughtful restoration: the decorated ceiling is particularly striking.

A dashing equine statue of Agramonte forms the centrepiece of **Parque Agramonte**, just to the south. The cathedral occupies one side of the park, and the Casa de la Trova, around a floral patio, has musical performances afternoon and evening.

A 10-minute walk west down Calle Cristo brings you to a dignified 18th-century church, **Santo Cristo del Buen Viaje**. Behind the church is a great sea of crosses and marble saints in a picturesque cemetery. A few blocks north is the triangular-shaped **Plaza del Carmen**, which has been beautifully restored and is notable for the life-size statues of local people passing the time of day. In one corner stands the **Convento de Nuestra Señora del Carmen**; dating from the early 19th century, the

Catching up with the news in Plaza del Carmen, Camagüey

restored church facade is one of the most beautiful in Cuba and is unique in Camagüey for having two towers.

Another splendid feature of Camagüey – and marvellously restored – is **Plaza San Juan de Dios**, an angular old cobblestoned square surrounded by brightly hued single-storey buildings dating from the 18th century, plus a lovely yellow church with a fine mahogany ceiling and altar, alongside a restored former hospital. It's one of Cuba's prettiest plazas. A few blocks south, near the river, is an impressive agricultural market. A lively place, it's open every day and stocked with a surprising array of meat and fresh produce.

PLAYA SANTA LUCÍA

An hour-and-a-half drive (110km/68 miles) from Camagüey on the north coast, remote **Playa Santa Lucía** ㉓ beckons sun worshippers with mid-range resort hotels strung along a particularly fine peninsular strip of sand. Each hotel backs directly onto the beach. A superb coral reef lies offshore, and diving here is excellent. Aside from a couple of roadside bars, however, nightlife is limited to hotel entertainment.

To counter the isolation of Playa Santa Lucía, the tourist authorities offer a wide range of excursions, including a rodeo at Rancho King, deep-sea fishing and boat and helicopter trips for days on the beach at such unspoiled cays as Cayo Sabinal and Cayo Saetía.

A bus service visits **Playa Los Cocos**, some 5km (3 miles) away; with sheltered aquamarine waters, it's a strong contender for the title of 'Cuba's most beautiful beach'. Adjacent is La Boca, a very small community of waterside shacks with fish restaurants.

ORIENTE: THE EAST

Prior to the Revolution, the east of Cuba was a single province known simply as **Oriente** ('East'), and most Cubans still refer to the region with this name. Oriente incorporates the post-revolutionary provinces of Holguín, Granma, Santiago de Cuba and Guantánamo, which are scenically and historically more interesting than most of central Cuba. The stunning landscapes vary from the north coast's exuberant banana and coconut groves clustered round thatched huts, little changed from earlier indigenous peoples' *bohíos*, to the towering peaks of the Sierra Maestra mountains and lush rainforest on the east coast. Some of Cuba's best beaches lie on the north coast of Oriente within sight of the mountains.

The wars of independence began in Oriente in the 1860s, and nearly a century later Castro concentrated his power base in the inaccessible Sierra Maestra. There are stirring monuments and museums recalling these periods in Santiago de Cuba, the latter dubbed a 'heroic city' for its many historic patriots.

The further east you travel in Cuba the more Caribbean it feels. Santiago de Cuba is renowned for its contributions to Cuban musical culture; the Oriente is the heartland of son, the traditional rural music that formed the roots of salsa, and many of the genre's greats (Trío Matamoros, La Vieja Trova Santiaguera and Elíades Ochoa, among others) got their start in Santiago.

HOLGUÍN PROVINCE

The province of Holguín begins bleakly around the busy capital but improves considerably as you travel north, where the countryside is lusher. **Guardalavaca** ㉔, 60km (37 miles) from Holguín, is an attractive resort, ringed by banana plantations. Watersports are excellent here and at the equally picturesque – but isolated – **Playa Esmeralda**, 2km (1 mile) west. All-inclusive hotels are dotted along the coast to the west, occupying horseshoe bays and sandy beaches such as Playa Pesquero Viejo and Playa Pesquero Nuevo.

There are plenty of possibilities for excursions in the vicinity of Guardalavaca. You can take a boat trip into the middle of Bahía de Naranjo to a simple aquarium, or arrange sailing and fishing trips from the marina. To the west is **Bahía de Bariay**, which has a monument claiming Columbus's landing (a fact contested chiefly by Baracoa, further east). Beyond the bay is **Gibara** ㉕ (27km/17 miles north of Holguín), a captivating if sleepy little port town, known for its annual festival for low-budget films.

About 6km (4 miles) south of Guardalavaca, on a hill amid a forest of palms and thatched homesteads, is **Chorro de Maita** ㉖ (Tue–Sun 9am–5pm), the Caribbean's most important excavated pre-Columbian burial ground. Fifty-six of the 108 skeletons found are on display. They date from 1490 to 1540 and lie exactly as they were found. All but one are Amerindian, buried in the Central American style with arms folded across stomachs. The one Spaniard lies in a Christian fashion with arms crossed on his chest.

Banana groves coat the hillsides along the scenic 30km (19-mile) route south to **Banes** 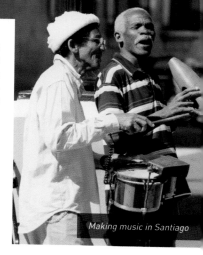, a town of wooden houses with corrugated roofs. Castro was married at the church here in 1948, and the town's interesting **Museo Indo-Cubano Bani** (Tue–Sat 9am–5pm, Sun 8am–noon, 2–5pm, Fri–Sun also 7–9pm) has some fascinating finds from the area.

Making music in Santiago

SANTIAGO DE CUBA

Many visitors prefer Cuba's second city (population 405,000) to the capital. **Santiago de Cuba** ㉘ (880km/546 miles southeast of Havana) is one of the oldest cities, with a wealth of colonial buildings. Unfailingly vibrant and seductive, it exudes a feel all its own. Enclosed by the Sierra Maestra mountains, Santiago can also be wickedly hot. *Santiagueros* negotiate their hilly streets by keeping to the shady sides, and they relax on overhanging balconies.

Santiago is Cuba's melting pot, with a friendly population of predominantly mulatto people: descendants of Spanish, French from Haiti, Jamaicans and huge numbers of African slaves. Afro-Cuban traditions remain strong, reflected in *carnaval*, which is still Cuba's best, and in music (walk down any street and a cacophony of sounds will emanate everywhere).

Founded in 1514, Santiago was the island's capital until 1553. It is regarded as a 'heroic city' *(ciudad héroe)*, and locals are proud of the city's rebellious past. Seminal events brought it centre-stage again during the 1950s, when it assumed a major role in the revolutionary struggle. The attack on Batista's forces at the Moncada Barracks in 1953 thrust Fidel Castro into the national limelight, and it was in Santiago's main square that he first declared victory, on 1 January 1959.

The city was badly damaged by Hurricane Sandy in 2012, losing most of its trees as well as many buildings, but subsequent repairs and a facelift to celebrate its 500th anniversary in 2015 mean the centre is now smart and attractive again.

Old Santiago

The most atmospheric part of the city is **Old Santiago**. Castro delivered his victory speech in the heart of the old town, from the balcony of city hall on **Parque Céspedes**. The attractive square is a genteel place with tall trees, gas lanterns and iron benches. Old Santiago's grid of streets unfolds here, a few blocks inland from the heavily industrialised harbour. Parque Céspedes is dominated by its twin-towered **cathedral**. A basilica was built on this spot in 1528, but what you see was rebuilt in the early 19th century after a series of earthquakes and fires.

On the west side of the plaza is **Casa de Diego Velázquez** (Mon–Thu and Sat 9am–5pm, Fri 2–5pm, Sun 9am–1pm). Noticeable for its black-slatted balconies, it was built in 1516 as the residence of the founder of Cuba's original seven *villas* (towns). The oldest house in Cuba and one of the oldest in the Americas, it is in remarkable condition. Housing the **Museo de**

Vintage car on a Santiago back street

Ambiente Histórico Cubano, its rooms overflow with period furniture and carved woodwork and encircle two lovely court-yards. Across the square is the elegant **Hotel Casa Granda**, which opened in 1914 and hosted many celebrity guests and gangsters before the Revolution. Its terrace bar on the fifth floor affords excellent views of the cathedral towers and the city beyond.

East from the square, **Calle Heredia** is the epicentre of Santiago culture and tourism. The city's famous **Casa de la Trova** (music hall), which has hosted nearly all legendary Cuban musicians, is the centrepiece of both. Starting in mid-morning, a succession of groups perform every style of Cuban music here, from *son* and *guarachas* to *boleros* and *salsa*. The intimate open-air space inside is the place to be in the eve-nings; at night the main groups play upstairs. Calle Heredia is lined by day with artisans and souvenir sellers.

Museo de Ambiente Histórico Cubano

Down the street is the **Museo El Carnaval** (Tue–Sun 9am–5pm), a museum containing instruments, photos and artefacts from Santiago's carnival. It also has Afro-Cuban music and dance (Sun–Fri at 4pm), as does the Artex store up the street. Also on Calle Heredia is the **Casa Natal de José María Heredia** (Tue–Sun 9am–5pm), the birthplace of the early 19th-century Cuban poet and a cultural centre and museum. A block south on Calle Bartolomé Masó, 358 (also called San Basilio) is the **Museo del Ron** (Mon–Sat 9am–5pm), which explains the history of rum in Santiago and has an atmospheric bar for a post-tour rum tasting.

Nearby, on Calle Pío Rosado, the **Museo Provincial Emilio Bacardí** (Tue–Sat 9am–5.15pm, Sun 9am–12.15pm) has an excellent collection of Cuban art, as well as some European works, some items from the wars of independence and an archaeological hall that features a 3,000-year-old Egyptian mummy, two Peruvian skeletons and a shrunken head. The museum, in a grandiose neoclassical building on a beguiling little street, is named for its benefactor and the town's former mayor, whose family founded the Bacardí rum empire.

One of Santiago's most delightful people-watching spots is **Plaza Dolores**, a shady plaza lined with colonial-era homes (several now house tourist restaurants). **Avenida José A.**

Saco (more commonly known as **Enramada**) is Santiago's main shopping thoroughfare. Its faded 1950s neon signs and ostentatious buildings recall more prosperous times. Cobbled **Calle Bartolomé Masó** (also known as San Basilio), just behind Heredia and the cathedral, is a delightful street that leads down to the picturesque Tivolí district.

In Tivolí you'll find the famous **Padre Pico** steps, named for a Santiaguero priest who aided the city's poor. Castro once roared fire and brimstone down on the Batista government here, but today you'll find more pacific chess and domino players who have set up all-hours tables on the steps. Take the steps up to the **Museo de la Lucha Clandestina**, the Museum of the Clandestine Struggle (Tue–Sun 9am–5pm). This excellent museum, in one of the city's finest colonial houses, focuses on the activities of the resistance movement under local martyr Frank País. Residents of Santiago were instrumental in supporting the Revolution, as were peasants in the Sierra Maestra. From the museum's balcony, there are tremendous views of Santiago and the bay (and, unfortunately, of plumes of pollution rising up from factories).

South of the museum is one of Santiago's best places to get sweaty in the evening. The **Casa de las Tradiciones**, a 'cultural centre' in a large colonial mansion with a central courtyard (Calle Jesús Rabí), has live *trova* and dancing. Known locally as La Casona, it's great fun, and local people usually outnumber tourists. Couples only.

Bacardí's bat

Bacardi moved its headquarters and production to Puerto Rico after the Revolution, and from there to Bermuda. But it was the fruit bats that nested in the rafters of the original rum factory in Santiago that gave Bacardi rum its world-famous bat logo.

Plaza de la Revolución

AROUND SANTIAGO

A good place to get your bearings on the suburbs of the city is from the rooftop bar of the lavish hotel Meliá Santiago, 3km (almost 2 miles) east of the city's centre. In the near distance you can make out the yellow **Moncada Barracks**, which Castro, along with around 100 rebels attacked on 26 July 1953. The date is now a rallying cry and public holiday, and the barracks have been converted into a school and museum, known both as the **Antiguo Cuartel Moncada** and the **Museo Histórico 26 de Julio** (Av. Moncada esq. Gen. Portuondo; Tue–Sat 9am–5pm, Sun 8am–noon; guided tour available in Spanish, English, French or Italian).

The museum tells the story of the road to revolution using dozens of memorable photographs. Also on display are various bloodstained rebel uniforms, some of Fidel's personal effects from his time in the mountains and '26 Julio' armbands (sporting the name of the resistance movement that developed after the Moncada attack). The bullet holes over the entrance were 'restored' from photos.

North of Moncada, by the bus station, is the **Plaza de la Revolución**, an open square at the corner of Av. las Américas and Av. de los Libertadores. Massive machetes (used by *mambí* independence fighters) thrust towards the sky in this monument to Antonio Maceo, a hero of the war of independence, who is seen riding triumphantly.

The fine **Cementerio Santa Ifigenia**, just north of the harbour (Av. Crombet, Reparto Juan Gómez), is the resting place of many Cuban heroes. The tombs to receive the most visitors, though, are those of Fidel Castro (1926–2016), whose ashes are interred in a simple boulder with a plaque marked simply 'Fidel', and of José Marti, whose vast octagonal mausoleum was designed so that the tomb catches the sun throughout the day. The two are close together and if visiting them it is worth waiting for the changing of the guard every half an hour, accompanied by martial music.

Seven kilometres (4 miles) from the city is the 17th-century **Castillo del Morro**, surveying the harbour mouth from a commanding clifftop position and now a World Heritage Site housing the Museo de la Piratería (daily 10am–7pm). Moated, thick-walled, and full of cannons, drawbridges and passageways, it is in fine condition. A guide will point out a torture room with a trap door in the floor, through which uncooperative prisoners and slaves were reportedly dropped into the sea below. The easiest way to get to El Morro is to hire a taxi.

A place of great import (and considerable beauty) is the triple-domed **Basílica del Cobre** ❷❾ (daily 6am–6pm; taxi from Santiago around CUC$20–30 round trip) named after the nearby copper mines that rise out of the forested foothills 18km (11 miles) west of Santiago. Cuban faithful make annual pilgrimages to the church to pay tribute to its statue of a black virgin, the Virgen de la Caridad (Virgin of Charity), Cuba's patron saint. According to legend, in 1606 three young fishermen struggling in their storm-tossed boat out in the bay were saved by the miraculous appearance of the

Basílica del Cobre

Virgin, who was holding a mulatto baby Jesus in one hand and a cross in the other. Pilgrims, often making the last of the trek on their knees, pray to her image and place mementos and offerings of thanks for her miracles; among them are small boats and prayers for those who have tried to escape Cuba on rafts. Except during Mass, the Virgin is kept on the second floor, encased in glass and cloaked in a glittering gold robe.

Day trips are offered by tour operators in Santiago up into the Sierra Maestra. Some go to **El Saltón**, a picturesque waterfall in the grounds of a small hotel. Alternatively you can hike up Pico Turquino (1,974m/6,476ft), the highest mountain.

East of Santiago is **Parque Baconao**, a biosphere reserve spread over 40km (25 miles). The local dark-sand beaches can be scrubby and the hotels themselves are isolated, but there's lots to explore in the park, and the Sierra de La Gran Piedra rises majestically above the coast. A tortuous side road 12km (7 miles) east along the coast ascends the mountains to **La Gran Piedra** ㉚ (Great Stone), where you can climb on foot for a bird's-eye view of eastern Cuba. About 2km (1 mile) beyond, a track leads to the **Cafetal-Museo La Isabelica**, a 19th-century coffee-plantation *finca* (country house). The museum (Mon–Sat 9am–4pm) is part of the Unesco World

Heritage Site that protects the architectural legacy of early 19th-century coffee farms.

GUANTÁNAMO PROVINCE

You can reach Cuba's remote, mountainous, far-eastern region from Santiago. The US military base of Guantánamo is synonymous with the 'war against terror', and while there's no immediately obvious reason to visit Guantánamo itself, it is a pleasant, well-kept provincial town. The province has only one true tourist draw, but it's a super one: the magical little town of Baracoa.

BARACOA

The dry, cactus-strewn landscape of the south coast begins to change as you follow the winding, spectacular 30km (18-mile) road 'La Farola' across the mountains to **Baracoa** ③ (150km/93 miles from Santiago), a picturesque little village known for its local chocolate and coconut factories.

☉ 'GITMO'

Guantánamo, known to American military personnel as 'Gitmo', is a curious anomaly in revolutionary Cuba. Where in the world is the US less likely to have a military base? Established in 1903 – making it the oldest overseas American naval base – the lease was effectively forced on the Cubans by an interventionist US administration. The US still sends its annual rent cheques (about US$4,000), which haven't been cashed since 1960. To do so would be to recognise the legitimacy of the American presence in Cuba.

Festive day

Baracoa really shines the week of 1 April, when heady street parties every night commemorate the date General Antonio Maceo disembarked at nearby Playa Duaba in 1895, marking the beginning of Cuba's War of Independence.

The tropical seaside town is surrounded by green hillsides covered with cocoa and coconut groves, and all around are palm-backed beaches. Baracoa lies smack in the middle of the wettest region in Cuba, and has no fewer than 10 rivers, all of them ripe for whitewater rafting. In the mountains to the north-west is the Parque Nacional Alejandro de Humboldt, a biosphere reserve named after the great German naturalist and explorer.

Baracoa was the first settlement to be established by Diego Velázquez in 1511. Columbus came here first, though, after landing at Bariay Bay in today's Holguín province in October 1492, and planted the Cruz de la Parra (Cross of the Vine) in the soil on his arrival. What is claimed to be this cross is on display in **Nuestra Señora de la Asunción**, the church on Plaza Independencia.

The town has suffered major hurricane damage in recent years, particularly on the seafront Malecón, but always picks itself up.

A good place to get your bearings is the hilltop **Hotel El Castillo**, a former castle looking out over red-tiled roofs, the town's expansive, oyster-shaped bay and the landmark mountain called El Yunque (The Anvil), named for its singular shape.

In the main square is a bust of Hatuey, the brave Indian leader who resisted early *conquistadores* until he was caught by the Spanish and burned at the stake. There's also a very lively Casa de la Trova here. It is worth wandering along the Malecón, the seaside avenue, from the snug **Fuerte Matachín** (an early 19th-century fort that has a small but informative municipal museum inside, daily 8am–4.30pm) to the Hotel La Rusa, which is named after a legendary Russian émigrée who over the years hosted celebrities such as Che Guevara and Errol Flynn.

In and around Baracoa are several dozen pre-Columbian archaeological sites related to the two major indigenous groups that once inhabited the region. The **Museo Arqueológico** (Mon–Fri 8am–5pm, Sat 8am–noon) in **Las Cuevas del Paraíso** up the hill from the village, contains a copy of the Taíno tobacco idol found nearby in 1903 (the original is in Havana).

Baracoa: the first Spanish settlement on Cuba, famous for its rain

Local musicians in Havana

WHAT TO DO

ENTERTAINMENT

Although cultural activity has been under state control since the Revolution and Havana no longer sizzles with the sleazy Mafia-funded casinos and clubs of the 1950s, both high culture and down-to-earth nightlife thrive in Cuba. Outside the resorts, it can be hard to pin down what's going on where, but informal musical performances are ubiquitous. In the resorts, nightlife is focused around hotels, ranging from decent live bands, dance and fashion shows to Beatles sing-alongs.

LIVE MUSIC PERFORMANCES

Cubans crave live music, and – with the surge in international popularity of traditional Cuban music – so do most visitors to Cuba. You certainly won't have to go out of your way to hear music performances. Roving groups of musicians can be found playing everywhere from airports to restaurants. Merely wandering the streets of Havana, Santiago or Trinidad, you're likely to stumble across a party with a live band, or even a back alley where some impromptu jamming is going on.

All the styles of Cuba's traditional music – *habaneras, son, boleros, guarachas, guajiras* and more – can be heard in every town's *casa de la trova*, usually a fine old building on or near the main square. Performances take place afternoons and evenings. Especially in the evenings and on weekends, the island's *casas de la trova* really swing. The most famous is in Santiago de Cuba, while those in towns like Trinidad, Baracoa, Camagüey and Holguín are great fun.

Getting the salsa rhythm

Aside from traditional acoustic music, Cuba revels in salsa. In Havana the salsa dance fan can choose from a number of venues every night. They feature top salsa groups, but cover charges are still quite low. Music hotspots include:

Havana. Casa de la Música Egrem (all types of music and dance including salsa; Avenida 35 and Calle 20, Miramar), Casa de la Música Galiano (lots of variety from rock to salsa, new bands and established big names; Calle Galiano 255, e/ Concordia y Neptuno, Centro), Teatro Nacional – El Delirio Habanero (piano bar, *nueva trova*, dancing to live band or disco; 5th floor, Paseo y Calle 39, Plaza de la Revolución) and Café Cantante (dancing to live bands or disco, often top bands; in the basement), and la Zorra y el Cuervo (jazz; Calles 23 y O, Vedado).

Trinidad. Casa de la Trova (traditional music; Fernando Echerri 29, e/ Jesús Menéndez y Patricio Lumumba), Casa de la Música (two venues on the Escalinata near the Plaza Mayor), Palenque de los Congos Reales (Afro-Cuban folkloric show during the day, son and salsa at night; Fernando Echerri half a block away towards the Plaza Mayor).

Santiago de Cuba. Casa de la Trova (*trova*, *son* and boleros, famous musicians play here; Calle Heredia), Casa de las Tradiciones (*trova*, *son* and boleros; Calle Rabí 154).

Baracoa. Casa de la Trova (Via Felix Ruene) and Casa de la Cultura (Maceo, 124).

☉ A MUSICAL MELTING POT

Salsa, rumba, mambo, *cha-cha-chá*, *son*, *danzón* – Cuba's rhythms are known the world over. Reflecting the mixed heritage of its people, Cuban music spontaneously combusted towards the end of the 1800s through the nexus of African and European cultures – in particular what's been described as the love affair between the African drum and the Spanish guitar. In a typical Cuban band today you'll hear Latin stringed instruments in harmony with congas, *timbales* and African bongos (all drums), *claves* (wooden sticks) and instruments made from hollow gourds such as the maracas and the *güiro*. Cuban percussionists are among the finest in the world.

First came *son* ('sound'), a style that originated in Oriente around the turn of the 20th century. *Son* permeates all Cuban music and is the direct forebear of salsa; it has a percussive swing that is intrinsically Cuban. Mixed with jazz influences, it led to the brass-band salsa of famous groups such as Los Van Van, Isaac Delgado and Irakere. *Cha-cha-chá* arrived in the 1950s, having developed from mambo, itself a blend of jazz and the sedate, European *danzón* of the ballroom. The strongly Afro-Cuban rumba is typified by heavy drumming and more celebratory, erotic dancing. *Trovas* (ballads) were sung in colonial times by troubadors in *casas de la trova*. After the revolution the *trova* evolved into the *nueva trova*, often with overtly political lyrics, made popular by such artists as Silvio Rodríguez and Pablo Milanés.

CABARET

A legacy of the high-rolling casino days in Cuba, cabarets have been kept alive and well as a magnet for tourist spending. Cavorting mulatta dancers in sparkling G-strings and pairs of strategically placed stars may not be most peoples' image of socialist doctrine – but this is Caribbean communism.

While the best shows (at the Tropicana clubs in both Havana and Santiago de Cuba) are rather expensive by Cuban standards, seeing at least one big song-and-dance production in the flesh (so to speak) is de rigueur.

The **Tropicana in Havana** (Calle 72 #4504 e/ 43 y 45, Marianao, tel: 07-267 1717; http://tropicanacabaret.com), founded in 1939, is indisputably the queen of cabarets. The likes of Nat King Cole performed here in pre-revolutionary times. With a 32-piece orchestra and a cast of over 200, in a dazzling open-air arena, the sheer scale of the spectacle will make your head spin. Tickets cost from CUC$70–90, including a quarter bottle of rum and a mixer. Book at your hotel reception, by phone from 10am–6pm, or buy tickets at the entrance between 8.30 and 9pm. The show starts at 10pm and lasts 1 hour 45 minutes, after which you can head to the club. Havana's next-best cabaret show, smaller and half the price, is Cabaret Parisien, at the Hotel Nacional (Calles 21 and O, Vedado, tel: 07-836 3663, burotur@gcnacio.gca.tur.cu; nightly at 10pm).

The **Tropicana in Santiago de Cuba** (Autopista Nacional km 1.5; tel: 22-642 579) fills an enormous complex on the city's northern outskirts. It is no less impressive than Havana's but tickets are less expensive (CUC$30 or group packages with transport and one drink included CUC$44 per person); get there for 9.30pm in time for the main show at 10pm.

DANCE

Afro-Cuban dance is often seen in resort hotels as part of the evening entertainment, but is best seen in theatres. The internationally renowned company, Clave y Guaguancó, perform Afro-Cuban dance, drumming and music and can be sometimes found performing in Callejón de Hamel (Centro Habana) on Sunday afternoons. The Conjunto Folklórico Nacional de Cuba puts on

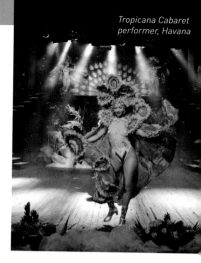

Tropicana Cabaret performer, Havana

rumba performances outside the Gran Palenque Bar, Calle 4 e/ Calzada y 5, on Saturday. Get there early, the box office opens at 2pm for a 3pm show.

The Ballet Nacional de Cuba was created in 1961 and has been supported by the Revolution ever since under the direction of prima ballerina Alicia Alonso (who will turn 100 in 2020). World famous and often on tour, when in Cuba they perform at the Gran Teatro on the Parque Central, Havana or the Teatro Nacional, Plaza de la Revolución. The Ballet de Camagüey is another classical ballet company, sometimes considered to be more innovative. Also worth seeing is the Danza Contemporánea de Cuba, which is based at the Teatro Nacional but also performs at other venues in Havana and nationwide.

Visitors to Santiago de Cuba should try to see the Ballet Folklórico Cutumba, a renowned troupe that delves into the world of Afro-Cuban spirituality and ritual. They perform at several theatres when in town and also offer dance classes. At the Museo del Carnaval there is an Afro-Cuban dance show by the Orishas at 4pm.

DISCOS

Discos pulsate to both Latin and Euro-American rhythms. The places to be are Habana Café (the disco in Havana's Hotel Meliá Cohiba) and the disco in Santiago's eponymous hotel. These are glitzy affairs, where foreigners get merry and approached by hustlers of all stripes. Situated in an old peanut oil factory, trendy Fabrica de Arte Cubano (Calle 26 esq. 11, Vedado; www.fabricadeartecubano.com) offers a unique blend of art, music, cinema, disco and dance. Expect long queues. Varadero has Palacio de La Rumba at the end of Avenue Las Américas, which is popular with a young crowd and has live salsa bands at weekends; or Mambo Club – on the Autopista Sur, further down the peninsula, by the Gran Hotel – which is similar but with live music. Both charge entrance.

In Trinidad, the Discoteca Ayala Las Cuevas really gets going at 1am, when the other music venues in town close. In Guardalavaca, head for open-air La Roca, set just above the beach.

BARS AND CAFÉS

Both bars and cafés are places to have a mojito, daiquiri or shot of *ron* (rum), smoke a Cohiba and – usually – hear some live Cuban rhythms. In Havana the bars not to miss are Hemingway haunts: La Bodeguita del Medio and El Floridita. Enjoyable café-bars in Havana include Café de Paris (Obispo y San Ignacio), Café O'Reilly (O'Reilly y San Ignacio), Bolabana (Calle 39 esq. 50, Playa) and El Patio (Plaza de la Catedral). There

Preparing mojitos

are also several places on Plaza Vieja, including Cervecería Taberna de La Muralla with home-brewed malt beer; and on the opposite corner, the Café Taberna at Mercaderes esq. Teniente Rey, done up in 1950s style and dedicated to the late, great Cuban singer, Beny Moré. Several hotels also have good bars, including Hotel Sevilla (made famous in Graham Greene's *Our Man in Havana*), Hotel Inglaterra's rooftop bar and Hotel Havana Libre's Turquino (with amazing views from the 25th floor).

In Santiago de Cuba, the terrace bar on the fifth floor of the Hotel Casa Granda has fine views and live music. A good place for a cold beer is Taberna de Dolores, which often has live music in its courtyard. At the corner of Calle Calvario is Café Isabelica, a venerable 24-hour bohemian haunt in a house three centuries old. Baracoa's Hotel Castillo has a bar with sensational views and frequent live music.

CLASSICAL REPERTOIRE

The classical arts are greatly valued in Cuba, and drama, opera, classical music recitals and above all ballet can be enjoyed in theatres all around Cuba. Opulent, old-fashioned theatres such as those in Cienfuegos, Camagüey and Matanzas and Havana's magnificent Gran Teatro, are sights in their own right.

The Gran Teatro in Havana, at Prado y San José (tel: 07-861 3096), has two main concert halls and puts on a wide repertoire of entertainment, from opera recitals to ballet. It is home to the internationally renowned Ballet Nacional de Cuba. Havana's International Ballet Festival is held every two years during the last week of October and first week of November.

At the Teatro Amadeo Roldán in Havana, at Calzada y D, Vedado, you can hear the Orquesta Sinfónica Nacional and visiting symphony orchestras. Other theatres and concert halls in Vedado include the Sala Hubert de Blanck, for classical and contemporary music concerts as well as drama and dance; Teatro El Sótano, for contemporary drama; Teatro Mella for modern dance and drama and Teatro Nacional de Cuba for concerts, drama and live bands in the Café Cantante and El Delirio Habanero. In 2014 the legendary Teatro Martí reopened, following a 40-year hiatus, with a programme of traditional Cuban music shows. Out in Miramar is the Teatro Karl Marx, used for grand occasions when large audiences can be accommodated.

Export permits

If you purchase anything that can be described as art – even a cheap watercolour at a flea market – you'll need an official export permit to get it out of the country without hassle or fear of confiscation. Most official galleries should be able to provide you with this – a purchase receipt will not usually be sufficient.

SHOPPING

Cuba has a reputation as a destination where there's little worth buying. You will see incredibly barren shops – window displays with bottles of cooking oil, shoe polish and a few plumbing parts. But there are plenty of things for visitors to buy. The dual currency system means that you pay for your goods in *pesos convertibles* (CUCs), while Cubans pay for their basic goods in

Shopping in Havana

pesos Cubanos, or *moneda nacional* (CUPs). Top on most people's lists are Cuba's greatest achievements (not including its health care system): cigars, rum and music. There is also an excellent selection of handicrafts, and tourist markets are now thriving in Cuba's major centres, even if much of what you'll find is related to Che Guevara – berets, T-shirts bearing his countenance and dolls, among many other 'revolutionary' items.

As for essentials, hotel and dollar shops (as the CUC shops are still called) carry mineral water, soap, shampoo, toilet paper and toothpaste, and these items are now sometimes available from small kiosk shops. However, it's still best to bring all your medicinal or cosmetic staples from home. Tiendas Panamericanas and Caracol are well-stocked stores, but probably the most impressive store in all Cuba is the Harris Bros. Company, a multistorey enterprise near the landmark Art Deco Bacardí building and the Capitolio.

Cuba's finest cigars

SOUVENIRS TO BUY

Cigars and rum. The biggest bargain in Cuba is probably a coveted box of premium cigars, which at home might cost four times more. Cigar factories have affiliated shops selling all brands of cigars; the original Partagás factory in Havana has a particularly good shop, as does the specialist cigar hotel in Old Havana: Hostal Conde de Villanueva at Mercaderes 202. You can also purchase cigars at shops such as Casa del Tabaco (Calle Obispo and Bernaza) and La Casa del Habano (Calle Mercaderes, 120) in Havana, at hotels and at the airport. You will find Habanos shops in several other towns (Trinidad's is on Lino Pérez, 296).

Bottles of Cuban **rum** also offer big savings. All tourist shops sell rum, whether aged from three to seven years *(añejo)* or low-grade *aguardiente* (from sugarcane alcohol) with humorous labels. Havana Club is the brand of choice and aficionados should visit the distillery's Museo del Ron (Av. del Puerto, 262 e/ Sol y Muralla) for a tour and rum tasting, as well as the shop attached. Above El Floridita, Havana's Casa del Ron has the most impressive selection of rums, including hundred-dollar vintages.

Music. Recordings of Cuban music are widely available. If you're in the market for Cuban recordings, look for the EGREM label, available in Artex stores (as well as others). Most are CUC$15 each. Recommended recordings include those by

⊘ EL PURO: THE CUBAN CIGAR

Before launching the US trade embargo against Cuba, President Kennedy reportedly had an aide round up a supply of his favourite Cuban cigars. Now that cigars have again become chic, almost everyone knows that Cuban *puros* are reputed to be the world's finest. Factories produce more than 350 million cigars a year, with 100 million for export. Before the Revolution there were more than 1,000 Cuban brands of cigars; today there are only about three dozen.

You can visit a number of cigar factories, where the rich aroma is overwhelming. *Torcedores* wrap the different types of leaves (some for taste, burn, etc) inside the wrapper leaves with dexterous ease. Sacks of tobacco leaves are sorted into bundles, cigars undergo quality control tests, and prestigious labels are applied. Handmade cigars vary in length from the 4.5-inch Demi Tasse to the 9.25-inch Gran Corona. As a rule, bigger cigars are of better quality and darker-coloured cigars taste sweeter. Back home, keep your cigars moist: place them in a humidor or put the box in a plastic bag with a damp sponge.

Buying a box of cigars can be daunting. People on the street will whisper 'You want cigar, my friend?' They may be hot, but they may also be inferior-quality fakes. Don't buy unless you know what you're doing.

Fakes are liable to confiscation by customs. In official shops, make sure you keep the two copies of the official receipt – one of these is for you and one is to be given to customs when leaving the country. Keep cigars in your hand luggage for inspection. You are allowed to take up to 20 loose cigars and up to 50 in their original sealed packaging, with the official hologram, out of the country without a receipt.

Trio Matamoros, Beny Moré, Celina González, La Vieja Trova Santiaguera, Los Compadres, Los Zafiros, El Cuarteto Patria, Los Van Van, Silvio Rodríguez, Chucho Valdés and Pablo Milanés, to name just a few of Cuba's most popular musicians.

Handicrafts. Local arts and crafts vary from tacky figurines to drawings of street scenes. You'll also find evocative posters and black-and-white photos of Fidel, Che and company. Fine handmade lace and crochet are available, principally in Trinidad. You might want to pick up a *guayabera*, the classic Cuban pleated, four-pocketed man's shirt, worn untucked. Boutique Quitrín (Obispo esq. San Ignacio in Old Havana) has the nicest cotton versions of the original white *guayabera*. Much of the silver-plated jewellery is also a good buy, but you should not purchase anything with black coral – it's endangered and illegal to import in many countries.

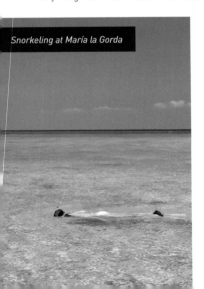

Snorkeling at María la Gorda

There are more interesting things to buy in Old Havana than in the rest of Cuba put together. A lively crafts market (daily 9am–5pm) is held next to ferry terminal on Desamparados. Plaza de Armas is busy with second-hand booksellers. The excellent Palacio de la Artesanía (at Calle Cuba, 64 e/ Peña Pobre y Cuarteles; open daily 10am–6pm, Sun until 1pm) is a souvenir supermarket. Outside Havana, Trinidad has the best array of crafts shops in the country. Several streets just south of the Plaza Mayor (around the *Casa de la Trova*), known as La Candonga, stage a vibrant daily crafts market, and you'll find good government-run crafts shops on Simón Bolívar. Santiago de Cuba's crafts mecca is among the shops and vendors along Calle Heredia.

SPORTS

WATERSPORTS

Watersports enthusiasts are in luck in Cuba. Virtually every resort offers windsurfing, sailing, scuba diving and snorkelling. As anywhere in the world, motorised sports are expensive. Watersports centres are almost always affiliated with a particular hotel, but anyone may rent the equipment.

Diving is the area of greatest interest and growth. Cuba claims to be surrounded by one of the world's largest coral reefs, and over 1,000 sunken wrecks. Facilities are generally excellent, and prices are the lowest in the Caribbean. Nearly every resort has at least one professional diving centre equipped with all the requisite equipment. Most centres offer week-long diving courses for an internationally recognised qualification, as well as two-day introductory courses.

Dozens of dive sites can be reached from resorts, typically a half-hour boat journey away. The diving centre at El Colony Hotel on the Isla de la Juventud offers the best facilities and diving, but it isn't well suited to beginners. Resorts catering to all levels of ability include Playa Santa Lucía, María la Gorda, Cayo Levisa, Cayo Largo, Varadero, Playa Girón, Playa Ancón, Cayo Coco and Guardalavaca.

Deep-sea fishing is one of Cuba's great attractions, as of yet not well known (or over-fished). Trips in search of marlin, wahoo, swordfish and tarpon or smaller fry can be arranged through **Marlin Naútica y Marinas** around the island at the Marina Hemingway, Marina Tarará, Varadero, Cayo Guillermo, Cayo Coco, Santa Lucía, Guardalavaca, Marina Santiago de Cuba, Marina Trinidad, Marina Cienfuegos, Jardines de la Reina, Isla de la Juventud and Cayo Largo del Sur. There is fly fishing in the Jardines de la Reina off the south coast, off Cayo Largo del Sur and in the salt flats of the Zapata peninsula. For **freshwater fishing**, Hanabanilla and Zaza (near Sancti Spíritus) lakes both hold impressively big, copious large-mouth bass, as do Maspotón in Pinar del Río, Laguna del Tesoro in the Zapata peninsula.

SPECTATOR SPORTS

The national sport is **baseball** (*béisbol*). Cuban teams are among the best in the world (several stars have defected to the US major leagues). While children improvise with a stick and a makeshift ball in every town's open spaces, the main cities have vast stadiums.

CUBA FOR CHILDREN

At resorts, water-loving babies will be happy; those aged 10 and up will be able to join in many of the activities. A few resort hotels (such as those at Cayo Coco) have children's clubs, and top hotels can arrange babysitting. Outside the resorts facilities are limited and transport can be problematic. Cubans adore children and will certainly make a fuss over yours. Travelling with young families in Cuba can be a remarkable – and eye-opening – experience. If you travel with very young children, be sure to take all the nappies and baby food you require, as these items are hard to find in Cuba. If travelling by hire car, you should supply your own car seat.

CALENDAR OF EVENTS

The Buró de Convenciones (Hotel Neptuno, Calle 3 e/70 y 74, Miramar; tel: 7-204 8273) has information and contact details for all of the festivals and conferences held throughout the year all over the country.

January New Year (1 January, public holiday): celebrated throughout the country and taking in Liberation Day, marking the end of the Batista dictatorship, with music, dancing and outdoor parties.

May May Day (1 May, public holiday): a big event with parades and speeches in all the Plazas de la Revolución in every town.

June Hemingway Marlin Fishing Tournament (Hemingway Marina, Havana): four-day competition begun in 1950 and won by Castro in 1960.

July (first week): Caribe Festival (Santiago de Cuba): street parades, concerts, lectures and fairs celebrating Afro-Caribbean culture.

18–27 July *Carnaval* (Santiago de Cuba): Cuba's most famous celebration, featuring *comparsas* (street dances); takes in Santiago's patron saint's day on the 25th, but stops temporarily on the 26th in memory of the attack on the Moncada barracks in 1953.

August *Carnaval* (Havana): parades, open-air concerts and street parties.

8 September Fiesta de la Virgen del Cobre: pilgrimage to the altar of Cuba's saint in El Cobre near Santiago de Cuba.

October–November Havana International Ballet Festival: a gathering of top ballet companies from around the world, begun in 1960 and held in alternate years.

December New Latin American Film Festival (Havana): the most important film festival in Latin America, held during the first two weeks of the month. International Jazz Festival (Havana): a week-long festival, which attracts top jazz artists from Cuba and around the world: performances, workshops, lectures and open rehearsals.

EATING OUT

It is a sad paradox that a land as fertile as Cuba should have such problems feeding its people. During the so-called Special Period of the early 1990s, food shortages became serious and distribution of harvested fruit and vegetables remains a problem. Ration books no longer provide enough to live on and are expected gradually to be phased out, leaving poor Cubans with uncertainty. However, those with plenty of money (tourists and a small number of Cubans) are immune from hardships and get the most and best of what little is available. Nevertheless, do not come to Cuba expecting memorable gastronomic experiences. Cuba once had a respectable *criollo* (Creole) cuisine, a fusion of Spanish and African culinary traditions. But many Cubans now have been reduced to eating simple box lunches and sandwiches. Many restaurants have no choice but to offer standard 'chicken or pork' main courses, along with rice and beans. Most hotels play it safe by offering international fare.

WHERE TO EAT

If you're based in a resort, you might face the potentially monotonous reality of eating almost all your meals at the hotel. Large hotels often have not only a main buffet restaurant but also an à la carte restaurant, a poolside *parrillada* (grill) and a beachside café.

State-run restaurants are of two types. Those for which you must pay in pesos *convertibles*, and those for which *pesos cubanos* are the accepted currency. The latter are usually cafeteria style for Cubans, have extremely limited menus and, generally, are of poor quality with long waits. In some isolated cities (like Bayamo) it is possible to eat in *peso cubano* establishments very cheaply, as long as you understand that perhaps only one item on the menu will be available and that Cuban diners might look at you as if to say, 'How did you get in here?' Often, however, they charge in *pesos convertibles* because you are a foreigner.

A third category is the *paladar*, a privately operated restaurant in a private home. These cater to anyone who pays in *pesos convertibles*. In 1995 the government legalised them, only to subsequently tax or fine many of them out of existence. In 2011 restrictions were relaxed in order to create jobs, allowing more to open, employ staff and increasing the maximum legal number of place settings from 12 to 50. The food is often better than in state-owned restaurants and the cost is more

Tables outside El Patio restaurant, Havana

reasonable. You'll be offered a three-course meal, sometimes with a beer or juice included, for a set price. *Paladares* are like small, simple restaurants, usually with menus, that just happen to be on the terrace or in someone's home.

If you are staying at a *casa particular* (see page 112), you can take advantage of the freshest and best *criollo* food. Families will cook whatever you want, or offer a few staple dishes. Usually you decide in the morning whether you want to eat in and they will shop and cook it for your evening meal. Fortified by a hearty breakfast of fresh fruit, eggs, coffee, juice and bread, these two meals will probably be enough, with just a snack at midday.

In all resort hotels and around Havana, cafés serve sandwiches (almost always ham and/or cheese), but otherwise snacks in Cuba are limited to bad street pizza and box lunches. Picnic food is an even more difficult proposition: hotel shops sell packs of biscuits and crisps, while private farmers' markets sell fruit for pesos.

WHAT TO EAT

At large hotels, particularly in the resorts, breakfast can be the best meal of the day: a buffet of fresh fruit, fruit juices, cheeses, meats and pancakes. Often there are also egg dishes made to order. In more modest hotels, sandwiches and omelettes are generally the staple fare.

Hotel buffets are also offered at lunch and dinner, and guests with large appetites will find these very good value. The food is 'international' rather than typically Cuban. The surfeit of choices (several salads, piles of bananas, chunks of watermelon, cakes galore, a choice of fish, meat and pasta) might make some travellers uncomfortable, given the limited supplies most Cubans put up with.

Most restaurants serve a Creole Cuban cuisine. Its main staple is rice and beans; you'll find either rice with kidney beans (*moros y cristianos*; 'Moors and Christians') or rice with black beans (*congrís*), the latter typically served in the east of Cuba. Meat is often *pollo asado* (roast chicken) or *cerdo asado* (roast pork). White fish is commonly presented under the generic label *pescado* and is typically fresh and simply grilled; numerous restaurants also serve lobster at a hefty price (CUC$25-30). Popular side dishes include root vegetables such as *malanga* and *yuca* (cassava) in addition to *maduros* or *tostones* (fried plantains). Common desserts are *pasta de guayaba con queso* (cheese with guava paste) and Coppelia ice cream, made all over the country.

WHAT TO DRINK

The national drink is *ron* (rum), produced from cane juice and molasses, the by-products of sugar manufacture. Un-aged rum, called *aguardiente* ('firewater'), has a very high alcoholic content. Five- or seven-year-old rum, darkened and flavoured in oak barrels, is drunk straight or on the rocks.

Cuban cocktails make use of one- or three-year-old white rum. A number have achieved folkloric status: Hemingway drank

Fruit at a street market

Thirst-quencher:
the mojito

his mojitos (sugar, lime juice, ice, fresh mint, rum and soda water) in La Bodeguita del Medio and his daiquiris (sugar, lime juice and rum blended into crushed ice) in El Floridita. Less exotic is the *Cuba libre*: simply rum and coke, served with a slice of lime.

National brands of beer include Bucanero, Cristal, Mayabe and Tínima, all very drinkable. Only the more expensive restaurants serve wine. Cuban wine is now produced with the help of Spanish technology, but is in its infancy and best avoided.

For soft drinks, try the wonderfully sweet *guarapo* (pure sugar cane juice) or *granizado* (a flavoured water-ice in a paper cone from ubiquitous streetside carts). In some towns, you may come across homemade cola stands, where they'll mix three shots of syrup with soda water. It's amazingly refreshing and only about 5 centavos.

Coffee is one of Cuba's main exports, but you don't always get export-quality coffee. In times of hardship it is mixed with chicory, a flavour many Cubans have got used to and now prefer. A *café* is served espresso style and traditionally drunk with unimaginable quantities of sugar; *café americano* is weaker and served in a large cup. *Café con leche* is half espresso/half milk. Coffee with a little cream in Cuba is often disappointingly grey.

TO HELP YOU ORDER...

Do you have a table?. **¿Tiene una mesa?**

May I see the menu, please? **¿Puedo ver la carta, por favor?**

What do you recommend? **¿Qué me aconseja?**

I'd like ... **Quisiera ...**

I'm a vegetarian **Soy vegetariano.**

beer **cerveza**
bread **pan**
butter **mantequilla**
cocktail **cóctel**
coffee **café**
dessert **postre**
fish **pescado**
fruit **fruta**
ice **hielo**
ice cream **helado**

meat **carne**
salad **ensalada**
sandwich **bocadito**
shellfish **mariscos**
soft drink **refresco**
tea **té**
vegetable **vegetales/ legumbres**
water **agua mineral**
wine **vino**

...AND READ THE MENU

arroz blanco white rice
asado roast/grilled
bistec steak
camarones shrimps/ prawns
cerdo/Puerco pork
congrí rice and beans
frijoles beans
frito fried
huevos eggs
jamón ham
jugo de fruta fruit juice

langosta lobster
naranja orange
pan tostado toast
papas potatoes
papas fritas chips (fries)
picadillo minced meat
platáno plantain
pollo chicken
queso cheese
tortilla/revoltillo omelette

PLACES TO EAT

We have used the following symbols to give an idea of the price for a three-course meal for one, excluding drinks, tips and shellfish (the latter is always the costliest on the menu).

$$$ over CUC$25
$$ CUC$12–25
$ under CUC$12

OLD HAVANA

La Barca $$–$$$ *Avenida del Puerto esq Obispo, tel: (7) 864 7777*. Open daily noon–midnight. Overlooking the harbour and the old yacht club, this is a pleasant open-air restaurant in the Habaguanex chain serving good Spanish food with lots of seafood. Alongside is a more upmarket seafood restaurant, Marinero El Templete, where Cuban artists exhibit their works. Each month, a different artist features, as well as illustrating the menu.

La Bodeguita del Medio $$$ *Empredado, 207 e/ San Ignacio y Cuba, tel: (7) 867 1374*. Open daily noon–midnight. Now in its seventh decade, this scruffy, graffiti-scrawled den has played host to celebrities from Sinatra to Salvador Allende. Now a stream of tourists sips mojitos, but the food and service suffers.

Café del Oriente $$$ *Plaza de San Francisco, tel: (7) 860 6686*. Open daily noon–midnight. This slick international restaurant in a beautiful colonial mansion is where to go for that dress-up, blow-out meal. Extensive wine list. Sit on the square for coffee or cocktails.

Café Taberna Beny Moré $$ *Mercaderes 531 esq. a Teniente Rey (corner of Plaza Vieja), tel: (7) 861 1637*. Open daily noon–midnight. In what was Havana's oldest café, named after its first owner, Juan Batista de Taberna, it has been made over with a Beny Moré theme. Live bands day and night; the atmosphere is better than the food.

Los Nardos $$$$ *Paseo de Martí 563, e/ Teniente Rey y Dragones, tel: (7) 863 2895.* Open daily noon–midnight. Quirky and popular, no reservations so wait in line. Decorated with soccer memorabilia and 1930s trophies. Huge portions of meat, fish and lobster. Upstairs with no queue are El Trofeo, serving Cuban and international food, or El Asturianito, for Cuban and Italian food, including good pizzas.

Nerei $$ *Calle 19, 110, e/ L y M, Vedado, tel: (7) 832 7860.* Open daily noon–midnight. Good Cuban dishes served in a dining room stuffed with antiques or outside on the terrace surrounded by plants. Roast suckling pig *(lechón asado)* is the house speciality.

Paladar La Julia $ *O'Reilly 506A, tel: (7) 862 7438.* Open daily noon–11pm. A traditional *paladar* offering huge portions of Cuban food, including good rice and beans. Popular, so come early or make a reservation.

El Patio $$–$$$ *Plaza de la Catedral, tel: (7) 867 1034.* Open daily noon–midnight. One of the capital's romantic settings for a meal, in one of Havana's most splendidly painted and restored colonial courtyards. Creole fare is decent, but it can't match the surroundings. The popular drinks terrace looks out on the Plaza de la Catedral.

Restaurant Van Van $ *58 San Juan de Dios, tel: (7) 860 2490.* Open daily 11am–midnight. Authentic Cuban food served amid colourful, music-inspired décor and in a friendly, lively atmosphere. The menu is slightly limited but the food is fresh.

CENTRO, VEDADO AND MIRAMAR

1830 $$$ *Malecón 12502 e/. Av. 20 y 22, Vedado, tel: (7) 838 3090.* Open noon–midnight. A popular restaurant right at the mouth of the river, a great location for weddings and family celebrations. International food well prepared. Dinner is followed by a cabaret at 10pm and lots of live music.

El Aljibe $$ *Av. 7 e/ 24 y 26, Miramar, tel: (7) 204 1583.* Open daily for lunch and dinner. One of the best dining experiences in the capital is at this thatched-roof restaurant out in Miramar, offering top-flight Creole cooking. The speciality is the all-you-can-eat lemony chicken (*pollo asado El Ajibe*), with salad, plantains, chips, rice and beans.

La Guarida $$ *Calle Concordia, 418, e/ Gervasio y Escobar, Centro Habana, tel: (7) 866 9047*, www.laguarida.com. Open daily noon–midnight. The most famous *paladar* in Havana, in the crumbling building where much of the Cuban film *Fresa y Chocolate* was filmed. Creative, wonderfully prepared food.

La Torre $$$ *M esq.17, Vedado, tel: (7) 838 3088.* Open daily noon–midnight. At the top of the FOCSA building with great views all over Havana. The restaurant has a high-class kitchen serving French and international food. Open for lunch and dinner, you can stay on till late for drinks at the bar.

VIÑALES

Casa de Don Tomás $–$$ *Salvador Cisneros 140, tel: (48) 796 300.* Open for lunch and dinner. Completely rebuilt after a hurricane destroyed the former handsome colonial building dating from 1879. Food average but it is a pleasant place to come for live music and a cocktail.

El Olivo $$ *Salvador Cisneros 89, tel: (48) 696 654.* Open noon–11pm. This Mediterranean *paladar* is a welcome change from rice and beans. Good fish, pasta, paella and even cheese. The service is slow but the food is tasty. Queues outside are testament to its popularity.

VARADERO

Albacora $–$$ *Calle 59 e/. Av 1ra y Playa, tel: (45) 668 050.* Open daily 9am–midnight. Pleasant setting on a terrace overlooking the sea and a good place to come for seafood.

Mansión Xanadú $$$ *Av. Las Américas, km 4.5, tel: (45) 668 482.* Open daily noon–10.30pm. Grand seaside mansion serving international dishes with variable success. Lunchtime snacks available on the terrace. On the third floor the Casa Blanca Panoramic Bar has cocktails and live music.

CIENFUEGOS

Palacio del Valle $$$ *Calle 37 esq. 2, Punta Gorda, tel: (43) 551 003.* Open daily 10am–11pm. Next to the Hotel Jagua, this ornate early 20th-century Moorish palace (see page 61) has a ground-floor restaurant serving reasonable seafood and paella. Rooftop bar.

TRINIDAD

Estela $–$$ *Calle Simón Bolívar, 557, tel: (41) 994 329.* Open Mon–Fri from 7pm. This *paladar* is probably the most popular place to eat so get there early. Tables are set in a walled garden among the shrubs. The food is fresh, imaginative and there is an extensive menu. Portions are generous and service is friendly.

San José $–$$ *Maceo No. 382 entre Colon y Smith, tel: (41) 994 702.* A trendy *paladar* which probably serves the best pizza on the island. Another good option is the fried plantains stuffed with beef and cheese. Make sure to arrive before 6pm as it gets busy later on. Excellent value for money.

Sol y Son $–$$ *Calle Simón Bolívar, 283, e/ Frank País y José Martí.* Open daily 7–11pm. A colonial house with an entryway that might be an antiques shop and peaceful courtyard, offering such dishes as *cerdo borracho* (drunken pork with rum) and stuffed fish.

CAMAGÜEY

1800 $$ *Plaza San Juan de Dios #113 entre San Rafael y San Juan de Dios; tel: (32) 283 619.* Situated on the city's most beautiful square, this lovely restaurant offers a good variety of tasty Cuban staples, seafood and tapas, plus an excellent buffet. Great atmosphere and music.

Campana de Toledo $ *Plaza San Juan de Dios, tel: (32) 286 812.* Open daily for lunch and dinner. Good – if not memorable – Spanish and Creole fare in one of the city's prettiest courtyards. Live music. Busy at lunch with tour parties.

GUARDALAVACA

El Ancla $$ *Playa Guardalavaca, Banes, tel: (24) 430 381*. Open daily 9am–10.30pm. Seafood platters and pastas and a waterside cocktail terrace in a fabulous site at the eastern end of the beach (cross the beach and river to reach it). A lovely spot for a lobster lunch.

SANTIAGO DE CUBA

El Morro $$–$$$ *Carretera del Morro, tel: (22) 691 576*. Open daily noon–10pm. In a superb clifftop location on a vine-covered terrace next to Castillo del Morro, this restaurant offers excellent Creole fare including shrimp and lobster along with the coastal views.

Santiago 1900 $–$$ *Bartolomé Masó, 354, e/ Hartmann y Pío Rosado, tel: (22) 623 507*. Open daily for lunch and dinner. This spectacular mansion has a beautiful courtyard and two terraces upstairs. You can pay in *pesos cubanos*, which makes a meal absurdly cheap. However, the *criollo* cooking is mostly hit or miss, as are the mojitos.

Zunzún $$$ *Avenida Manduley 159 esq Calle 7, Vista Alegre, tel: (22) 641 528*. Open daily noon–9pm. Elegant dining with marble floors and crystal chandeliers. The food is good, particularly the lobster, and the service is attentive.

BARACOA

La Colonial $ *José Martí 123, tel: (21) 645 391*. Open daily for dinner. Of Baracoa's many good *paladares*, this is one of the nicest, with a seductive decor and ambience, a pretty courtyard and such local fare as coconut-flavoured fish-and-rice dishes and sweet *cucurucho* (shredded coconut with fruit flavouring). Vegetarian options available. Good service.

A–Z TRAVEL TIPS

A SUMMARY OF PRACTICAL INFORMATION

A

ACCOMMODATION

Standards and facilities have improved dramatically over the past few years. Cuba's new or restored hotels in beach resorts and in Havana typically have pools, restaurants, buffets, boutiques, air conditioning and satellite TV. Top resort hotels offer round-the-clock entertainment, while simpler resort hotels offer some in-house entertainment and invariably have a pool. Elsewhere, there are large, Soviet-style concrete eyesores located on the outskirts of towns, but there are now a number of small, attractive boutique hotels in town centres in renovated old hotels with plenty of character.

Casas particulares – private accommodation in Cuban homes – are inexpensive alternatives that can be the most rewarding way of experiencing Cuba. Not only do you get to know the owners, but there is usually a better standard of service, cleanliness and comfort than in the equivalent or higher value hotel room. The food served is fresher and often cooked better. *Casas particulares* must be registered with the authorities and should display a blue, anchor-shaped sign on or above the front door.

Outside such high periods as Christmas, New Year and Easter, you don't always need advance reservations, but it helps. Your host will often come to the bus station to pick you up so you don't get lost or diverted to another *casa*. For reservations from abroad it is worth checking www.casaparticularcuba.org.

I'd like a room with twin beds/double bed **Quisiera una habitación con dos camas/cama matrimonial**
What's the price? **¿Cuál es el precio?**
Is breakfast included? **¿El desayuno está incluído?**
Is there a private homestay near here? **¿Conoce una casa particular por aquí?**

AIRPORTS (see Getting there)

Cuba's main airport is Havana's José Martí International Airport (tel: (7) 266 4644 (7) 33 5777; http://havana.airportcuba.net), located 20km (12 miles) south of downtown Havana. Hotel and long distance bus reservations can be made at the airport's Infotur office. Varadero's Juan Gualberto Gómez Airport is 22km (14 miles) west of Varadero. Santiago de Cuba's Antonio Maceo Airport is located 6km (4 miles) south of that city. There are also international airports in Camagüey, Cayo Coco, Cayo Largo, Holguín, Santa Clara, Varadero, Cienfuegos, Santiago de Cuba and Manzanillo.

On arrival, if you're on a package holiday a bus will transfer you to your hotel. Independent travellers can book transfers through agencies in their own country; otherwise take a taxi or a bus from Terminal 1 (the domestic flights terminal); buses run until 8pm and payment is by CUPs. From the airport, it costs CUC$25 to downtown Havana by taxi (usually less to return); CUC$10–15 to the centre of Santiago. It's a 40-minute trip from José Martí airport to central Havana. You must pay a departure tax at all airports: CUC$25.

B

BICYCLE HIRE

With the scarcity of public transport, millions of Cubans ride bikes. Most resorts have bikes and mopeds to hire. Many rental bikes are old and have few gears, and serious cyclists intending to tour the country should bring their bikes, as well as plenty of parts and spare tubes. Alternatively, you could try a bike tour with a Canadian-based company WoWCuba (www.wowcuba.com), which also has a branch in Havana.

BUDGETING FOR YOUR TRIP

Compared with the rest of Latin America, Cuba can be surprisingly expensive, but it compares well with the rest of the Caribbean.

Transport to Cuba. The airfare is likely to be your greatest expenditure, especially if coming from Europe or Asia. It's cheapest to travel outside of high season (mid-Dec to mid-Apr) or on a package tour.

Accommodation. Hotels in Havana, Santiago and major resorts are expensive, comparable to North America and Europe. In resorts, all-inclusive deals (meals, drinks and entertainment) can be a good option. Private houses *(casas particulares)* are generally inexpensive.

Meals and drinks. Eating out is rarely very expensive, about CUC$25 per person in a smartish restaurant, but there are many restaurants and *paladares* where you can eat well for around CUC$15 or less. If you are going to drink wine, this puts the price up quite a lot. In a bar, beer costs around CUC$1.50, mojitos CUC$3–6, depending on location.

Local transport. Urban public transport is cheap and improving but still crowded and inefficient. Taxis and *bicitaxis* are the best way to get about within cities and resorts; they are inexpensive.

Incidentals. Entertainment in cabarets and discos is expensive for Cuba (CUC$10–90), and drinks in such nightspots are also much more expensive than in bars and cafés. Gifts like prestigious hand-rolled cigars are expensive, even if much cheaper than they are abroad.

C

CAMPING

There are official campsites in isolated locations all over the island, but they offer basic huts rather than tents. In each major town ask for the Campismo office for local campsites, most of which are used by Cubans on holiday. There are also 21 campsites, hotels or parking sites for tourists using camper vans, with water, power and waste disposal, dotted around the island. Not all of them are available to foreigners, however. Book through an agency abroad, which will issue a voucher for you to present to Campertour (Calle 3 y Malecón, Vedado).

CAR HIRE

There are good reasons for not hiring a car in Cuba. It can be expensive, petrol (gasoline) is pricey by North American standards (although not when compared to the UK), and rental firms are often inefficient and difficult to deal with in the event of car damage or other problems. If you wish to hire a car in one place and return it in another, you must pay the cost of having it returned to its origin. Long-distance buses are reliable and, along with tour buses, go to most places of interest, but only a hire car will allow you to go anywhere you wish, when you wish. To hire a car, you must be at least 21 and have had a year's driving experience. You will need a national or international licence.

Cuba has none of the major international rental agencies. However, there are good local hire firms with offices throughout the island. Here are the main ones: Vía Rentacar (www.carrentalcuba.com), Havanautos (www.havanautos.cu), Cubacar (www.cubacar.info/englisch/) and Rex (www.rex-carrental.com). Rates range from CUC$45 to $100 per day for unlimited mileage. Insurance must be paid locally even if you have prepaid the car hire abroad. If there is any damage to the car, you must pay the first few hundred dollars-worth of repair unless you prove the accident wasn't your fault. You must leave a cash or open credit-card guarantee to cover for this eventuality. Inspect the car before you set off to identify existing dents and scratches.

> I'd like to rent a car for a day/a week **Quisiera alquilar un auto/carro por un día/una semana**
> Fill it up. **Llénelo, por favor.**

CLIMATE

Cuba has a subtropical climate: hot and humid. The chart below shows the average daily temperature in Havana. For beach lovers and sightseers, November to May is the ideal time to visit, though there is plenty of sunshine year-round. Hurricane season lasts from June until the end of November. The more active should avoid the height of summer, when it's debilitatingly hot and wet. The mountains are cooler and the south and east drier and warmer. Oriente, the area around Santiago, can be wickedly hot – much hotter than the western region.

	J	F	M	A	M	J	J	A	S	O	N	D
°C	22	22	23	25	26	27	28	28	27	26	24	22
°F	72	72	73	77	79	81	82	82	81	79	75	72

CLOTHING

During the day you'll rarely need more than shorts or a skirt and a T-shirt (and swimsuit). At night in winter, a light sweater or jacket may be needed. In upmarket hotels, restaurants and nightclubs you are required to dress equally smartly.

CRIME AND SAFETY (see also Emergencies and Police)

Cuba is a remarkably safe place in which to travel – one of the safest anywhere. The crime that does exist is generally directed at possessions rather than people, so place temptation out of sight. Most top hotels provide safes, though usually with a rental charge.

In Havana, be sensible and take the same precautions you would in any unfamiliar city. At night keep to busy and well-lit streets (or walk in the middle of the road if there is no street lighting). There is much less crime outside the capital, but in Santiago you must take the same precautions as you would in Havana.

I want to report a theft. **Quiero denunciar un robo.**
my wallet/handbag/passport **mi cartera/bolso/pasaporte**
safe (deposit box) **caja fuerte**

D

DRIVING

Road conditions. There is little traffic outside of town centres. Most main roads are paved and in fairly good condition, although they are not well signposted. The Autopista Nacional (motorway) runs from Havana west to Pinar del Río and east to Jatibonico, just before Ciego de Avila. From there a good road heads east to Santiago de Cuba. A number of rural roads are not paved. Beware of potholes: some are big enough to cause real damage. Other hazards are cyclists, hidden railway crossings and wandering livestock. Driving at night is not advisable; Cubans often drive with headlights on full beam and animals may wander onto the road.

Rules and regulations. To drive, you must be 21 and have a valid driver's licence. Drive on the right. Speed limits, strictly enforced, are 100km/h (62mph) on the highway (motorway), 90km/h (56mph) on other open roads, 60km/h (37mph) on smaller rural roads and 40km/h (25mph) in urban areas. You are likely to get an on-the-spot fine if caught breaking the speed limit. Insurance is mandatory, as is wearing seatbelts. It's common practice to sound your horn when passing to let vehicles without rearview mirrors know what's happening.

Fuel (gasolina). Cupet stations are spread throughout the country and are open 24 hours. They are not self-service. Petrol or diesel must be paid for in CUC$. The quality of regular petrol is poor, and many rental companies insist that you purchase expensive 'especial' fuel.

stop **pare**
caution **cuidado**
no parking **no parqueo**
give way (yield) **ceda el paso**

one-way **dirección única**
danger **peligro**
car registration papers **permiso de circulación**
driver's licence **licencia de manejar**
How do I get to ... ? **¿Cómo se puede ir a ... ?**
Is this the right street for ... ? **¿Es ésta la calle que va a ... ?**
Full tank, please. **Llénelo, por favor.**
My car has broken down. **Mi carro tiene problemas mecánicos.**
I have a flat tire. **Tengo la goma ponchada.**
May I park here? **¿Se puede aparcar aquí?**
Is this the highway (road) to ... ? **¿Es ésta la carretera hacia ... ?**

E

ELECTRICITY

Electrical appliances in hotels and *casas particulares* operate on either 110 volts or 220 volts. Most outlets accept flat-pin plugs, some round-pin plugs. Take an adapter; a converter might also be necessary.

What's the voltage? **¿Cuál es el voltaje?**
adaptor/a battery **un adaptador/una pila**

EMBASSIES

Canada: Calle 30, no. 518, e/ 5 y 7, Miramar, Havana, tel: (7) 204 2516, (7) 204 7079; www.canadainternational.gc.ca.
UK: Calle 34, no. 702/4, esq 7, Miramar, Havana, tel: (7) 214 2200; www.gov.uk. The UK embassy also represents New Zealand interests and will help Australian and Irish citizens in an emergency.

US: Since the renewal of diplomatic relations between the US and Cuba, the Interests Section (in the Swiss embassy) has become the US embassy: Calzada e/ L y M, Vedado, Havana, tel: (7) 839 4100.

EMERGENCIES (see also Health and medical care and Police)

Asistur, a state-run organisation, helps foreigners with medical or financial problems and is affiliated with a number of international travel insurance companies. For a 10 percent commission, they can negotiate a cash advance if provided with bank details overseas. They can also help to find lost luggage and issue travel documents. Asistur's main office is at Paseo del Prado, 208 e/ Colón y Trocadero, Old Havana, tel: (7) 866 4499, www.asistur.cu. There are also offices in Cayo Coco, Guardalavaca, Santiago and Varadero. All offices open 24 hours.

Useful telephone numbers: Police 106, Fire 105, Ambulance 104, Information 113. These numbers may not work in remote areas so ask your hotel or *casa particular* or call Asistur, where you will be put through to someone who speaks English.

G

GETTING THERE (see also Airports)

Most flights into Cuba are charters, arriving at Havana, Varadero and several other airports convenient to beach resorts such as Cayo Coco, Playa Santa Lucía and Guardalavaca. From Canada, scheduled flights to Cuba leave from Montreal or Toronto, taking around four hours. There are also charters from Vancouver, Halifax and Ottawa. From Europe, Cubana flies from London, Paris, Moscow, Madrid and Rome; Air France flies to Havana from Paris; Iberia flies from Madrid and Virgin Atlantic flies from London. From Australia and New Zealand, the options include travelling through Canada, Mexico or other points in Latin America.

Scheduled flights are now operating (in addition to charters) from the US to Cuba. American Airlines, Jet Blue, Delta,

Southwest and Sun Country are the main carriers, flying from Miami, Atlanta, Chicago, Philadelphia, Minneapolis and Fort Lauderdale.

Those wishing to circumvent travel restrictions from the US usually go through Canada (Toronto, Montreal, Vancouver), Mexico (Mexico City, Mérida, Cancún), Bahamas (Nassau) or Jamaica (Kingston, Montego Bay). Havanatur, www.havanatur.com is an online travel service which handles tourist cards as well as roundtrip air tickets on Cubana Aviación.

Similar arrangements can be made through Canadian, Jamaican and Mexican airlines and travel agencies.

GUIDES AND TOURS

Most still come to Cuba on package tours, which may include a group excursion or two. If you wish to travel independently and have found a hotel-airfare package that is cheaper than separate arrangements or airfare alone, you are not obligated to go along with the group once in Cuba. Plenty of people check into their resort hotels and take off on their own.

The most popular and straightforward way of exploring Cuba is on group excursions. However, these trips – available in any tourist hotel and led by English-speaking tour guides – may insulate you from the most interesting aspects of Cuban life. You can reach virtually the whole island from any resort on excursions; most are flexible and will allow you to break up a daytrip and stay overnight if you wish to explore on your own.

Freelance 'guides', offering to take you to *casas particulares* and *paladares* (privately run lodgings and restaurants) or obtain cigars and prostitutes, are omnipresent in Cuba.

Another way to explore the island, albeit a more expensive one, is on a Harley Davidson with La Poderosa Tours (www.lapoderosatours.com), run by the son of Che Guevara. Prices for a seven-day tour start from US$3,250.

H

HEALTH AND MEDICAL CARE (see also Emergencies)

Cuba has an excellent national health system. There are no mandatory vaccinations required for travel to Cuba; nonetheless, some health professionals recommend vaccinations against typhoid and hepatitis A.

Although Cuban water is chlorinated, tap water is not generally safe to drink. Bottled mineral water *(agua mineral)* is widely available and recommended. The most likely source of food poisoning is from unhygienic hotel buffet food. Cuban food is very plain, and upset stomachs are less common than in many other countries.

The Cuban sun can burn fair-skinned people within minutes. Use plenty of sunscreen and wear a hat. It's also easy to become dehydrated, so be sure to drink plenty of water. Mosquitoes are a menace from dusk to dawn in coastal resorts. Air conditioning helps keep them at bay, but apply insect repellent.

If you need to see a doctor, contact your hotel's reception desk. Large resort hotels have their own doctor. All the island's main resorts have an international clinic *(clínica internacional)*, as do Havana, Santiago de Cuba, Cienfuegos and Trinidad. Medical treatment in Cuba is excellent and free for Cubans. Foreigners, however, must pay. Such treatment is expensive, so proper insurance is essential; it is mandatory to have health insurance before you arrive in Cuba.

Every town has an all-night pharmacy *(farmacia)*. The range of medicines has become severely limited. Resorts have better-stocked international pharmacies, though prices can be astronomical.

I'm sick. **Estoy enfermo(a)**.
Where's the nearest hospital?**¿Dónde está el hospital más cercano?**
Call a doctor/dentist. **Llame a un médico/dentista.**

HITCH-HIKING

Although hitching a ride in Cuba is easy and safe, it is not recommended because of the possibility that police may fine your benefactor on suspicion that he's earning dollars illegally. If you're looking to hitch, the biggest problem you'll encounter is the paucity of vehicles (at least outside the major cities).

L

LANGUAGE

The official language is Spanish, Increasing numbers of Cubans are learning English (French, Italian and other languages), and many people in the tourist industry are fluent, but you will most likely need some Spanish, especially outside tourist hotels and major resorts. The *Berlitz Latin American Spanish Phrase Book & Dictionary* includes over 1,200 phrases useful for travellers.

LGBTQ TRAVELLERS

The hardline Cuban policy on homosexuality has lessened in recent years (sex between consenting adults was legalised in 1979) and there is generally a more tolerant attitude. It is still not the most LGBTQ-friendly place to visit, although there are a growing number of openly gay people – mostly in the capital and in some small, laid-back places such as Viñales and Baracoa.

M

MAPS

The best road map of Cuba is 'Guía de Carreteras' by the Directorio Turístico de Cuba (on sale in Cuba for CUC$12). Other maps are 'Cuba: ITM 190' (ITMB), 'Cuba' (Globetrotter Travel Map) and 'Cuba' (Nelles Map). Hotels and bookshops in Havana and Santiago sell reasonable maps and the Infotur desk at Havana airport is a good place to look on arrival.

MEDIA

You will not receive much outside news in Cuba, although many tourist hotels offer CNN. You might find a stray European newspaper at major hotels in Havana or resorts, but it's not likely. The main national newspaper, *Granma*, is the mouthpiece of the government. A weekly *Granma* international edition is published in English, French, Portuguese and German, with cultural features of tourist appeal. Four- and five-star hotels (particularly in Havana) often carry foreign publications from *Time* to *Cosmopolitan*.

Cuban national television is broadcast on five state-owned national channels. Foreign films (usually American) are shown on Thursday, Friday, Saturday and Sunday. Soaps, usually Brazilian, Colombian, Mexican or Cuban, are extremely popular. Tourist hotels all have satellite TV and more than 20 channels.

Just about everyone in Cuba has a radio, and loud music is a constant background sound wherever you go. There are six state-owned national radio stations and each province has its own station as well. Radio Reloj (Clock Radio) gives round-the-clock news on AM to the infuriating background noise of a ticking clock; Radio Havana Cuba broadcasts news and features on short wave. Voice of America broadcasts from 6pm on 7070, short wave. Radio Martí, Voice of America's Spanish-language propaganda service, broadcasts from Miami, and often changes its frequency to avoid jamming, but without much success.

MONEY

Currency. Although Raúl Castro has announced his intention to unify the currency, at the moment Cuba still has two currencies, the *peso cubano* (CUP), or national peso, and the *peso convertible* (CUC), or convertible peso. The latter is the one which tourists use most of the time, as it is fully exchangeable for foreign currencies. Tourists have to use the *peso convertible* for all payments such as restaurant bills, hotel bills (if not paid in advance), transport and souvenirs. The only time *pesos cubanos* are needed is in very out of the way places, for street food, snacks or in a rural market, or if you take a local bus. Local town buses cost 20–40 centavos and you are unlikely to need to exchange more than US$5 into *pesos cubanos* for a two-week stay. Spend all your CUCs before you leave the island, as they can't be exchanged outside Cuba. The only place in Cuba where you can change pesos into other currencies is at Havana airport.

Currency exchange. For accounting purposes, the *peso convertible* is fixed at US$1 = CUC$1, but there is a 10 percent tax on all US dollar exchange transactions. You are advised to bring euros, sterling or Canadian dollars, which do not attract the tax. Bring plenty of cash and make sure that the notes are clean and undamaged; any with writing on them or tears will be rejected. There are banks and *casas de cambio* (exchange houses, called a CADECA) where you can exchange your money. If you want to buy *pesos cubanos*, the rate is CUC$1 = CUP25.

Credit cards *(tarjetas de crédito)*. An increasing number of outlets accept credit cards (Access/MasterCard, Visa and others), including many tourist shops, upmarket hotels and restaurants, airlines, petrol stations and car hire companies. Nevertheless, nobody should rely solely on credit cards, as not everybody accepts them and, even if they do, telephone lines are sometimes out of action so payments cannot be processed. Cuba remains a largely cash *(divisa)* economy. Getting change from big notes is often difficult, so it is worthwhile keeping a stock of 10s, 5s and single notes in your wallet.

ATMs. Cuba has a growing network of automatic teller machines in cities. Your hotel will know if ATMs are in place by the time of your trip. Several banks (Banco Financiero is one) and CADECAs give over-the-counter cash advances on credit or debit cards on production of a passport, but charge high commission.

May I pay with a credit card? **¿Se puede pagar con tarjeta?**
How much is that? **¿Cuánto es?**

O

OPENING HOURS

Offices are usually open weekdays from 8.30am to 5 or 6pm, with a one-hour lunch break. Some are open on Saturday mornings, from 8am to noon or 1pm. Banks are typically open weekdays from 8.30am to 3pm.

Some museums open daily, but most close for one day (usually Monday) and also close on Sunday at noon or 1pm. Typical museum hours are 9am (sometimes 8am or 10am) until 5pm (sometimes 4pm or 6pm). Regardless of when you go, you'll find several closed for renovations; make inquiries before travelling a long way.

Restaurants do not typically stay open late; most close their doors around 10pm or even earlier. The great exception is *paladares*, which are usually open from noon to 11pm or midnight.

Farmers' markets open early, from around 7am or even earlier, and close when traders decide to leave – usually between 4 and 6pm. CUC retail stores (often referred to as dollar stores) are all over Cuba; most open Mon–Sat 10am–5pm but may stay open later. CUC supermarkets usually open Mon–Sat 9am–6pm and Sun 9am–1pm. Many of the bigger stores open 9am–9pm.

P

POLICE

Most police are helpful and friendly, even though they occasionally harass Cubans (or, more specifically, anyone of dark skin colour who might be assumed to be Cuban) accompanying foreigners. If you are robbed, make sure you get a police report, a time-consuming affair.

POST OFFICES

You can buy stamps *(sellos)* with *pesos convertibles* at hotels, although this costs more than if you buy them with *pesos cubanos* at post offices. Some stamps are not sticky and you have to ask a post office or hotel desk for glue. Cuba's post system is unreliable and slow. Postcards *(tarjetas postales)* sent to Europe take from two weeks to a month or more to arrive.

Post offices are generally open weekdays 8am to 5pm and Saturday 9am to 3pm. You'll find post offices in every rural town; cities have several branches. In Havana, the best one to use is the one in the Hotel Havana Libre in Vedado (Calles L and 23). More efficient mailing services are available through DHL Worldwide Express, with offices in several cities. In Havana, there's one in the Hotel Havana Libre.

PUBLIC HOLIDAYS

The following days are public holidays in Cuba:

1 January Anniversary of the Triumph of the Revolution: Liberation Day
19 April Anniversary of the Bay of Pigs victory
1 May International Workers' Day (Labour Day)
25–27 July National Rebellion Day (26 July)
10 October Independence Day

R

RELIGION

Roman Catholicism in Cuba is strongly intertwined with Afro-Cuban religions such as *santería* (see page 33). Many aspects of these religious practices can be experienced by visitors. The government blunted the power and influence of the Catholic Church in the early 1960s, but mass is still said in churches throughout the island, and since the Pope's visits to Cuba in 1998, 2012 and 2015 there has been a resurgence of Catholic practice.

T

TELEPHONES

Cuba's country code is 53. In addition, each area of the island has its own area code (for Havana it is 7). To make an international call from Cuba dial 119, then the country code, the area code and the phone number.

To make a domestic call, add the area code (for example, 7 for Havana). For interprovincial calls you first have to dial the appropriate prefix (0 to and from Havana, 01 for all other provinces), followed by the area code, then the number itself. When phoning Cuba from abroad, drop the 0 or 01. Dial 113 for the free domestic telephone enquiries service.

Top hotels have direct-dial facilities for all calls. Elsewhere you can make domestic calls on a direct line, but you will need to go through the hotel operator for international calls. International calls from Cuba are very expensive (CUC$2.20–4.40 per minute). As they do everywhere in the world, hotels charge a significant surcharge on calls.

Public phones which take coins (20 centavos or 1 peso Cubano) are now rare; most have been converted to take pre-paid phone cards *(tarjetas)*. Tourists are supposed to buy them in CUC$, in denominations of CUC$10–50, while Cubans pay in CUP$. The state telecommunications company is ETECSA, also known as Telepunto, which offers a full range of services.

Mobile phones can be rented through Cubacel, which can be found at ETECSA and Telepunto offices. They cost about CUC$8 a day to hire, plus a CUC$3 activation fee, and call charges are high. You can use your own phone in Cuba (where there is a signal) and texting is often cheaper, quicker and easier than queuing to use the internet at ETECSA. All mobile numbers begin with 5 and have 8 digits. To call a mobile from Havana dial 0 and then the number, from other provinces dial 01 and then the number. Area codes are not needed.

I'd like make a telephone call ... **Quisiera hacer una llamada ...**
to England/Canada/ United States. **a Inglaterra/Canadá/ los Estados Unidos.**
reverse-charge call **cobro revertido**
Can you get me this number in ... ? **¿Puede comunicarme con este número en ... ?**
phone card **tarjeta telefónica**

TIME ZONES

Cuba is five hours behind GMT. It operates on Eastern Standard Time in winter and Daylight Saving Time (one hour later) from April to October.

San Francisco	**Cuba**	New York	London	Sydney
9am	**noon**	noon	5pm	2am

TIPPING

Taxi drivers, waiters and hotel staff should be tipped in CUCs – this is the only access to convertible currency that they get. Ten percent is usual for taxi drivers and restaurant staff. You should leave CUC$1 a day for a hotel chambermaid.

TOILETS

It's often best to carry a roll of toilet paper with you at all times in Cuba, as many establishments do not provide their own. Those that do often demand a few cents for providing it – so it's worth carrying some small change.

TOURIST INFORMATION

There are official Cuban government tourism offices in Canada and Britain but not in the US:

Canada: 1200 Bay Street, Suite 305, Toronto, Ontario M5R 2A5, tel: (416) 362 0700; www.gocuba.ca.

UK: 167 High Holborn, London WC1V 6PA, tel: (020) 7240 6655; www.travel2cuba.co.uk.

In Cuba itself, there is no centralised system providing tourism information, and reliable information is sometimes hard to come by. Instead, you must rely upon hotels and travel agencies, whose primary function is to sell excursion packages. In Cuba all hotels have a tourism desk (buró de turismo).

Infotur is the only tourist information service, although other state tour operators will help. The main office is at Obispo, 521 e/ Bernaza y Villegas in Old Havana, tel: (7) 866 3333. Other branches are at the airport terminals; Av. Las Terrazas e/ 11 y 12, Santa María del Mar, Playas del Este, tel: (7) 797 1261; Av. 5 y 112, Miramar, tel: (7) 204 7036; and Obispo y San Ignacio, Old Havana, tel: (7) 863 6884.

TRANSPORT

Taxis. There is only one state taxi company, Cubataxi, tel: (7) 855 5555 in Havana. You can call them or pick them up from designated ranks (usually outside hotels, major museums, bus stations and airports). They are metered and fares are paid in *pesos convertibles*. Private taxis (which might or might not be licensed) also circulate. The lumbering vintage American cars with taxi signs (*colectivos* or *máquinas*) have fixed routes and are usually reserved for Cubans, although the smarter versions, owned by the Grancar company, are state-owned and geared towards tourists – in Havana call (7) 338 417980.

You can hire any taxi for a single fare or a day. Many owners of private cars *(particulares)* also operate legally as freelance taxi drivers, although it is illegal for them to carry tourists. Owners face large fines if caught, so it's best to ride in official taxis.

Buses (*guaguas*, pronounced 'wah-wahs'). Buses are the backbone of Cuba's public transport system, but urban buses in Havana are not a great option for tourists. There are too few of them, they're uncomfortable, they're usually full when they do arrive, there are long queues and there is a risk of being pickpocketed. A better option for tourists is the hop-on, hop-off service called the HabanaBusTour, with two routes, one from the Almacenes San José on Av del Puerto to Vedado, Plaza de la Revolución and Miramar (CUC$10 per day) and the other from the Parque Central out to Playas del Este via the Castillo del Morro (CUC$5). A similar service runs from Varadero to Matanzas; from Trinidad to Playa Ancón; and around Viñales.

For travel between cities, towns and resorts of major tourist interest, however, there is a company named Víazul (Av. 26 e/ Av. Zoológico y Ulloa, Nuevo Vedado; tel: (7) 883 6092; www.viazul.com). It operates air-conditioned tour buses to Varadero, Viñales/Pinar del Río, Cienfuegos, Trinidad, Santa Clara, Sancti Spíritus, Ciego de Ávila, Camagüey, Holguín, Las Tunas, Bayamo and Santiago de Cuba. Prices range from US$10 (Havana to Varadero Airport) to US$51 (Havana to Santiago). If you're not hiring a car in Cuba but travelling independently, Víazul is the way to go. It's far more efficient, faster and more reliable than trains. Another company, Astro, also runs long-distance buses but they are for Cubans.

Trains *(trenes)*. Journeys are extremely slow, schedules unreliable, and breakdowns are frequent. There are no express trains, almost all are local services that stop at every station. Trains usually run only on alternate days or a couple of times a week to most destinations. The train between Havana and Santiago de Cuba takes at least 15 hours, usually many more. It runs every other day, with stops at Santa Clara, Camagüey and Santiago (CUC$30, cash only). In Havana you can make bookings at the Estación Central, Arsenal y Ejido (tel: (7) 861 1920).

Domestic flights. Flying in Cuba is the quickest and most reliable form of transport for long trips. It's also good value (flights range from about CUC$43–143 each way). Flights fill up fast, so book in advance from your home country if possible. Cubana, the national airline, provides domestic flights to 13 destinations from the capital, including to Baracoa, Camagüey, Ciego de Ávila, Cienfuegos, Guantánamo, Holguín, Nueva Gerona (Isla de la Juventud), Santiago and Varadero. Frequency varies enormously, from several daily flights to Santiago to twice weekly to Baracoa. Tickets can be purchased in Cubana offices around the country or from the main office in Havana on Calle 23 (La Rampa), no. 64 esq. Infanta (tel: (7) 834 4446), or at the airport, Terminal 3 (tel: (7) 649 0410).

Bicycle taxis. Havana's *cocotaxis* are yellow three-wheeled buggies powered by motorcycle engines. They are just as plentiful as car taxis in Havana and cost 50 centavos per kilometre. *Bicitaxis*, pedicabs, are a fun way to traverse the city on short trips. Note that only some *bicitaxis* are licensed to carry foreigners; unlicensed ones should not be used.

Horse carts *(coches)*. Due to fuel shortages, in virtually every city except Havana and Santiago there are horses pulling covered carts and plush little carriages up and down the main streets. Ironically, horse carriages acting as taxis have become a tourist attraction in the resorts.

> When's the next bus/train to...? **¿Cuándo sale el próximo autobús/tren para...?**
> What's the fare to...? **¿Cuánto es la tarifa a...?**
> A ticket to... **Un billete para...**
> single (one-way) **ida**
> return (roundtrip) **ida y vuelta**

V

VISAS AND ENTRY REQUIREMENTS

All visitors entering Cuba must show a passport valid for at least six months beyond the date of arrival in Cuba. In addition, visitors must have a tourist card (tarjeta de turista), issued by the Cuban Consulate directly or, more commonly, through a travel agent. This will be valid for the length of your planned visit, but can be extended (once) up to the date shown on your return aeroplane ticket – as long as the total time you are in the country does not exceed 60 days. Immigration officials stamp your tourist card, not your passport. Do not lose it – you must show it when you leave the country.

Visas for US citizens. These are handled by the Cuban Embassy in Washington, DC. Travel to Cuba for tourist activities remains prohibited by the US state; however visas are issued under one of 12 categories for travel. For details, visit https://cu.usembassy.gov.

WEBSITES

Although few Cubans have access to the internet, Cuba is surprisingly well served by the web. From sites about the US embargo and travel restrictions to traveller recommendations, there is a wealth of information. A few sites worth exploring include the following:

www.dtcuba.com Cuban Tourist Directory site

www.cubaweb.cu Official government site

www.cubatravel.cu Official tourist site

www.cuba.com English/Spanish website packed with information

http://www.visitcuba.com/ Website with lots of information about Cuba and its culture

http://www.cuba-junky.com A comprehensive site for all Cuba lovers.

www.casaparticularcuba.org Accommodation booking service

www.lahabana.com A guide to the city and its arts and culture

RECOMMENDED HOTELS

The very best hotels are joint ventures with private firms from Spain, Canada and other countries. These are of an international standard. Many others, though, are a notch or two down from what you'd expect in Europe, North America or Asia. In Old Havana hotels in renovated colonial mansions are run by Habaguanex (www.habaguanexhotels.com) and are beautiful places to stay. At the inexpensive level, hotels around the island are often lacking in ambience and amenities.

Casas particulares – accommodation in private homes – are not only a better-quality and much cheaper alternative to the inexpensive hotels; they allow you a glimpse into unguarded Cuban life. They generally cost CUC$15–35 per room, depending on the location and the season. Your hosts usually also offer breakfast and evening meals at a small extra cost. You'll find a very abbreviated list of recommended private-home *casas* following the regular hotel listings below; however, others are very easy to find.

The price categories below, in US dollars, are for a standard double room, excluding meals, in high season (mid-December to mid-April, July to August). Prices drop by 15–30 percent during other months. All accommodation is paid for in *pesos convertibles*. Only top hotels accept credit cards. For reservations it's best to call directly and get a confirmation number.

$$$$	over $150
$$$	$100–150
$$	$50–100
$	under $50

HAVANA

Old Havana

Ambos Mundos $$ *Obispo 153 esq. Mercaderes, Habana Vieja, tel: (7) 860 9530, www.gaviotahotels.com.* Hemingway wrote much of *For Whom the*

Bell Tolls in room 511 of this historic hotel (opened in 1920). It's in the heart of Old Havana, on one of its most picturesque streets. The rooms are adequate in size, nicely decorated, but not all have windows to the outside. On the ground floor is an airy, lovely piano bar and the rooftop bar offers great views. 52 rooms.

Hotel Florida $$ *Calle Obispo 252 esq. Cuba, Habana Vieja, tel: (7) 862 4127,* www.hotelfloridahabana.com. A marvellous colonial mansion built in 1836, achieves affordable luxury. It originally became a hotel in 1885 but reopened only in 1999. It is elegant, with plush public rooms, a lovely courtyard, and a great location just a couple of blocks from the Plaza de Armas. Some rooms have balconies. Piano bar, lobby bar and restaurant. 25 rooms.

Hotel Mercure Sevilla $$$ *Trocadero, 55 e/ Zulueta y Animas, Habana Vieja, tel: (7) 860 8560,* www.hotelmercuresevillahabana.com. This restored turn-of-the-20th-century establishment, of Spanish and Moroccan inspiration has a sumptuous lobby, magnificent rooftop restaurant and other excellent dining options. Guests have included Al Capone, Josephine Baker and Enrico Caruso, and scenes from Greene's *Our Man in Havana* were set here. Rooms are comfortable and stylish. Good pool, gymnasium, billiards/snooker, sauna, massage and solarium. 178 rooms.

Hotel Santa Isabel $$$$ *Calle Baratillo, 9 e/ Obispo y Narciso López, Habana Vieja, tel: (7) 801 1201,* www.habaguanexhotels.com. This small, quiet, gorgeously restored hotel is an 18th-century palace right on the Plaza de Armas. Sumptuous rooms have period furniture, and the hotel features a lovely courtyard and great views from the roof. Recent guests have included former US President Jimmy Carter, Sting and Jack Nicholson. Breakfast is served overlooking the Plaza. 27 rooms and suites.

Hostal Valencia $$ *Oficios, 53 esq. Obrapía, Habana Vieja, tel: (7) 867 1037,* www.habaguanexhotels.com. In an 18th-century mansion between Plaza de Armas and Plaza Vieja, this small Spanish-style yellow colonial is utterly charming. One of the city's best deals, it features rooms (no air conditioning) surrounding a delightful green courtyard. Book well in advance. 12 rooms.

Vedado

Hotel Nacional de Cuba $$$ *Calle O esq. 21, Vedado, tel: (7) 836 3564*, www.hotelnacionaldecuba.com. A classic feature of New Havana, this landmark 1930 hotel rises above the Malecón. Former guests include Hemingway, Churchill, Frank Sinatra, Ava Gardner, Errol Flynn, Marlon Brando and gangsters Meyer Lansky and Lucky Luciano. Rooms are large, and most have sea views. It has a stunning dining room, two pools, a nightly cabaret show, gardens, terraces and bars. Prices include breakfast. 467 rooms.

Tryp Habana Libre $$$ *Calle L e/. 23 y 25, tel: (7) 834 6281*, www.melia-cuba.com. An iconic tower hotel which opened in 1958 as the Hilton but was renamed in 1959 when it became the Revolutionary headquarters for a few months. Fascinating photos of that time line the hotel lobby. It is now a luxury hotel with lots of facilities including a shopping mall, airline offices, coffee shop, good restaurants and the Cabaret Turquino on the 25th floor with a roof which opens so you can dance under the stars. 569 rooms.

PINAR DEL RÍO PROVINCE

Horizontes La Ermita $$ *Carretera de la Ermita, km 2, Viñales, tel: (48) 796 250*, www.hotelescubanacan.com. This contemporary, low-slung hotel of Spanish colonial design is lacking in service and is simply and minimally furnished, but it has some of the finest views in the country, particularly from the swimming pool. All rooms open onto private balconies with chairs where the verdant valley and spectacular sunsets fill the horizon. An enjoyable 20-minute walk from Viñales town. 62 rooms.

Horizontes Los Jazmines $$ *Carretera de Viñales, km 23.5 (3km from Viñales), tel: (48) 796 205*, www.hotelescubanacan.com. This pretty hotel on the edge of the beautiful Viñales valley has stupendous panoramic views. Bedrooms have balconies and air conditioning. The pool can get a bit crowded. Horse-riding is available, and there are organised tours. 62 rooms and 16 small *cabañas*.

Isla de la Juventud

El Colony $$ *Carretera de Sigueanea, km 16, tel: (46) 398 181*, www.hotelelcolony.com. On the coast, 42km (26 miles) southwest of Nueva Gerona, this is an isolated 1950s tourist enclave of exclusive interest to divers. The hotel is adequate but the diving is superb. Lots of activities. 77 rooms and 24 bungalows.

Cayo Largo

Sol Pelícano $$$$ *Cayo largo del sur, 12345, tel: (45) 248 333*, www.hotel-solpelicano.com All the hotels on Cayo Largo del Sur are all-inclusive, booked as packages from abroad. This 4-star hotel has all the facilities you could possibly need for a successful beach holiday, offering activities such as diving and lots of entertainment for children. 307 modern, functional rooms and junior suites.

MATANZAS PROVINCE

Varadero

Meliá Las Américas $$$$ *Carretera Las Morlas, Playa Las Américas, tel: (45) 667 600*, www.meliacuba.com. This swanky 5-star hotel is a highly-ranked all-inclusive golf and beach resort offering international quality and facilities. Adults only. 332 rooms and suites.

Meliá Varadero $$$$ *Autopista del Sur, Playa Las Américas, tel: (45) 667 013*, www.meliacuba.com. Located next to the Plaza Las Americas Convention Center and Shopping Center and the Varadero Golf Club. This is an all-inclusive mega-complex with tons of amenities: fountain, pool, five restaurants, nightclub, shops and more. Direct beach access. 490 rooms.

Starfish Cuatro Palmas Varadero $$$ *Avenida 1ra e/ 60 y 64, tel: (45) 667 040*, www.starfishcuatropalmas-varadero.com. An attractive beachside complex with colonial-style villas and bungalows on either side of the road. Some of the rooms (which can be a little worn) are arranged around an excellent pool. 282 rooms with air conditioning. Convenient for down town, nightlife and restaurants.

Zapata Peninsula

Villa Horizontes Guamá $ *Laguna del Tesoro, Ciénaga de Zapata, tel: (45) 915 551,* www.hotelescubanacan.com. Reached by boat, this is one of the most distinctive places to stay in Cuba, set out as a replica Taíno village. Thatched huts are spread over interconnected islands in the middle of a swamp. Mosquito repellent essential. Good for birdwatching. Crocodile on the menu.

CENTRAL CUBA

Cienfuegos

La Unión $$$ *Ave 31 esq. 54, tel: (43) 551 020,* www.meliacuba.de/kuba-hotels/hotel-la-union. The building dates from 1869 and has been restored into a hotel, making this one of the nicest places to stay in the area, but its town centre location means it can be noisy. Facilities include a business centre, gym, courtyard, pool (which can get very crowded), car rental, restaurant and bars.

Trinidad

Iberostar Grand Hotel Trinidad $$$ *José Martí 262 y Lino Pérez, tel: (41) 996 070,* www.iberostar.com. Centrally located, this is the best hotel in the area. Good service, good food, lovely renovated old building. 40 rooms, some with balconies overlooking the plaza, but no pool or terrace.

Cayo Coco

Tryp Cayo Coco $$$ *Cayo Coco, tel: (33) 301 300,* www.meliacuba.com. One of Cuba's most attractive resort hotels, a replica of a colonial village amid palm gardens and by a dazzling white beach. The pastel-coloured villas are interwoven by a magnificent sculpted pool. Watersports, diving centre, restaurants, and shops are all available. 508 rooms.

Cayo Guillermo

Iberostar Daiquirí $$$ *Cayo Guillermo, tel: (33) 301 650*, www.iberostar. com. A good, popular, all-inclusive family hotel, with bright, recently refurbished rooms, each with its own balcony. The hotel is set on a long, narrow beach with shallow sea. Good food, buffet or themed restaurants, nice pool, excellent service. 312 rooms.

Camagüey

Gran Hotel $$ *Calle Maceo, 67, tel: (32) 292 093*, www.meliacuba.com. This colonial building in the heart of town has been a hotel since 1939. Handsome lobby, pleasant piano bar and nice suites. Most rooms have balconies, but those overlooking the street can be noisy. 72 rooms.

Playa Santa Lucía

Bravo Caracol $$$ *Playa Santa Lucía, tel: (32) 365 158*, www.galahotels. com. The resort's prettiest hotel has flower gardens and two-storey villas with fancy bedrooms, each with balcony, sea view and sitting area. Lots of activities and facilities. 150 rooms.

ORIENTE: THE EAST

Guardalavaca

Paradisus Río de Oro Resort and Spa $$$$ *Playa Esmeralda, tel: (24) 430 090*, www.meliacuba.com.com. This all-inclusive resort is the best in the area and one of the most luxurious hotels in Cuba, situated on a pretty bay. Four very good restaurants including Japanese and Creole.

Santiago de Cuba

Hotel Casa Granda $$$ *Heredia, 201 (on Parque Céspedes), tel: (22) 686 600/653 021*, www.galahotels.com. A grand white building in the heart of Santiago, overlooking the main plaza, this classic hotel is a great place for people-watching, but the rooms are tired and dingy. In its heyday Joe

Louis and Graham Greene's 'Man in Havana' stayed here. Terrace bar with great views. 58 rooms.

Hotel E San Basilio $$ *San Basilio 403 e/ Calvario y Carnicería, tel: (22) 651 702.* Central and convenient for shops and sites of interest, this boutique hotel is simple but charming. Restaurant, lobby bar, and only 8 rooms.

Meliá Santiago de Cuba $$$$ *Av. de las Américas y Calle M, tel: (22) 647 777,* www.meliacuba.com. Santiago's most ostentatious hotel, 3km (2 miles) from the centre. Six bars, luxury pool, indulgent buffets and snazzy nightclub. 302 rooms.

Baracoa

Hotel El Castillo $$ *Calixto García, Loma del Paraíso, tel: (21) 645 165.* One of Cuba's most charming hotels, converted from one of Baracoa's old forts. Perched on a cliff, it has a fine pool, gardens, mountain views, helpful staff and spacious bedrooms. A real bargain. 34 rooms.

Hostal La Habanera $$ *Maceo 68 esq. Frank País, tel: (21) 645 273.* This pretty pink building in the town centre was converted to a hotel in 2003 and is designed on traditional lines with an internal courtyard and balconies. Small and stylish, it also has the best restaurant food in Baracoa. 10 rooms.

CASAS PARTICULARES (PRIVATE LODGINGS)
Havana

Casa Federico $ *Cárcel 156 e/ San Lázaro y Prado, Old Havana, tel: (7) 861 7817,* email: llanesrenta@yahoo.es. Spacious rooms in an apartment just off the Malecón. Good breakfasts, the only drawback is the climb up the 64 stairs. Friendly and helpful hosts.

Evora Rodríguez $ *Prado 20 e/. San Lázaro y Cárcel, Old Havana, tel: (7) 861 7932,* email: evorahabana@yahoo.com. Amazing apartment on ninth floor with tremendous views up the Prado and over the harbour to the fortresses. Huge rooms with large bathrooms, big windows open to sea breezes, making it light and airy. English spoken, good breakfast.

Melba and Alberto $ *Galiano 115, Apt 81, e/. Animas y Trocadero, Centro,* tel: (7) 863 5178, email: barracuda1752@yahoo.es. Rooms in an apartment on the eighth floor with great views from the balconies and worlds away from the down-at-heel street life of Centro. Comfortable rooms with use of kitchenette. Excellent meals offered.

Trinidad

Casa Colonial Muñoz $ *José Martí, 401, e/ Fidel Claro y Santiago Escobar,* tel: (41) 993 673, www.casa.trinidadphoto.com. Colonial house built in 1800 with a shady patio and roof terrace, and large rooms furnished with antiques. Knowledgeable English-speaking hosts with children, their pet dogs and horse. One of the finest *casas* in Cuba. Horse riding can be arranged.

Casa López-Santander $ *Camilo Cienfuegos 313, e/ Jesús Menéndez y Julio Antonio Mella,* tel: (41) 993 541. Rooms in an attractive home dating from 1916, with a porch and striking neoclassical facade. Two blocks from Plaza Santa Ana; a 10-minute walk to the Plaza Mayor. Parking, and pleasant patio area.

Hostal Isabel Cristina Prada $ *Fernando Echerri 31, esq. Patricio Lumumba,* tel: (41) 993 054. A colonial house in the centre, near Plaza Mayor. One room has its own street entrance. It's in the main party street, though, so not good if you want an early night.

Santiago de Cuba

Casa Colonial Maruchi $ *San Félix 357 e/. San Germán y Trinidad,* tel: (22) 620 767, email: maruchib@yahoo.es. Ideal location in the heart of the old city, lovely colonial house around central courtyard garden. The two guest rooms have high ceilings, exposed timbers and contemporary décor. English spoken.

Casa Colonial Tania $ *Santa Rita 101, e/ Padre Pico y Callejón Santiago,* tel: *(22) 624 490,* email: aquiles@cultstgo.cult.cu. Central yet quiet colonial house with high ceilings. Two rooms, each with bathroom, one double, one twin, fridge, air conditioning, and terrace with harbour views. Meals available.

Casa Dulce $ *San Basilio, 552, esq. Clarín,* tel: *(22) 625 479,* email: gdcastillo20@yahoo.es. Apartment upstairs on the corner, with large windows to catch the breeze. Comfortable room, charming English-speaking hostess, and a pleasant roof terrace with spectacular views of the city.

Viñales

Villa Los Pinos $ *Salvador Cisneros, 36,* tel: *(48) 796 097.* Colonial house built in 1892, on the main street. The bedroom has independent access, two double beds, air conditioning and a good bathroom. English and French spoken by knowledgeable couple.

Santa Clara

Casa Mercy $ San *Cristóbal 4 e/. Cuba y Colón,* tel: *(42) 216 941,* email: arnaldomm@uclv.edu.cu. Charming hosts offer two spacious rooms overlooking the street in this comfortable house which is very central. Pleasant roof terrace for cocktails, excellent food offered and any diet accommodated.

Hostal Florida Center $ *Candelaria, 56 e/ Colón y Maceo,* tel: *(42) 208 161.* Colonial house on one level around a leafy courtyard. The charming host is an excellent cook. The rooms contain antique furniture but have modern luxuries as well.

Baracoa

Casa Colonial Lucy $ *Céspedes, 29 e/ Rubert López y Maceo,* tel: *(21) 643 548.* Pretty colonial house run by the efficient Lucy, who can arrange excursions and knows what is going on. Lovely rooms and a pleasant roof terrace with terrific views over the town to the sea. Good food available, local specialities served.

DICTIONARY

ENGLISH–SPANISH

adj adjective **adv** adverb **BE** British English **n** noun **prep** preposition **v** verb

A

abbey la abadía
accept v aceptar
access el acceso
accident el accidente
accommodation el alojamiento
account la cuenta
acupuncture la acupuntura
adapter el adaptador
address la dirección
admission la entrada
after después;
~**noon** la tarde;
~**shave** el bálsamo para después del afeitado
age la edad
agency la agencia
AIDS el sida
air el aire; ~
conditioning el aire acondicionado;
~ **pump** el aire;
~**line** la compañía aérea; ~**mail** el correo aéreo; ~**plane** el avión; ~**port** el aeropuerto
aisle el pasillo; ~ **seat** el asiento de pasillo
allergic alérgico; ~
reaction la reacción alérgica

allow v permitir
alone solo
alter v (clothing) hacer un arreglo
alternate route el otro camino
aluminum foil el papel de aluminio
amazing increíble
ambulance la ambulancia
American estadounidense
amusement park el parque de atracciones
anemic anémico
anesthesia la anestesia
animal el animal
ankle el tobillo
antibiotic el antibiótico
antiques store la tienda de -antigüedades
antiseptic cream la crema antiséptica
anything algo
apartment el apartamento
appendix (body part) el apéndice
appetizer el aperitivo
appointment la cita
arcade el salón de juegos recreativos

area code el prefijo
arm el brazo
aromatherapy la aromaterapia
around (the corner) doblando (la esquina)
arrivals (airport) las llegadas
arrive v llegar
artery la arteria
arthritis la artritis
arts las letras
Asian asiático
aspirin la aspirina
asthmatic asmático
ATM el cajero automático
attack el asalto
attend v asistir
attraction (place) el sitio de interés
attractive guapo
Australia Australia
Australian australiano
automatic automático;
~ **car** coche automático
available disponible

B

baby el bebé; ~
bottle el biberón;
~ **wipe** la toallita;
~**sitter** el/la canguro
back la espalda;

~**ache** el dolor de espalda; ~**pack** la mochila
bag la maleta
baggage el equipaje;
~ **claim** la recogida de equipajes; ~
ticket el talón de equipaje
bakery la panadería
ballet el ballet
bandage la tirita
bank el banco
bar el bar
barbecue la barbacoa
barber la peluquería de caballeros
baseball el béisbol
basket (grocery store) la cesta
basketball el baloncesto
bathroom el baño
battery (car) la batería
battery la pila
battleground el campo de batalla
be v ser, estar
beach la playa
beautiful precioso
bed la cama; ~ **and breakfast** la pensión
begin v empezar
before antes de

beginner principiante
behind detrás de
beige beis
belt el cinturón
berth la litera
best el/la mejor
better mejor
bicycle la bicicleta
big grande
bigger más grande
bike route el sendero
para bicicletas
bikini el biquini; **~ wax** la depilación
de las ingles
bill v (charge) cobrar;
~ n (money) el bil-
lete; **~** n (of sale) el
recibo
bird el pájaro
birthday el
cumpleaños
black negro
bladder la vejiga
bland soso
blanket la manta
bleed v sangrar
blood la sangre; **~ pressure** la tensión
arterial
blouse la blusa
blue azul
board v embarcar
boarding pass la
tarjeta de embarque
boat el barco
bone el hueso
book el libro;
~store la librería
boots las botas
boring aburrido
botanical garden el
jardín botánico
bother v molestar

bottle la botella; **~ opener** el abrebotellas
bowl el cuenco
box la caja
boxing match la pelea
de boxeo
boy el niño;
~friend el novio
bra el sujetador
bracelet la pulsera
brakes (car) los frenos
break v romper
break-in (burglary)
el allanamiento de
morada
breakdown la avería
breakfast el desayuno
breast el seno;
~feed dar el pecho
breathe v respirar
bridge el puente
briefs (clothing) los
calzoncillos
bring v traer
British británico
broken roto
brooch el broche
broom la escoba
brother el hermano
brown marrón
bug el insecto
building el edificio
burn v (CD) grabar
bus el autobús; **~ station** la estación de
autobuses; **~ stop** la
parada de autobús; **~ ticket** el billete de
autobús; **~ tour** el
recorrido en autobús
business los negocios;
~ card la tarjeta de
negocios; **~ cent-**

er el centro de
negocios; **~ class** la
clase preferente;
~ hours el horario
de atención al público
butcher el carnicero
buttocks las nalgas
buy v comprar
bye adiós

C

cabaret el cabaré
cabin (house) la
cabaña; **~ (ship)** el
camarote
cable car el teleférico
cafe la cafetería
call v llamar; **~** n la
llamada
calories las calorías
camera la cámara;
digital ~ la cámara
digital; **~ case** la
funda para la cámara;
~ store la tienda de
fotografía
camp v acampar; **~ stove** el hornillo;
~site el cámping
can opener el
abrelatas
Canada Canadá
Canadian canadiense
cancel v cancelar
candy el caramelo
canned goods las
conservas
canyon el cañón
car el coche; **~ hire [BE]** el alquiler de
coches; **~ park [BE]**
el aparcamiento;
~ rental el alquiler
de coches; **~ seat** el

asiento de niño
carafe la garrafa
card la tarjeta; **ATM ~** la tarjeta de
cajero automático;
credit ~ la tarjeta de
crédito; **debit ~** la
tarjeta de débito;
phone ~ la tarjeta
telefónica
**carry-on (piece of
hand luggage)** el
equipaje de mano
cart (grocery store) el
carrito; **~ (luggage)** el
carrito para el equipaje
carton el cartón; **~ of
cigarettes** el cartón
de tabaco
case (amount) la caja
cash v cobrar; **~** n
el efectivo; **~ ad-
vance** sacar dinero
de la tarjeta
cashier el cajero
casino el casino
castle el castillo
cathedral la catedral
cave la cueva
CD el CD
cell phone el teléfono
móvil
Celsius el grado
centígrado
centimeter el
centímetro
certificate el
certificado
chair la silla; **~ lift** el
telesilla
change v (buses)
cambiar; **~** n (money)
el cambio
charcoal el carbón

charge v (credit card) cobrar; ~ n (cost) el precio

cheap barato

cheaper más barato

check v (on something) revisar; ~ v (luggage) facturar; ~ n (payment) el cheque; ~-in (airport) la facturación; ~-in (hotel) el registro; ~ing account la cuenta corriente; ~-out (hotel) la salida

Cheers! ¡Salud!

chemical toilet el váter químico

chemist [BE] la farmacia

cheque [BE] el cheque

chest (body part) el pecho; ~ pain el dolor de pecho

chewing gum el chicle

child el niño; ~ seat la silla para niños

children's menu el menú para niños

children's portion la ración para niños

Chinese chino

chopsticks los palillos chinos

church la iglesia

cigar el puro

cigarette el cigarrillo

class la clase; **business** ~ la clase preferente; **economy** ~ la clase económica; **first** ~ la primera clase

classical music la música clásica

clean v limpiar; ~ adj limpio; ~ing product el producto de limpieza; ~ing supplies los productos de limpieza

clear v (on an ATM) borrar

cliff el acantilado

cling film [BE] el film transparente

close v (a shop) cerrar

closed cerrado

clothing la ropa; ~ store la tienda de ropa

club la discoteca

coat el abrigo

coffee shop la cafetería

coin la moneda

colander el escurridor

cold n (sickness) el catarro; ~ adj (temperature) frío

colleague el compañero de trabajo

cologne la colonia

color el color

comb el peine

come v venir

complaint la queja

computer el ordenador

concert el concierto; ~ hall la sala de conciertos

condition (medical) el estado de salud

conditioner el suavizante

condom el preservativo

conference la conferencia

confirm v confirmar

congestion la congestión

connect v (internet) conectarse

connection (internet) la conexión; ~ (flight) la conexión de vuelo

constipated estreñido

consulate el consulado

consultant el consultor

contact v ponerse en contacto con

contact lens la lentilla de contacto; ~ solution el líquido de lentillas de contacto

contagious contagioso

convention hall el salón de congresos

conveyor belt la cinta transportadora

cook v cocinar

cooking gas el gas butano

cool (temperature) frío

copper el cobre

corkscrew el sacacorchos

cost v costar

cot el catre

cotton el algodón

cough v toser; ~ n la tos

country code el código de país

cover charge la entrada

crash v (car) estrellarse

cream (ointment) la pomada

credit card la tarjeta de crédito

crew neck el cuello redondo

crib la cuna

crystal el cristal

cup la taza

currency la moneda; ~ exchange el cambio de divisas; ~ exchange office la casa de cambio

current account [BE] la cuenta corriente

customs las aduanas

cut v (hair) cortar; ~ n (injury) el corte

cute mono

cycling el ciclismo

D

damage v causar daño

damaged ha sufrido daños

dance v bailar; ~ club la discoteca

dangerous peligroso

dark oscuro

date (calendar) la fecha

day el día

deaf sordo

debit card la tarjeta de débito

deck chair la tumbona

declare v declarar

decline v (credit card) rechazar

deeply hondo

degrees (temperature) los grados

delay v retrasarse

delete v (**computer**) borrar
delicatessen la charcutería
delicious delicioso
denim tela vaquero
dentist el dentista
denture la dentadura
deodorant el desodorante
department store los grandes almacenes
departures (airport) las salidas
deposit v depositar; ~ n (**bank**) el depósito bancario; ~ v (**reserve a room**) la fianza
desert el desierto
dessert el postre
detergent el detergente
develop v (**film**) revelar
diabetic diabético
dial v marcar
diamond el diamante
diaper el pañal
diarrhea la diarrea
diesel el diesel
difficult difícil
digital digital; ~ **camera** la cámara digital; ~ **photos** las fotos digitales; ~ **prints** las fotos digitales
dining room el comedor
dinner la cena
direction la dirección
dirty sucio
disabled discapacitado; ~ **accessible**

[BE] el acceso para discapacitados
discharge (bodily fluid) la secreción
disconnect (computer) desconectar
discount el descuento
dish (kitchen) el plato; ~**washer** el lavavajillas; ~**washing liquid** el líquido lavavajillas
display v mostrar; ~ **case** la vitrina
disposable desechable; ~ **razor** la cuchilla desechable
dive v bucear
diving equipment el equipo de buceo
divorce v divorciar
dizzy mareado
doctor el médico
doll la muñeca
dollar (U.S.) el dólar
domestic nacional; ~ **flight** el vuelo nacional
door la puerta
dormitory el dormitorio
double bed la cama de matrimonio
downtown el centro
dozen la docena
drag lift el telesquí
dress (piece of clothing) el vestido; ~ **code** las normas de vestuario
drink v beber; ~ n la bebida; ~ **menu** la carta de bebidas;

~**ing water** el agua potable
drive v conducir
driver's license number el número de permiso de conducir
drop (medicine) la gota
drowsiness la somnolencia
dry cleaner la tintorería
dubbed doblada
during durante
duty (tax) impuesto; ~-**free** libre de impuestos
DVD el DVD

E

ear la oreja; ~**ache** el dolor de oído
earlier más temprano
early temprano
earrings los pendientes
east el este
easy fácil
eat v comer
economy class la clase económica
elbow el codo
electric outlet el enchufe eléctrico
elevator el ascensor
e-mail v enviar un correo electrónico; ~ n el correo electrónico; ~ **address** la dirección de correo electrónico
emergency la emergencia; ~ **exit** la salida de urgencia

empty v vaciar
enamel (jewelry) el esmalte
end v terminar
English el inglés
engrave v grabar
enjoy v disfrutar
enter v entrar
entertainment el entretenimiento
entrance la entrada
envelope el sobre
equipment el equipo
escalators las escaleras mecánicas
e-ticket el billete electrónico
EU resident el/la residente de la UE
euro el euro
evening la noche
excess el exceso
exchange v (**money**) cambiar; ~ v (**goods**) devolver; ~ n (**place**) la casa de cambio; ~ **rate** el tipo de cambio
excursion la excursión
excuse v (**to get past**) pedir perdón; ~ v (**to get attention**) disculparse
exhausted agotado
exit v salir; ~ n la salida
expensive caro
expert (skill level) experto
exposure (film) la foto
express rápido; ~ **bus** el autobús rápido; ~ **train** el tren rápido

extension (phone) la extensión
extra adicional; **~ large** equis ele (XL)
extract v **(tooth)** extraer
eye el ojo
eyebrow wax la depilación de cejas

F

face la cara
facial la limpieza de cutis
family la familia
fan (appliance) el ventilador; **~ (souvenir)** el abanico
far lejos; **~sighted** hipermétrope
farm la granja
fast rápido; **~food** la comida rápida
faster más rápido
fat free sin grasa
father el padre
fax v enviar un fax; **~** n el fax; **~number** el número de fax
fee la tasa
feed v alimentar
ferry el ferry
fever la fiebre
field (sports) el campo
fill v llenar; **~out** v **(form)** rellenar
filling (tooth) el empaste
film (camera) el carrete
fine (fee for breaking law) la multa

finger el dedo; **~nail** la uña del dedo
fire fuego; **~ department** los bomberos; **~door** la puerta de incendios
first primero; **~class** la primera clase
fit (clothing) quedar bien
fitting room el probador
fix v **(repair)** reparar
flashlight la linterna
flight el vuelo
floor el suelo
flower la flor
folk music la música folk
food la comida
foot el pie
football [BE] el fútbol
for para/por
forecast el pronóstico
forest el bosque
fork el tenedor
form el formulario
formula (baby) la fórmula infantil
fort el fuerte
fountain la fuente
free gratuito
freezer el congelador
fresh fresco
friend el amigo
frying pan la sartén
full completo; **~service** el servicio completo; **~time** a tiempo completo

G

game el partido
garage (parking) el garaje; **~ (repair)** el taller
garbage bag la bolsa de basura
gas la gasolina; **~ station** la gasolinera
gate (airport) la puerta
gay gay; **~ bar** el bar gay; **~ club** la discoteca gay
gel (hair) la gomina
get to v ir a
get off v **(a train/bus/ subway)** bajarse
gift el regalo; **~ shop** la tienda de regalos
girl la niña; **~friend** la novia
give v dar
glass (drinking) el vaso; **~ (material)** el vidrio
glasses las gafas
go v **(somewhere)** ir a
gold el oro
golf golf; **~ course** el campo de golf; **~ tournament** el torneo de golf
good n el producto; **~** adj bueno; **~afternoon** buenas tardes; **~evening** buenas noches; **~ morning** buenos días; **~bye** adiós
gram el gramo
grandchild el nieto

grandparent el abuelo
gray gris
green verde
grocery store el supermercado
ground la tierra; **~floor** la planta baja; **~cloth** la tela impermeable
group el grupo
guide el guía; **~book** la guía; **~ dog** el perro guía
gym el gimnasio
gynecologist el ginecólogo

H

hair el pelo; **~ dryer** el secador de pelo; **~salon** la peluquería; **~brush** el cepillo de pelo; **~cut** el corte de pelo; **~spray** la laca; **~style** el peinado; **~stylist** el estilista
half medio; **~ hour** la media hora; **~kilo** el medio kilo
hammer el martillo
hand la mano; **~ luggage [BE]** el equipaje de mano; **~bag [BE]** el bolso
handicapped discapacitado; **~accessible** el acceso para discapacitados
hangover la resaca
happy feliz
hat el sombrero
have v tener

head (body part) la cabeza; **~ache** el dolor de cabeza; **~phones** los cascos
health la salud; **~ food store** la tienda de alimentos naturales
heart el corazón; **~ condition** padecer del corazón
heat v calentar; **~** n el calor
heater [heating BE] la calefacción
hello hola
helmet el casco
help v ayudar; **~** n la ayuda
here aquí
hi hola
high alto; **~chair** la trona; **~way** la autopista
hiking boots las botas de montaña
hill la colina
hire v [BE] alquilar; **~ car [BE]** el coche de alquiler
hitchhike v hacer autostop
hockey el hockey
holiday [BE] las vacaciones
horse track el hipódromo
hospital el hospital
hostel el albergue
hot (temperature) caliente; **~ (spicy)** picante; **~ spring** el agua termale; **~ water** el

agua caliente
hotel el hotel
hour la hora
house la casa; **~hold goods** los artículos para el hogar; **~keeping services** el servicio de limpieza de habitaciones
how (question) cómo; **~ much (question)** cuánto cuesta
hug v abrazar
hungry hambriento
hurt v **(have pain)** tener dolor
husband el marido

I

ibuprofen el ibuprofeno
ice el hielo; **~ hockey** el hockey sobre hielo
icy adj helado
identification el documento de identidad
ill v **(to feel)** encontrarse mal
in dentro
include v incluir
indoor pool la piscina cubierta
inexpensive barato
infected infectado
information (phone) el número de teléfono de información; **~ desk** el mostrador de información
insect el insecto; **~ bite** la picadura de

insecto; **~ repellent** el repelente de insectos
insert v introducir
insomnia el insomnio
instant message el mensaje instantáneo
insulin la insulina
insurance el seguro; **~ card** la tarjeta de seguro; **~ company** la compañía de seguros
interesting interesante
intermediate el nivel intermedio
international (airport area) internacional; **~ flight** el vuelo internacional; **~ student card** la tarjeta internacional de estudiante
internet la internet; **~ cafe** el cibercafé; **~ service** el servicio de internet; **wireless ~** el acceso inalámbrico
interpreter el/la intérprete
intersection el cruce
intestine el intestino
introduce v presentar
invoice [BE] la factura
Ireland Irlanda
Irish irlandés
iron v planchar; **~** n **(clothes)** la plancha
Italian italiano

J

jacket la chaqueta
jar el bote

jaw la mandíbula
jazz el jazz; **~ club** el club de jazz
jeans los vaqueros
jet ski la moto acuática
jeweler la joyería
jewelry las joyas
join v acompañar a
joint (body part) la articulación

K

key la llave; **~ card** la llave electrónica; **~ ring** el llavero
kiddie pool la piscina infantil
kidney (body part) el riñón
kilo el kilo; **~gram** el kilogramo; **~meter** el kilómetro
kiss v besar
kitchen la cocina; **~ foil [BE]** el papel de aluminio
knee la rodilla
knife el cuchillo

L

lace el encaje
lactose intolerant alérgico a la lactosa
lake el lago
large grande; **~er** más grande
last último
late (time) tarde; **~er** más tarde
launderette [BE] la lavandería
laundromat la lavandería

laundry la colada; **~ facility** la lavandería; **~ service** el servicio de lavandería
lawyer el abogado
leather el cuero
to leave v salir
left (direction) la izquierda
leg la pierna
lens la lente
less menos
lesson la lección
letter la carta
library la biblioteca
life la vida; **~ jacket** el chaleco salvavidas; **~guard** el socorrista
lift n (overhead) la luz; v (cigarette) dar fuego; **~bulb** la bombilla
lighter el mechero
like v gustar; **I like** me gusta
line (train) la línea
linen el lino
lip el labio
liquor store la tienda de bebidas alcohólicas
liter el litro
little pequeño
live v vivir
liver (body part) el hígado
loafers los mocasines

local de la zona
lock v cerrar; **~** n el cerrojo
locker la taquilla
log on v (computer) iniciar sesión
log off v (computer) cerrar sesión
long largo; **~ sleeves** las mangas largas; **~-sighted [BE]** hipermétrope
look v mirar
lose v (something) perder
lost perdido; **~ and found** la oficina de objetos perdidos
lotion la crema hidratante
louder más alto
love v querer; **~** n el amor
low bajo; **~er** más bajo
luggage el equipaje; **~ cart** el carrito de equipaje; **~ locker** la consigna automática; **~ ticket** el talón de equipaje; **hand ~ [BE]** el equipaje de mano
lunch la comida
lung el pulmón

M

magazine la revista
magnificent magnífico
mail v enviar por correo; **~** n el correo; **~box** el buzón de correo
main principal; **~**

attractions los principales sitios de interés; **~ course** el plato principal
make up a prescription v [BE] despachar medicamentos
mall el centro comercial
man el hombre
manager el gerente
manicure la manicura
manual car el coche con transmisión manual
map el mapa
market el mercado
married casado
marry v casarse
mass (church service) la misa
massage el masaje
match la cerilla
meal la comida
measure v (someone) medir
measuring cup la taza medidora
measuring spoon la cuchara medidora
mechanic el mecánico
medicine el medicamento
medium (size) mediano
meet v (someone) conocer
meeting la reunión; **~ room** la sala de reuniones
membership card la tarjeta de socio

memorial (place) el monumento conmemorativo
memory card la tarjeta de memoria
mend v zurcir
menstrual cramps los dolores menstruales
menu la carta
message el mensaje
meter (parking) el parquímetro
microwave el microondas
midday [BE] el mediodía
midnight la medianoche
mileage el kilometraje
mini-bar el minibar
minute el minuto
missing desaparecido
mistake el error
mobile móvil; **~ home** la caravana; **~ phone [BE]** el teléfono móvil
mobility la movilidad
money el dinero
month el mes
mop la fregona
moped el ciclomotor
more más
morning la mañana
mosque la mezquita
mother la madre
motion sickness el mareo
motor el motor; **~ boat** la lancha motora; **~cycle** la motocicleta; **~way [BE]** la autopista

mountain la montaña;
~ bike la bicicleta
de montaña
mousse (hair) la
espuma para el pelo
mouth n la boca
movie la película; **~
theater** el cine
mug v asaltar
muscle (body part) el
músculo
museum el museo
music la música; **~
store** la tienda de
música

N

nail la u¯na; **~ file** la
lima de uñas; **~
salon** el salon de
manicura
name el nombre
napkin la servilleta
nappy [BE] el pañale
nationality la
nacionalidad
nature preserve la
reserva natural
(be) nauseous v tener
náuseas
near cerca;
~-sighted miope;
~by cerca de aquí
neck el cuello
necklace el collar
need v necesitar
newspaper el
periódico
newsstand el quiosco
next próximo
nice adj amable
night la noche; **~club**
la discoteca
no no

non sin; **~-alco-
holic** sin alcohol;
~-smoking para no
fumadores
noon el mediodía
north el norte
nose la nariz
note [BE] el billete
nothing nada
notify v avisar
**novice (skill
level)** principiante
now ahora
number el número
nurse el enfermero/la
enfermera

O

office la oficina; **~
hours (doctor's)** las
horas de consulta;
**~ hours (other of-
fices)** el horario de
oficina
off-licence [BE] la
tienda de bebidas
alcohólicas
oil el aceite
OK de acuerdo
old adj viejo
on the corner en la
esquina
once una vez
one uno; **~-way
ticket** el billete
de ida; **~-way
street** la calle de
sentido único
only solamente
open v abrir; **~** adj
abierto
opera la ópera; **~
house** el teatro de
la ópera

opposite frente a
optician el oculista
orange (color) naranja
orchestra la orquesta
order v pedir
outdoor pool la
piscina exterior
outside fuera
over sobre; **~
the counter
(medication)** sin
receta; **~look
(scenic place)** el
mirador; **~night** por
la noche
oxygen treatment la
oxigenoterapia

P

p.m. de la tarde
pacifier el chupete
pack v hacer las
maletas
package el paquete
paddling pool [BE] la
piscina infantil
pad [BE] la compresa
pain el dolor
pajamas los pijamas
palace el palacio
pants los pantalones
pantyhose las medias
paper el papel; **~
towel** el papel de
cocina
paracetamol [BE] el
paracetamol
park v aparcar;
~ n el parque;
~ing garage el
párking; **~ing lot** el
aparcamiento
**parliament build-
ing** el palacio de las

cortes
part (for car) la pieza;
~-time a tiempo
parcial
pass through v estar
de paso
passenger el pasajero
passport el pasaporte;
~ control el control
de pasaportes
password la
contraseña
pastry shop la
pastelería
path el camino
pay v pagar; **~
phone** el teléfono
público
**peak (of a moun-
tain)** la cima
pearl la perla
pedestrian el peatón
pediatrician el
pediatra
pedicure la pedicura
pen el bolígrafo
penicillin la penicilina
penis el pene
per por; **~ day** por
día; **~ hour** por
hora; **~ night** por
noche; **~ week** por
semana
perfume el perfume
period (menstrual) la
regla; **~ (of time)** la
época
permit v permitir
petite las tallas
pequeñas
petrol la gasolina; **~
station** la gaso-
linera
pewter el peltre

pharmacy la farmacia
phone v
   hacer una llamada;
   ~ n el teléfono; ~
   call la llamada de
   teléfono; ~ **card** la
   tarjeta telefónica; ~
   number el número
   de teléfono
photo la foto;
   ~**copy** la fotocopia;
   ~**graphy** la foto-
   grafía
pick up v (**some-
   thing**) recoger
picnic area la zona
   para picnic
piece el trozo
Pill (birth control) la
   píldora
pillow la almohada
**personal identifica-
   tion number
   (PIN)** la clave
pink rosa
piste la pista; ~
   map [BE] el mapa
   de pistas
pizzeria la pizzería
place v (**a bet**) hacer
   una apuesta
plane el avión
plastic wrap el film
   transparente
plate el plato
**platform [BE]
   (train)** el andén
platinum el platino
play v jugar; ~ n
   (**theater**) la obra de
   teatro; ~**ground** el
   patio de recreo;
   ~**pen** el parque
please por favor

pleasure el placer
plunger el desa-
   tascador
plus size la talla
   grande
pocket el bolsillo
poison el veneno
poles (skiing) los
   bastones
police la policía; ~
   report el certificado
   de la policía; ~ **station** la comisaría
pond el estanque
pool la piscina
pop music la música
   pop
portion la ración
post [BE] el correo;
   ~ **office** la oficina
   de correos; ~**box
   [BE]** el buzón de
   correos; ~**card** la
   tarjeta postal
pot la olla
pottery la cerámica
**pounds (British
   sterling)** las libras
   esterlinas
pregnant embarazada
prescribe v recetar
prescription la receta
press v (**cloth-
   ing**) planchar
price el precio
print v imprimir
problem el problema
produce las frutas y
   verduras; ~ **store** la
   frutería y verdulería
prohibit v prohibir
pronounce v
   pronunciar
public el público

pull v (**door sign**) tirar
purple morado
purse el bolso
push v (**door
   sign**) empujar;
   ~**chair [BE]** el
   cochecito de niño

Q

quality n la calidad
question la pregunta
quiet adj tranquilo

R

racetrack el circuito
   de carreras
racket (sports) la
   raqueta
**railway station
   [BE]** la estación de
   trenes
rain la lluvia;
   ~**coat** el chubas-
   quero; ~**forest** el
   bosque pluvial;
   ~**y** adv lluvioso
rap (music) el rap
rape v violar; ~ n la
   violación
rash la erupción
   cutánea
razor blade la hoja de
   afeitar
reach v localizar
ready listo
real auténtico
receipt el recibo
receive v recibir
reception la recepción
recharge v recargar
recommend v
   recomendar
recommendation la
   recomendación

recycle v reciclar
red rojo
refrigerator n la
   nevera
region la región
registered mail el
   correo certificado
regular normal
relationship la
   relación
rent v alquilar
rental car el coche de
   alquiler
repair v arreglar
repeat v repetir
reservation la
   reserva;
   ~ **desk** la taquilla
reserve v reservar
restaurant el
   restaurante
restroom el servicio
retired jubilado
return v (**some-
   thing**) devolver; ~ n
   [BE] la ida y vuelta
rib (body part) la
   costilla
right (direction) derecha; ~ **of way** prioridad de paso
ring el anillo
river n el río
road map el mapa de
   carreteras
rob v atracar
robbed atracado
romantic romántico
room la habitación;
   ~ **key** la llave de
   habitación; ~ **ser-
   vice** el servicio de
   habitaciones
round-trip ida y vuelta

route la ruta
rowboat la barca de remos
rubbish [BE] la basura; **~ bag [BE]** la bolsa de basura
rugby el rugby
ruins las ruinas
rush la prisa

S

sad triste
safe *n* la caja fuerte; **~** *adj* seguro
sales tax el IVA
same mismo
sandals las sandalias
sanitary napkin la compresa
saucepan el cazo
sauna la sauna
save (computer) guardar
savings (account) la cuenta de ahorro
scanner el escáner
scarf la bufanda
schedule *v* programar; **~** *n* el horario
school el colegio
science la ciencia
scissors las tijeras
sea el mar
seat el asiento
security la seguridad
see *v* ver
self-service el autoservicio
sell *v* vender
seminar el seminario
send *v* enviar
senior citizen jubilado
separated (marriage) -separado

serious serio
service (in a restaurant) el servicio
sexually transmitted disease (STD) la enfermedad de transmisión sexual
shampoo el champú
sharp afilado
shaving cream la crema de afeitar
sheet la sábana
ship *v* enviar
shirt la camisa
shoe store la zapatería
shoes los zapatos
shop *v* comprar
shopping ir de compras; **~ area** la zona de compras; **~ centre [BE]** el centro comercial; **~ mall** el centro comercial
short corto; **~ sleeves** las mangas cortas; **~s** los pantalones cortos; **~-sighted [BE]** miope
shoulder el hombro
show *v* enseñar
shower la ducha
shrine el santuario
sick enfermo
side el lado; **~ dish** la guarnición; **~ effect** el efecto secundario; **~ order** la guarnición
sightsee *v* hacer turismo
sightseeing tour el recorrido turístico

sign *v* **(name)** firmar
silk la seda
silver la plata
single (unmarried) soltero; **~ bed** la cama; **~ prints** una copia; **~ room** una habitación individual
sink el lavabo
sister la hermana
sit *v* sentarse
size la talla
skin la piel
skirt la falda
ski *v* esquiar; **~** *n* el esquí; **~ lift** el telesquí
sleep *v* dormir; **~er car** el coche cama; **~ing bag** el saco de dormir
slice *v* cortar en rodajas
slippers las zapatillas
slower más despacio
slowly despacio
small pequeño
smaller más pequeño
smoke *v* fumar
smoking (area) la zona de fumadores
snack bar la cafetería
sneakers las zapatillas de deporte
snorkeling equipment el equipo de esnórquel
snow la nieve; **~board** la tabla de snowboard; **~shoe** la raqueta de nieve; **~y** nevado
soap el jabón

soccer el fútbol
sock el calcetín
some alguno
soother [BE] el chupete
sore throat las anginas
sorry lo siento
south el sur
souvenir el recuerdo; **~ store** la tienda de recuerdos
spa el centro de salud y belleza
Spain España
Spanish el español
spatula la espátula
speak *v* hablar
special (food) la especialidad de la casa
specialist (doctor) el especialista
specimen el ejemplar
speeding el exceso de velocidad
spell *v* deletrear
spicy picante
spine (body part) la columna vertebral
spoon la cuchara
sports los deportes; **~ massage** el masaje deportivo
sporting goods store la tienda de deportes
sprain el esguince
square cuadrado; **~ kilometer** el kilómetro cuadrado; **~ meter** el metro cuadrado
stadium el estadio

stairs las escaleras
stamp v (a
  ticket) picar;
  ~ n (**postage**) el
  sello
start v empezar
starter [BE] el
  aperitivo
station la estación;
  bus ~ la estación
  de autobuses; **gas
  ~** la gasolinera;
  muster ~ [BE] el
  punto de reunión;
  petrol ~ [BE] la
  gasolinera; **subway
  ~** el metro; **train
  ~** la estación de tren
statue la estatua
stay v quedarse
steal v robar
steep empinado
sterling silver la
  plata esterlina
sting el escozor
stolen robado
stomach el estómago;
  ~ache el dolor de
  estómago
stop v pararse; ~ n la
  parada
storey [BE] la planta
stove el horno
straight recto
strange extraño
stream el arroyo
stroller el cochecito
student el estudiante
study v estudiar
stunning impresio-
  nante
subtitle el subtítulo
subway el metro; ~
  station la estación

de metro
suit el traje
suitcase la maleta
sun el sol; **~block** el
  protector solar total;
  ~burn la quemadura
  solar; **~glasses** las
  gafas de sol;
  ~ny soleado;
  ~screen el protec-
  tor solar; **~stroke**
  la insolación
super (**fuel**) súper;
  ~market el super-
  mercado
surfboard la tabla
  de surf
surgical spirit [BE] el
  alcohol etílico
swallow v tragar
sweater el jersey
sweatshirt la
  sudadera
sweet (**taste**) dulce;
  ~s [BE] los cara-
  melos
swelling la hinchazón
swim v nadar;
  ~suit el bañador
symbol (**keyboard**) el
  símbolo
synagogue la
  sinagoga

T

table la mesa
tablet (**medicine**) el
  comprimido
take v llevar; ~ **away**
  [BE] para llevar
tampon el tampón
tapas bar el bar de
  tapas
taste v probar

taxi el taxi
team el equipo
telephone el teléfono
temporary provisional
tennis el tenis
tent la tienda de
  campaña; ~ **peg** la
  estaca; ~ **pole** el
  mástil
terminal (**airport**) la
  terminal
terracotta la ter-
  racotta
terrible terrible
text v (**send a
  message**) enviar
  un mensaje de texto;
  ~ n (**message**) el
  texto
thank v dar las gracias
  a; ~ **you** gracias
that eso
theater el teatro
there ahí
thief el ladrón
thigh el muslo
thirsty sediento
this esto
throat la garganta
ticket el billete; ~
  office el despacho
  de billetes; **~ed pas-
  senger** el pasajero
  con billete
tie (**clothing**) la
  corbata
time el tiempo; **~table**
  [BE] el horario
tire la rueda
tired cansado
tissue el pañuelo de
  papel
tobacconist el
  estanco

today hoy
toe el dedo del pie;
  ~nail la uña del pie
toilet [BE] el servicio;
  ~ **paper** el papel
  higiénico
tomorrow mañana
tongue la lengua
tonight esta noche
too demasiado
tooth el diente;
  ~brush el cepillo de
  dientes; **~paste** la
  pasta de dientes
total (**amount**) el
  total
tough (**food**) duro
tourist el turista; ~ **information office** la
  oficina de turismo
tour el recorrido
  turístico
tow truck la grúa
towel la toalla
tower la torre
town la ciudad; ~ **hall**
  el ayuntamiento; ~
  map el mapa de
  ciudad; ~ **square** la
  plaza
toy el juguete; ~
  store la tienda de
  juguetes
track (**train**) el andén
traditional tradicional
traffic light el
  semáforo
trail la pista; ~
  map el mapa de
  la pista
trailer el remolque
train el tren; ~
  station la estación
  de tren

transfer *v* cambiar
translate *v* traducir
trash la basura
travel *v* viajar; ~ **agency** la agencia de viajes; ~ **sickness** el mareo; ~**er's check [cheque BE]** el cheque de viaje
tree el árbol
trim (hair cut) cortarse las puntas
trip el viaje
trolley [BE] el carrito
trousers [BE] los pantalones
T-shirt la camiseta
turn off *v* apagar
turn on *v* encender
TV la televisión
type *v* escribir a máquina
tyre [BE] la rueda

U

United Kingdom (U.K.) el Reino Unido
United States (U.S.) los Estados Unidos
ugly feo
umbrella el paraguas
unattended desatendido
unconscious inconsciente
underground [BE] el metro; ~ **station [BE]** la estación de metro
underpants [BE] los calzoncillos

understand *v* entender
underwear la ropa interior
university la universidad
unleaded (gas) la gasolina sin plomo
upper superior
urgent urgente
use *v* usar
username el nombre de usuario
utensil el cubierto

V

vacancy la habitación libre
vacation las vacaciones
vaccination la vacuna
vacuum cleaner la aspiradora
vaginal infection la infección vaginal
valid validez
valley el valle
valuable valioso
VAT [BE] el IVA
vegetarian vegetariano
vehicle registration el registro del coche
viewpoint [BE] el mirador
village el pueblo
vineyard la viña
visa (passport document) el visado
visit *v* visitar; ~**ing hours** el horario de visita
visually impaired la persona con

discapacidad visual
vitamin la vitamina
V-neck el cuello de pico
vomit *v* vomitar

W

wait *v* esperar; ~ *n* la espera; ~**ing room** la sala de espera
waiter el camarero
waitress la camarera
wake *v* despertarse; ~**up call** la llamada despertador
walk *v* caminar; ~ *n* la caminata; ~**ing route** la ruta de senderismo
wallet la cartera
warm *v* **(something)** calentar; ~ *adj* **(temperature)** calor
washing machine la lavadora
watch el reloj
waterfall la cascada
weather el tiempo
week la semana; ~**end** el fin de semana; ~**ly** semanal
welcome *v* acoger
well bien; ~**-rested** descansado
west el oeste
what (question) qué
wheelchair la silla de ruedas; ~ **ramp** la rampa para silla de ruedas
when (question) cuándo

where (question) dónde
white blanco; ~ **gold** el oro blanco
who (question) quién
widowed viudo
wife la mujer
window la ventana; ~ **case** el escaparate
windsurfer el surfista
wine list la carta de vinos
wireless inalámbrico; ~ **internet** el acceso inalámbrico a internet; ~ **internet service** el servicio inalámbrico a internet; ~ **phone** el teléfono móvil
with con
withdraw *v* retirar; ~**al (bank)** retirar fondos
without sin
woman la mujer
wool la lana
work *v* trabajar
wrap *v* envolver
wrist la muñeca
write *v* escribir

Y

year el año
yellow amarillo
yes sí
yesterday ayer
young joven
youth hostel el albergue juvenil

Z

zoo el zoológico

SPANISH–ENGLISH

A

a tiempo completo full-time
a tiempo parcial part-time
la abadía abbey
el abanico fan (souvenir)
abierto *adj* open
el abogado lawyer
abrazar *v* hug
el abrebotellas bottle opener
el abrelatas can opener
el abrigo coat
abrir *v* open
el abuelo grandparent
aburrido boring
acampar *v* camp
el acantilado cliff
el acceso access; **~ inalámbrico a internet** wireless internet; **~ para discapacitados** handicapped- [disabled-BE] accessible
el accidente accident
el aceite oil
aceptar *v* accept
acoger *v* welcome
acompañar a *v* join
la acupuntura acupuncture
el adaptador adapter
adicional extra
adiós goodbye
las aduanas customs
el aeropuerto airport
afilado sharp
la agencia agency; **~ de viajes** travel agency
agotado exhausted
el agua water; **~ caliente** hot water; **~ potable** drinking water
las aguas termales hot spring
ahí there
ahora now
el aire air, air pump; **~ acondicionado** air conditioning
el albergue hostel; **~ juvenil** youth hostel
alérgico allergic; **~ a la lactosa** lactose intolerant
algo anything
el algodón cotton
alguno some
alimentar *v* feed
el allanamiento de morada break-in (burglary)
la almohada pillow
el alojamiento accommodation
alquilar *v* rent [hire BE]; **el ~ de coches** car rental [hire BE]
alto high
amable nice
amarillo yellow
la ambulancia ambulance
el amigo friend
el amor *n* love
el andén track [platform BE] (train)
anémico anemic
la anestesia anesthesia
las anginas sore throat
el anillo ring
el animal animal
antes de before
el antibiótico antibiotic
el año year
apagar *v* turn off
el aparcamiento parking lot [car park BE]
aparcar *v* park
el apartamento apartment
el apéndice appendix (body part)
el aperitivo appetizer [starter BE]
aquí here
el árbol tree
la aromaterapia aromatherapy
arreglar *v* repair
el arroyo stream
la arteria artery
la articulación joint (body part)
los artículos goods; **~ para el hogar** household good
la artritis arthritis
asaltar *v* mug
el asalto attack
el ascensor elevator [lift BE]
asiático Asian
el asiento seat; **~ de niño** car seat; **~ de pasillo** aisle seat
asistir *v* attend
asmático asthmatic
la aspiradora vacuum cleaner
la aspirina aspirin
atracado robbed
atracar *v* rob
Australia Australia
australiano Australian
auténtico real
el autobús bus; **~ rápido** express bus
automático automatic
la autopista highway [motorway BE]
el autoservicio self-service
la avería breakdown
el avión airplane, plane
avisar *v* notify
ayer yesterday
la ayuda *n* help
ayudar *v* help
el ayuntamiento town hall
azul blue

B

bailar *v* dance
bajarse *v* get off (a train, bus, subway)

bajo low
el ballet ballet
el baloncesto basketball
el bálsamo para después del afeitado aftershave
el banco bank
el bañador swimsuit
el baño bathroom
el bar bar; **~ de tapas** tapas bar; **~ gay** gay bar
barato cheap, inexpensive
la barbacoa barbecue
la barca de remos rowboat
el barco boat
los bastones poles (skiing)
la basura trash [rubbish BE]
la batería battery (car)
el bebé baby
beber *v* drink
la bebida *n* drink
beis beige
el béisbol baseball
besar *v* kiss
el biberón baby bottle
la biblioteca library
la bicicleta bicycle; **~ de montaña** mountain bike
el billete *n* bill (money); **~** ticket; **~ de autobús** bus ticket; **~ de ida** one-way (ticket); **~ de ida y vuelta** round trip [return BE]; **~ electrónico** e-ticket

el biquini bikini
blanco white
la blusa blouse
la boca mouth
el bolígrafo pen
la bolsa de basura garbage [rubbish BE] bag
el bolsillo pocket
el bolso purse [handbag BE]
los bomberos fire department
la bombilla lightbulb
borrar *v* clear (on an ATM); **~** *v* delete (computer)
el bosque forest; **~ pluvial** rainforest
las botas boots; **~ de montaña** hiking boots
el bote jar
la botella bottle
el brazo arm
británico British
el broche brooch
bucear to dive
bueno *adj* good
buenas noches good evening
buenas tardes good afternoon
buenos días good morning
la bufanda scarf
el buzón de correo mailbox [postbox BE]

C

la cabaña cabin (house)
el cabaré cabaret

la cabeza head (body part)
la cafetería cafe, coffee shop, snack bar
la caja case (amount); **~ fuerte** *n* safe
el cajero cashier; **~ automático** ATM
el calcetín sock
la calefacción heater [heating BE]
calentar *v* heat, warm
la calidad quality
la calle de sentido único one-way street
calor hot, warm (temperature)
las calorías calories
los calzoncillos briefs [underpants BE] (clothing)
la cama single bed; **~ de matrimonio** double bed
la cámara camera; **~ digital** digital camera
la camarera waitress
el camarero waiter
el camarote cabin (ship)
cambiar *v* change, exchange, transfer
el cambio *n* change (money); **~ de divisas** currency exchange
caminar *v* walk
la caminata *n* walk
el camino path
la camisa shirt
la camiseta T-shirt
el cámping campsite

el campo field (sports); **~ de batalla** battleground; **~ de golf** golf course
Canadá Canada
canadiense Canadian
cancelar *v* cancel
el/la canguro babysitter
cansado tired
el cañón canyon
la cara face
los caramelos candy [sweets BE]
la caravana mobile home
el carbón charcoal
el carnicero butcher
caro expensive
el carrete film (camera)
el carrito cart [trolley BE] (grocery store); **~ de equipaje** luggage cart
la carta letter
la carta *n* menu; **~ de bebidas** drink menu; **~ para niños** children's menu; **~ de vinos** wine list
la cartera *n* wallet
el cartón carton; **~ de tabaco** carton of cigarettes
la casa house; **~ de cambio** currency exchange office
casado married
casarse *v* marry
la cascada waterfall
el casco helmet

los cascos headphones
el casino casino
el castillo castle
el catarro cold (sickness)
la catedral cathedral
el catre cot
causar daño v damage
el cazo saucepan
el CD CD
la cena dinner
el centímetro centimeter
el centro downtown area; **~ comercial** shopping mall [centre BE]; **~ de negocios** business center; **~ de salud y belleza** spa
el cepillo de pelo hair brush
la cerámica pottery
cerca near; **~ de aquí** nearby
la cerilla n match
cerrado closed
cerrar v close, lock; **~ sesión** v log off (computer)
el cerrojo n lock
el certificado certificate; **~ de la policía** police report
la cesta basket (grocery store)
el chaleco salvavidas life jacket
el champú shampoo
la chaqueta jacket
la charcutería delicatessen

el cheque n check [cheque BE] (payment); **~ de viaje** traveler's check [cheque BE]
el chicle chewing gum
chino Chinese
el chubasquero raincoat
el chupete pacifier [soother BE]
el cibercafé internet cafe
el ciclismo cycling
el ciclomotor moped
la ciencia science
el cigarrillo cigarette
la cima peak (of a mountain)
el cine movie theater
la cinta transportadora conveyor belt
el cinturón n belt
el circuito de carreras racetrack
la cita appointment
la ciudad town
la clase class; **~ económica** economy class; **~ preferente** business class
la clave personal identification number (PIN)
el club de jazz jazz club
cobrar v bill (charge); **~** v cash; **~** v charge (credit card)
el cobre copper
el coche n car; **~ de alquiler** rental [hire BE] car; **~ automáti-**

co automatic car; **~ cama** sleeper [sleeping BE] car; **~ con transmisión manual** manual car
el cochecito stroller [pushchair BE]
la cocina kitchen
cocinar v cook
el código de país country code
el codo elbow
la colada laundry
el colegio school
la colina hill
el collar necklace
la colonia cologne
el color color
la columna vertebral spine (body part)
el comedor dining room
comer v eat
la comida food, lunch, meal; **~ rápida** fast food
la comisaría police station
cómo how
el compañero de trabajo colleague
la compañía company; **~ aérea** airline; **~ de seguros** insurance company
comprar v buy, shop
la compresa sanitary napkin [pad BE]
el comprimido tablet (medicine)
con with; **~ plomo** leaded (gas)
el concierto concert

conducir v drive
conectarse v connect (internet)
la conexión connection (internet); **~ de vuelo** connection (flight)
la conferencia conference
confirmar v confirm
el congelador freezer
la congestión congestion
conocer v meet (someone)
la consigna automática luggage locker
el consulado Consulate
el consultor consultant
contagioso contagious
la contraseña password
el control de pasaportes passport control
el corazón heart
la corbata tie (clothing)
el correo n mail [post BE]; **~ aéreo** airmail; **~ certificado** registered mail; **~ electrónico** n e-mail
cortar v cut (hair); **~ en rodajas** to slice
cortarse las puntas v trim (hair cut)
el corte v cut (injury); **~ de pelo** haircut
corto short

costar v cost

la costilla rib (body part)

la crema cream; ~ antiséptica antiseptic cream; ~ de afeitar shaving cream; ~ hidratante lotion

el cristal crystal

el cruce intersection

cuándo when (question)

cuánto cuesta how much

el cubierto utensil

la cuchara spoon; ~ medidora measuring spoon

la cucharadita teaspoon

la cuchilla desechable disposable razor

el cuchillo knife

el cuello neck; ~ de pico V-neck; ~ redondo crew neck

el cuenco bowl

la cuenta account; ~ de ahorro savings account; ~ corriente checking [current BE] account

cuero leather

la cueva cave

el cumpleaños birthday

la cuna crib

D

dar to give; ~ el pecho breastfeed; ~ fuego light (ciga-

rette); ~ las gracias a v thank

de from, of; ~ acuerdo OK; ~ la mañana a.m.; ~ la tarde p.m.; ~ la zona local

declarar v declare

el dedo finger; ~ del pie toe

deletrear v spell

delicioso delicious

la dentadura denture

el dentista dentist

dentro in

la depilacion wax; ~ de cejas eyebrow wax; ~ de las ingles bikini wax

deportes sports

depositar v deposit

el depósito bancario deposit (bank)

la derecha right (direction)

el desatascador plunger

desatendido unattended

el desayuno breakfast

descansado wellrested

desconectar v disconnect (computer)

el descuento discount

desechable disposable

el desierto desert

el desodorante deodorant

despachar medicamentos v fill [make up BE] a prescription

el despacho de billetes ticket office

despacio slowly

despertarse v wake

después after

el detergente detergent

detrás de behind (direction)

devolver v exchange, return (goods)

el día day

diabético diabetic

el diamante diamond

la diarrea diarrhea

el diente tooth

el diesel diesel

difícil difficult

digital digital

el dinero money

la dirección direction

la dirección address; ~ de correo electrónico e-mail address

discapacitado handicapped [disabled BE]

la discoteca club (dance, night); ~ gay gay club

disculparse v excuse (to get attention)

disfrutar v enjoy

disponible available

divorciar v divorce

doblada dubbed

doblando (la esquina) around (the corner)

la docena dozen

el documento de identidad identification

el dólar dollar (U.S.)

el dolor pain; ~ de cabeza headache; ~ de espalda backache; ~ de estómago stomachache; ~ de oído earache; ~ de pecho chest pain

los dolores menstruales menstrual cramps

dónde where (question)

dormir v sleep

el dormitorio dormitory

la ducha shower

dulce sweet (taste)

durante during

el DVD DVD

E

la edad age

el edificio building

el efectivo cash

el efecto secundario side effect

el ejemplar specimen

embarazada pregnant

embarcar v board

la emergencia emergency

el empaste filling (tooth)

empezar v begin, start

empinado steep

empujar v push (door sign)

en la esquina on the corner

el encaje lace

encender v turn on

el enchufe eléctrico electric outlet

encontrarse mal *v* be ill

la enfermedad de transmisión sexual sexually transmitted disease (STD)

el enfermero/la enfermera nurse

enfermo sick

enseñar *v* show

entender *v* understand

la entrada admission/ cover charge; ~ entrance

entrar *v* enter

el entretenimiento entertainment

enviar *v* send, ship; ~ **por correo** *v* mail; ~ **un correo electrónico** *v* e-mail; ~ **un fax** *v* fax; ~ **un mensaje de texto** *v* text (send a message)

envolver *v* wrap

la época period (of time)

el equipaje luggage [baggage BE]; ~ **de mano** carry-on (piece of hand luggage)

el equipo team

el equipo equipment; ~ **de buceo** diving equipment; ~ **de esnórquel** snorkeling equipment

equis ele (XL) extra large

el error mistake

la erupción cutánea rash

las escaleras stairs; ~ **mecánicas** escalators

el escáner scanner

el escaparate window case

la escoba broom

el escozor sting

escribir *v* write; ~ **a máquina** *v* type

el escurridor colander

el esguince sprain

el esmalte enamel (jewelry)

eso that

la espalda back

España Spain

el español Spanish

la espátula spatula

la especialidad de la casa special (food)

el especialista specialist (doctor)

la espera *n* wait

esperar *v* wait

la espuma para el pelo mousse (hair)

el esquí *n* ski

esquiar *v* ski

los esquís acuáticos water skis

esta noche tonight

la estaca tent peg

la estación station; ~ **de autobuses** bus station; ~ **de metro** subway [underground BE] station; ~ **de tren** train [railway BE] station

el estadio stadium

el estado de salud condition (medical)

los Estados Unidos United States (U.S.)

estadounidense American

el estanco tobacconist

el estanque pond

estar *v* be; ~ **de paso** *v* pass through

la estatua statue

el este east

el estilista hairstylist

esto this

el estómago stomach

estrellarse *v* crash (car)

estreñido constipated

estudiando studying

el estudiante student

estudiar *v* study

el euro euro

el exceso excess; ~ **de velocidad** speeding

la excursión excursion

experto expert (skill level)

la extensión extension (phone)

extraer *v* extract (tooth)

extraño strange

F

fácil *adj* easy

la factura bill [invoice BE]

la facturación check-in (airport)

facturar check (luggage)

la falda skirt

la familia family

la farmacia pharmacy [chemist BE]

el fax *n* fax

la fecha date (calendar)

feliz *adj* happy

feo *adj* ugly

el ferry ferry

la fianza deposit (to reserve a room)

la fiebre fever

el film transparente plastic wrap [cling film BE]

el fin de semana weekend

firmar *v* sign (name)

la flor flower

la fórmula infantil formula (baby)

el formulario form

la foto exposure (film); ~ photo; ~**copia** photocopy; ~**grafía** photography; ~ **digital** digital photo

la fregona mop

los frenos brakes (car)

frente a opposite

fresco fresh

frío *adj* cold (temperature)

las frutas y verduras produce

la frutería y verdulería produce store

el fuego fire

la fuente fountain

fuera outside

el fuerte fort

fumar *v* smoke

la funda para la cámara camera case
el fútbol soccer [football BE]

G

las gafas glasses; **~ de sol** sunglasses
el garaje garage (parking)
la garganta throat
la garrafa carafe
el gas butano cooking gas
la gasolina gas [petrol BE]; **~ sin plomo** unleaded gas
la gasolinera gas [petrol BE] station
gay gay
el gerente manager
el gimnasio gym
el ginecólogo gynecologist
la gomina gel (hair)
la gota drop (medicine)
grabar v burn (CD); **~** v engrave
gracias thank you
los grados degrees (temperature); **~ centígrado** Celsius
el gramo gram
grande large
los grandes almacenes department store
la granja farm
gratuito free
gris gray
la grúa tow truck
el grupo group
guapo attractive

guardar v save (computer)
la guarnición side dish, order
el guía guide
la guía guide book; **~ de tiendas** store directory
gustar v like; **me gusta** I like

H

ha sufrido daños damaged
la habitación room; **~ individual** single room; **~ libre** vacancy
hablar v speak
hacer v have; **~ una apuesta** v place (a bet); **~ un arreglo** v alter; **~ una llamada** v phone; **~ las maletas** v pack; **~ turismo** sightseeing
hambriento hungry
helado icy
la hermana sister
el hermano brother
el hielo ice
el hígado liver (body part)
la hinchazón swelling
hipermétrope far-sighted [long-sighted BE]
el hipódromo horse-track
el hockey hockey; **~ sobre hielo** ice hockey
la hoja de afeitar ra-

zor blade
hola hello
el hombre man
el hombro shoulder
hondo deeply
la hora hour
el horario n schedule [timetable BE]
los horarios hours; **~ de atención al público** business hours; **~ de oficina** office hours; **~ de visita** visiting hours
las horas de consulta office hours (doctor's)
el hornillo camp stove
el horno stove
el hospital hospital
el hotel hotel
hoy today
el hueso bone

I

el ibuprofeno ibuprofen
la ida y vuelta round-trip [return BE]
la iglesia church
impresionante stunning
imprimir v print
el impuesto duty (tax)
incluir v include
inconsciente unconscious
increíble amazing
la infección vaginal vaginal infection
infectado infected
el inglés English

iniciar sesión v log on (computer)
el insecto bug
la insolación sunstroke
el insomnio insomnia
la insulina insulin
interesante interesting
internacional international (airport area)
la internet internet
el/la intérprete interpreter
el intestino intestine
introducir v insert
ir a v go (somewhere)
ir de compras v go shopping
Irlanda Ireland
irlandés Irish
el IVA sales tax [VAT BE]
la izquierda left (direction)

J

el jabón soap
el jardín botánico botanical garden
el jazz jazz
el jersey sweater
joven young
las joyas jewelry
la joyería jeweler
jubilado retired
jugar v play
el juguete toy

K

el kilo kilo; **~gramo** kilogram; **~metraje** mileage

el **kilómetro** kilometer; ~ **cuadrado** square kilometer

L

el **labio** lip
la **laca** hairspray
el **ladrón** thief
el **lago** lake
la **lana** wool
la **lancha motora** motor boat
largo long
el **lavabo** sink
la **lavadora** washing machine
la **lavandería** laundromat [launderette BE]
lavar v wash
el **lavavajillas** dishwasher
la **lección** lesson
lejos far
la **lengua** tongue
la **lente** lens
las **lentillas de contacto** contact lens
las **letras** arts
las **libras esterlinas** pounds (British sterling)
libre de impuestos duty-free
la **librería** bookstore
el **libro** book
la **lima de uñas** nail file
limpiar v clean
la **limpieza de cutis** facial
limpio adj clean
la **línea** line (train)
el **lino** linen
la **linterna** flashlight

el **líquido** liquid; ~ **de lentillas de contacto** lens solution; ~ **lavavajillas** dishwashing liquid
listo ready
la **litera** berth
el **litro** liter
la **llamada** n call; ~ **de teléfono** phone call; ~ **despertador** wake-up call
llamar v call
la **llave** key; ~ **de habitación** room key; ~ **electrónica** key card
el **llavero** key ring
las **llegadas** arrivals (airport)
llegar v arrive
llenar v fill
llevar v take; ~ **en coche** lift (to give a ride)
la **lluvia** rain
lluvioso rainy
lo siento sorry
localizar v reach
la **luz** light (overhead)

M

la **madre** mother
magnífico magnificent
el **malestar estomacal** upset stomach
la **maleta** bag, suitcase
la **mandíbula** jaw
las **mangas cortas** short sleeves
las **mangas largas** long sleeves
la **manicura** manicure
la **mano** hand
la **manta** blanket
mañana tomorrow; la ~ morning
el **mapa** map; ~ **de carreteras** road map; ~ **de ciudad** town map; ~ **de la pista** trail [piste BE] map
el **mar** sea
marcar v dial
mareado dizzy
el **mareo** motion [travel BE] sickness
el **marido** husband
marrón brown
el **martillo** hammer
más more; ~ **alto** louder; ~ **bajo** lower; ~ **barato** cheaper; ~ **despacio** slower; ~ **grande** larger; ~ **pequeño** smaller; ~ **rápido** faster; ~ **tarde** later; ~ **temprano** earlier
el **masaje** massage; ~ **deportivo** sports massage
el **mástil** tent pole
el **mecánico** mechanic
el **mechero** lighter
la **media hora** half hour
mediano medium (size)
la **medianoche** midnight
el **medicamento** medicine

el **médico** doctor
medio half; ~ **kilo** half-kilo; ~**día** noon [midday BE]
medir v measure (someone)
mejor best
menos less
el **mensaje** message; ~ **instantáneo** instant message
el **mercado** market
el **mes** month
la **mesa** table
el **metro** subway [underground BE]
el **metro cuadrado** square meter
la **mezquita** mosque
el **microondas** microwave
el **minibar** mini-bar
el **minuto** minute
el **mirador** overlook [viewpoint BE] (scenic place)
mirar v look
la **misa** mass (church service)
mismo same
los **mocasines** loafers
la **mochila** backpack
molestar v bother
la **moneda** coin, currency
mono cute
la **montaña** n mountain
el **monumento conmemorativo** memorial (place)
morado purple

el mostrador de información information desk

mostrar v display

la moto acuática jet ski

la motocicleta motorcycle

movilidad mobility

la mujer wife, woman

la multa fine (fee for breaking law)

la muñeca doll; ~ wrist

el músculo muscle

el museo museum

la música music; ~ **clásica** classical music; ~ **folk** folk music; ~ **pop** pop music

el muslo thigh

N

nacional domestic

la nacionalidad nationality

nada nothing

nadar v swim

las nalgas buttocks

naranja orange (color)

la nariz nose

necesitar v need

los negocios business

negro black

nevado snowy

la nevera refrigerator

el nieto grandchild

la niña girl

el niño boy, child

el nivel intermedio intermediate

no no

la noche evening,

night

el nombre name; ~ **de usuario** username

normal regular

las normas de vestuario dress code

el norte north

la novia girlfriend

el novio boyfriend

el número number; ~ **de fax** fax number; ~ **de permiso de conducir** driver's license number; ~ **de teléfono** phone number; ~ **de teléfono de información** information (phone)

O

la obra de teatro n play (theater)

el oculista optician

el oeste west

la oficina office; ~ **de correos** post office; ~ **de objetos perdidos** lost and found; ~ **de turismo** tourist information office

el ojo eye

la olla pot

la ópera opera

el ordenador computer

la oreja ear

la orina urine

el oro gold; ~ **amarillo** yellow gold; ~ **blanco** white gold

la orquesta orchestra

oscuro dark

el otro camino alternate route

la oxigenoterapia oxygen treatment

P

padecer del corazón heart condition

el padre father

pagar v pay

el pájaro bird

el palacio palace; ~ **de las cortes** parliament building

los palillos chinos chopsticks

la panadería bakery

los pantalones pants [trousers BE]; ~ **cortos** shorts

el pañal diaper [nappy BE]

el pañuelo de paper tissue

el papel paper; ~ **de aluminio** aluminum [kitchen BE] foil; ~ **de cocina** paper towel; ~ **higiénico** toilet paper

el paquete package

para for; ~ **llevar** to go [take away BE]; ~ **no fumadores** non-smoking

el paracetamol acetaminophen [paracetamol BE]

la parada n stop; ~ **de autobús** bus stop

el paraguas umbrella

pararse v stop

el párking parking garage

el parque playpen; ~ **park**; ~ **de atracciones** amusement park

el partido game; ~ **de fútbol** soccer [football BE]; ~ **de voleibol** volleyball game

el pasajero passenger; ~ **con billete** ticketed passenger

el pasaporte passport

el pase de acceso a los remontes lift pass

el pasillo aisle

la pasta de dientes toothpaste

la pastelería pastry shop

el patio de recreo playground

el peatón pedestrian

el pecho chest (body part)

el pediatra pediatrician

la pedicura pedicure

pedir v order

el peinado hairstyle

el peine comb

la película movie

peligroso dangerous

el pelo hair

el peltre pewter

la peluquería de caballeros barber

la peluquería hair salon

los pendientes earrings

el pene penis

la penicilina penicillin

la pensión bed and breakfast

pequeño small

perder v lose (something)

perdido lost

el perfume perfume

el periódico newspaper

la perla pearl

permitir v allow, permit

el perro guía guide dog

la persona con discapacidad visual visually impaired person

la picadura de insecto insect bite

picante spicy

picar v stamp (a ticket)

el pie foot

la piel skin

la pierna leg

la pieza part (for car)

los pijamas pajamas

la pila battery

la píldora Pill (birth control)

la piscina pool; ~ **cubierta** indoor pool; ~ **exterior** outdoor pool; ~ **infantil** kiddie [paddling BE] pool

la pista trail [piste BE]

la pizzería pizzeria

el placer pleasure

la plancha n iron (clothes)

planchar v iron

la planta floor [storey BE]; ~ **baja** ground floor

la plata silver; ~ **esterlina** sterling silver

el platino platinum

el plato dish (kitchen); ~ **principal** main course

la playa beach

la plaza town square

la policía police

la pomada cream (ointment)

ponerse en contacto con v contact

por for; ~ per; ~ **día** per day; ~ **favor** please; ~ **hora** per hour; ~ **la noche** overnight; ~ **noche** per night; ~ **semana** per week

el postre dessert

el precio price

precioso beautiful

el prefijo area code

la pregunta question

presentar v introduce

el preservativo condom

la primera clase first class

primero first

los principales sitios de interés main attraction

principiante beginner, novice (skill level)

la prioridad de paso right of way

la prisa rush

el probador fitting room

probar v taste

el problema problem

el producto good; ~ **de limpieza** cleaning product

programar v schedule

prohibir v prohibit

el pronóstico forecast

pronunciar v pronounce

el protector solar sunscreen

provisional temporary

próximo next

el público public

el pueblo village

el puente bridge

la puerta gate (airport); ~ door; ~ **de incendios** fire door

el pulmón lung

la pulsera bracelet

el puro cigar

Q

qué what (question)

quedar bien v fit (clothing)

quedarse v stay

la queja complaint

la quemadura solar sunburn

querer v love (someone)

quién who (question)

el quiosco newsstand

R

la ración portion; ~ **para niños** children's portion

la rampa para silla de ruedas wheelchair ramp

el rap rap (music)

rápido express, fast

la raqueta racket (sports); ~ **de nieve** snowshoe

la reacción alérgica allergic reaction

recargar v recharge

la recepción reception

la receta prescription

recetar v prescribe

rechazar v decline (credit card)

recibir v receive

el recibo receipt

reciclar v recycling

recoger v pick up (something)

la recogida de equipajes baggage claim

la recomendación recommendation

recomendar v recommend

el recorrido tour; ~ **en autobús** bus tour; ~ **turístico** sightseeing tour

recto straight

el recuerdo souvenir

el regalo gift

la región region

el registro check-in (hotel); ~ **del coche** vehicle registration

la regla period (menstrual)

el Reino Unido United Kingdom (U.K.)

la relación relationship

rellenar v fill out (form)

el reloj watch; **~ de pared** wall clock

el remolque trailer

reparar v fix (repair)

el repelente de insectos insect repellent

repetir v repeat

la resaca hangover

la reserva reservation; **~ natural** nature preserve

reservar v reserve

el/la residente de la UE EU resident

respirar v breathe

el restaurante restaurant

retirar v withdraw; **~ fondos** withdrawal (bank)

retrasarse v delay

la reunión meeting

revelar v develop (film)

revisar v check (on something)

la revista magazine

el riñón kidney (body part)

el río river

robado stolen

robar v steal

el robo theft

la rodilla knee

rojo red

romántico romantic

romper v break

la ropa clothing; **~ interior** underwear

rosa pink

roto broken

el rugby rugby

la rueda tire [tyre BE]; **~ pinchada** flat tire [tyre BE]

las ruinas ruins

la ruta route; **~ de senderismo** walking route

S

la sábana sheet

el sacacorchos corkscrew

el saco de dormir sleeping bag

la sala room; **~ de conciertos** concert hall; **~ de espera** waiting room; **~ de reuniones** meeting room

la salida check-out (hotel)

la salida n exit; **~ de urgencia** emergency exit

las salidas departures (airport)

salir v exit, leave

el salón room; **~ de congresos** convention hall; **~ de juegos recreativos** arcade; **~ de manicura** nail salon

¡Salud! Cheers!

la salud health

las sandalias sandals

sangrar v bleed

la sangre blood

el santuario shrine

la sartén frying pan

la sauna sauna

el secador de pelo hair dryer

la secreción discharge (bodily fluid)

la seda silk

sediento thirsty

la seguridad security

el seguro insurance

seguro safe (protected)

el sello n stamp (postage)

el semáforo traffic light

la semana week

semanal weekly

el seminario seminar

el sendero trail; **~ para bicicletas** bike route

el seno breast

sentarse v sit

separado separated (marriage)

ser v be

serio serious

el servicio restroom [toilet BE]; **~** service (in a restaurant); **~ completo** full-service; **~ de habitaciones** room service; **~ inalámbrico a internet** wireless internet service; **~ de internet** internet service; **~ de lavandería** laundry

service; **~ de limpieza de habitaciones** housekeeping service

la servilleta napkin

sí yes

el sida AIDS

la silla chair; **~ para niños** child seat; **~ de ruedas** wheelchair

el símbolo symbol (keyboard)

sin without; **~ alcohol** non-alcoholic; **~ grasa** fat free; **~ receta** over the counter (medication)

la sinagoga synagogue

el sitio de interés attraction (place)

el sobre envelope

el socorrista lifeguard

el sol sun

solamente only

soleado sunny

solo alone

soltero single (marriage)

el sombrero hat

la somnolencia drowsiness

sordo deaf

soso bland

el suavizante conditioner

el subtítulo subtitle

sucio dirty

la sudadera sweatshirt

el suelo floor

el sujetador bra

súper super (fuel)

superior upper
el supermercado grocery store, supermarket
la supervisión supervision
el sur south
el surfista windsurfer

T

la tabla board; ~ **de snowboard** snowboard; ~ **de surf** surfboard
la talla size; ~ **grande** plus size; ~ **pequeña** petite size
el taller garage (repair)
el talón de equipaje luggage [baggage BE] ticket
el tampón tampon
la taquilla locker; ~ reservation desk
tarde late (time)
la tarde afternoon
la tarjeta card; ~ **de cajero automático** ATM card; ~ **de crédito** credit card; ~ **de débito** debit card; ~ **de embarque** boarding pass; ~ **internacional de estudiante** international student card; ~ **de memoria** memory card; ~ **de negocios** business card; ~ **postal** postcard; ~ **de seguro** insurance card; ~ **de socio** membership card; ~ **telefónica** phone card
la tasa fee
el taxi taxi
la taza cup; ~ **medidora** measuring cup
el teatro theater; ~ **de la ópera** opera house
la tela impermeable groundcloth [groundsheet BE]
el teleférico cable car
el teléfono telephone; ~ **móvil** cell [mobile BE] phone; ~ **público** pay phone
la telesilla chair lift
el telesquí ski/drag lift
la televisión TV
el templo temple (religious)
temprano early
el tenedor fork
tener v have; ~ **dolor** v hurt (have pain); ~ **náuseas** v be nauseous
el tenis tennis
la tensión arterial blood pressure
la terminal terminal (airport)
terminar v end
la terracotta terracotta
terrible terrible
el texto n text (message)

el tiempo time; ~ **weather**
la tienda store; ~ **de alimentos naturales** health food store; ~ **de antigüedades** antique store; ~ **de bebidas alcohólicas** liquor store [off-licence BE]; ~ **de campaña** tent; ~ **de deportes** sporting goods store; ~ **de fotografía** camera store; ~ **de juguetes** toy store; ~ **de música** music store; ~ **de recuerdos** souvenir store; ~ **de regalos** gift shop; ~ **de ropa** clothing store
las tijeras scissors
la tintorería dry cleaner
el tipo de cambio exchange rate
tirar v pull (door sign)
la tirita bandage
la toalla towel
la toallita baby wipe
el tobillo ankle
el torneo de golf golf tournament
la torre tower
la tos n cough
toser v cough
el total total (amount)
trabajar v work
tradicional traditional
traducir v translate
traer v bring

tragar v swallow
el traje suit
tranquilo quiet
el tren train; ~ **rápido** express train
triste sad
la trona highchair
el trozo piece
la tumbona deck chair
el turista tourist

U

último last
la universidad university
uno one
la uña nail; ~ **del dedo** fingernail; ~ **del pie** toenail
urgente urgent
usar v use

V

las vacaciones vacation [holiday BE]
vaciar v empty
la vacuna vaccination
la vagina vagina
la validez valid
valioso valuable
el valle valley
el valor value
el vaquero denim
los vaqueros jeans
el vaso glass (drinking)
el váter químico chemical toilet
vegetariano vegetarian
la vejiga bladder
vender v sell
el veneno poison

venir _v_ come
la ventana window
el ventilador fan (appliance)
ver _v_ see
verde green
el vestido dress (piece of clothing)
el viaje trip
el vidrio glass (material)

viejo old
la viña vineyard
la violación _n_ rape
violar _v_ rape
el visado visa (passport document)
visitar _v_ visit
la vitamina vitamin
la vitrina display case
viudo widowed
vivir _v_ live

vomitar _v_ vomit
el vuelo flight; ~ **internacional** international flight; ~ **nacional** domestic flight

Z

la zapatería shoe store
las zapatillas slip-pers; ~ **de deporte** sneaker
los zapatos shoes
la zona area; ~ **de compras** shopping area; ~ **de fumadores** smoking area; ~ **para picnic** picnic area
el zoológico zoo
zurcir _v_ mend

INDEX

Berlitz pocket guide

CUBA

Fourteenth Edition 2019

Editor: Helen Fanthorpe
Author: Klaudyna Cwynar
Head of DTP and Pre-Press: Rebeka Davies
Picture Editor: Tom Smyth
Cartography Update: Carte
Update Production: Apa Digital
Photography Credits: 123RF 80, 89;
Dreamstime 4MC, 5TC, 16, 91, 96; Getty
Images 5MC; iStock 1, 4TC, 4ML, 7, 7R, 21,
52, 67; Mockford & Bonetti/Apa Publications
19; Shutterstock 4TL, 5T, 6L, 6R, 58;
Sylvaine Poitau/Apa Publications 5M, 5MC,
5M, 11, 12, 14, 24, 26, 29, 31, 32, 35, 36,
38/39, 40, 41, 43, 44, 47, 49, 51, 53, 55, 57, 60,
63, 64, 69, 70, 73, 75, 76, 78, 83, 84, 86, 93,
94, 101, 103, 104
Cover Picture: iStock

Distribution

UK, Ireland and Europe: Apa Publications
(UK) Ltd; sales@insightguides.com
United States and Canada: Ingram
Publisher Services; ips@ingramcontent.com
Australia and New Zealand: Woodslane;
info@woodslane.com.au
Southeast Asia: Apa Publications (SN) Pte;
singaporeoffice@insightguides.com
Worldwide: Apa Publications (UK) Ltd;
sales@insightguides.com

**Special Sales, Content Licensing
and CoPublishing**
Insight Guides can be purchased in bulk
quantities at discounted prices. We can
create special editions, personalised jackets
and corporate imprints tailored to your
needs. sales@insightguides.com;
www.insightguides.biz

Contact us
Every effort has been made to provide
accurate information in this publication,
but changes are inevitable. The publisher
cannot be responsible for any resulting loss,
inconvenience or injury. We would appreciate
it if readers would call our attention to any
errors or outdated information. We also
welcome your suggestions; please contact
us at: berlitz@apaguide.co.uk
www.insightguides.com/berlitz